D0176141

Palisades.
Pure Romance.

FICTION THAT FEATURES CREDIBLE CHARACTERS AND

ENTERTAINING PLOT LINES, WHILE CONTINUING TO UPHOLD

STRONG CHRISTIAN VALUES. FROM HIGH ADVENTURE

TO TENDER STORIES OF THE HEART, EACH PALISADES

ROMANCE IS AN UNDILUTED STORY OF LOVE,

FROM BEGINNING TO END!

MISTLETOE

BARBARA JEAN HICKS

LORENA McCOURTNEY

KAREN M. BALL

PALISADES

This is a work of fiction. The characters, incidents, and dialogues are products of the author's imagination and are not to be construed as real. Any resemblance to actual events or persons, living or dead, is entirely coincidental.

MISTLETOE
published by Palisades
a part of the Questar publishing family

© 1996 Tea for Two by Barbara Jean Hicks
© 1996 Feliz Navidad by Lorena McCourtney
© 1996 An Unlikely Angel by Karen M.Ball

International Standard Book Number: 1-57673-013-1

Cover illustration by George Angelini
Cover designed by Mona Weir-Daly
Edited by Shari MacDonald

Printed in the United States of America

For information:
QUESTAR PUBLISHERS, INC.
POST OFFICE BOX 1720
SISTERS, OREGON 97759

96 97 98 99 00 01 02 03 — 10 9 8 7 6 5 4 3 2 1

For unto us a Child is born,
Unto us a Son is given;
And the government will be upon His shoulder.
And His name will be called
Wonderful, Counselor, Mighty God,
Everlasting Father, Prince of Peace.

ISAIAH 9:6 (NKJV)

Tea for Two

BARBARA JEAN HICKS

CHAPTER

One

❧

Labor Day

D addy needs a *wife,*" the young girl said emphatically to her elderly companion. She set her delicate china teacup in its saucer. "I can watch out for him summers and holidays, but what about the rest of the year?" The gray eyes beneath the brim of her hat were clouded with concern. "He's too *comfortable* just sitting around the bookstore all day. He's getting that tattered look, y'know?"

She glanced across the open courtyard at the small building next door. A dilapidated table on the porch was stacked with used paperbacks. The girl had printed the sign herself, just this morning: *50¢ Each or 3 for $1.00.* "Like one of his old books," she added, picking up a triangle of cucumber sandwich.

The elderly woman, her carriage imposing even when she was seated, filled the girl's teacup from the china pot on the table. Her age-spotted hands shook only slightly. "Nothing wrong with 'comfortable,'" she said tartly.

Nine-year-old Angel, the girl in the hat, knew her companion well enough not to be offended by her tone. "I know, Gran-Gabby. But...well, maybe *comfortable* isn't the right word." Angel wanted to be a writer when she grew up, and using the right word was already important to her.

Gran-Gabby pursed her lips and squinted at her young friend. "The word you're looking for is *resigned*. There's a difference. If you're going to be a writer, be precise."

"*Resigned*. Yes, that's it exactly." Angel was pleased until she remembered the point of her comment. "But Gran-Gabby, isn't there anything we can *do*?"

Gran-Gabby, dark eyes still bright in her weathered face, nodded curtly. "There is. I've been cogitating on the situation all summer." She leaned forward, resting a hand on the stack of books that lay between them, and whispered conspiratorially, "My great-niece Lettie would be perfect for your father!" Sitting back, she lifted her china teacup in a regal pose.

"Lettie *Weatherspoon?!* Really, Gran-Gabby?" Of all the people in the world Angel wanted to meet in person—and there were many—her favorite author was at the top of the list. "You never told me she's single!"

"No reason to till now." Gran-Gabby paused for a sip of tea, watching Angel over the rim of the cup as the girl waited impatiently for her to continue. "We've got to work fast," she finally said, setting the teacup in its saucer with a rattle. "Lettie thinks she wants to marry some buffoon who can't make up his mind about her." Gran-Gabby raised a perfectly penciled brow and added haughtily, "I say if he can't make up his mind, he isn't good enough for Lettie!"

Angel unconsciously twisted a strand of curly blonde hair around a finger. "But Lettie Weatherspoon lives in Seattle! That's—" She stopped to calculate, closing one eye and wrinkling her forehead in concentration. Math didn't come as easily as writing. "Well, anyhow, a long way from Nevada City, California. How could they ever get together long enough to fall in love?"

The older woman waved her hand dismissively. "Doesn't

take so long to fall in love, so long as the principals—that is, Lettie and your father—are *ready* for it." She paused, glancing toward the bookstore across the courtyard. Parker McPhee stood at the window, bearded chin in hand, looking lost.

When she turned back, Angel was watching her expectantly. She leaned forward once again. "That's where you and I come in," she said firmly.

Parker stood at the open window overlooking the courtyard between his bookstore and Gabrielle's Tea Garden. The sunshine, the cloudless sky, and the warm breeze filling the wind sock that hung from his porch would have been enough, under normal circumstances, to insure his customary cheerfulness. Instead, his shoulders slumped and his head drooped, and the feeling of despondency with which he'd wakened this morning seemed to be increasing at rather an alarming rate.

As if sensing his owner's low spirits, the large orange cat in his arms meowed and pushed his head into the crook of Parker's arm, an affectionate gesture his master always found comforting.

"Hey, Riley," he said to the cat, not caring that there were customers browsing in the stacks who could hear him. "At least I don't have to tell *you* goodbye." The red tabby longhair looked up at him solemnly, his round copper eyes unblinking, and waved a paw. Parker lifted his fingers to ruffle the long fur under the cat's chin and was gratified to hear its loud, distinctive purr, like an engine badly in need of a tune-up. "Even as spoiled as you are, I don't know what I'd do without you."

He sank into the overstuffed chair in front of the window, settled Riley on his lap, and gazed across the courtyard at the table where Angel sat with Gabrielle Weatherspoon—"Miss Gabby," as she'd been known in Nevada City for twenty-five years. Angel and a very few other select friends called the dowager "Gran-Gabby."

His young daughter daintily lifted her teacup to her lips, prompting a stab of inexplicable longing in Parker's heart. She looked so grown up in her flowered sundress and straw hat that he felt suddenly quite aged. Wasn't it just yesterday she'd been a tomboy in shorts and a T-shirt, needing him to help her up from the sidewalk and gently tend to her skinned knee?

His heart ached for the moments of her childhood he'd missed and for the moments of her future he would never share. Her immediate future in particular: Marci and William would be here in an hour to take her back to the city. The summer had gone too fast.

Angel and Miss Gabby had their heads together now, and his daughter was furiously taking notes. A stack of books lay between them, strewn haphazardly across the table. He wondered what they were up to. The two of them were thick as thieves: his nine-year-old daughter and the eccentric proprietress of Gabrielle's, who was in her seventies—an odd friendship that didn't surprise Parker in the least. Angel had an innate curiosity, like his own, that drew her to eccentrics, and the spinster Miss Gabby, despite her stern exterior, had a mothering streak wider than a lot of real mothers he knew. Including, unfortunately, Angel's own.

His gaze shifted to the elegant Queen Anne Victorian edifice behind his daughter and her comrade, crowning the hill above Broad Street. The grand house overlooked the tiny California gold town, tucked away in the mountains of the Sierra Nevada range, like a queen overlooking her kingdom. Or, Parker thought with the hint of a smile, like a giant ice cream sundae ready to melt down the streets, as Angel had suggested the first time she'd seen it. Miss Gabby had painted the house like a Neapolitan confection, in shades of chocolate, strawberry, and

12

vanilla. The ice-cream colors gave the house a fairy tale feel, lifting it above the everyday just as the fancy English teas Miss Gabby served there lifted the restaurant's guests out of the ordinary.

The siding was painted cocoa brown, the scalloped shingles of the gables a paler shade of the same. Stone steps led from the street to a wide porch which wrapped around the house. On the side facing his bookstore, the porch had been enclosed to form a glass solarium that opened onto a flagstone patio garden, creating an alfresco dining room for Gabrielle's. The porch rails, the French windows of the solarium, and the filigreed casements upstairs and down sparkled like vanilla cream against the chocolate walls. Shades of rosy pink and a deep berry accented the Victorian details of the nineteenth-century architecture.

Even in the midst of historic downtown Nevada City, famous for the charm and character of its Victorian gingerbread, Gabrielle's Tea Garden stood out like a lady among maidservants. No wonder the restaurant had been written up in every West Coast travel magazine. And no wonder Angel wanted to say her farewell to Miss Gabby there over afternoon tea.

The sound of the bell over his shop door broke into his reverie. "Hey, McPhee!" It was Cosmo, the contradictory teenager he'd hired on Miss Gabby's recommendation to help him out in the store. Cosmo's hair was long on top, shaved at the sides and neck, and dyed deep purple. He wore a small gold ring in his left ear, and his right forearm sported a tattoo of his own design which incorporated the images of several endangered species. Despite his somewhat formidable appearance, he was a more responsible and conscientious employee than many adults Parker had had the misfortune to manage.

"You look like the cat died," Cosmo declared as he plopped down in the armchair next to Parker.

"You have such a way with words, Coz," Parker said dryly. He rubbed his hand along Riley's tummy. The sleeping tabby was stretched out across his lap with his short thick legs splayed. "Does this cat look dead to you?"

"Truthfully?"

Parker grinned. Cosmo never failed to cheer him. "Never mind." He stood, depositing Riley on the plump brocade cushion of the armchair. The cat opened one copper eye, closed it again, and rumbled loudly for a moment before falling asleep again.

"Thanks for coming in on such short notice, Coz. I want to spend a few minutes with Angel before she leaves for her mother's. Think you can handle the store by yourself?"

Cosmo gave him a confident thumbs-up. "No problem."

"I'll be just outside if you need me."

"Go on. Get outta here."

Angel and Miss Gabby were so engrossed in their project they didn't notice Parker's approach until his shadow fell across the table. "So I'll write a letter every week," Angel was saying.

"Good," Miss Gabby answered. "And don't forget—Oh, hello, Parker." She closed the book she'd been perusing. Angel quickly turned her notebook over.

"All right," Parker said sternly, raising his dark, bushy eyebrows. He slid into an empty chair as he pulled it up to the table. "Just what are you two girls hiding from me now?"

Miss Gabby snorted. "So I'm a *girl* now, am I, Parker McPhee? Full of the blarney *you* are today."

"Young at heart, Miss Gabby. You'll never get old," he said gallantly. He turned to his daughter. "So, Angel, you're going to write your Gran-Gabby every week. How about your dear old dad, too, since you're abandoning ship for the city?"

"Dad! It's not like I'm never going to see you again. You're coming to San Francisco next weekend, right?"

"True. It just *feels* like I'm never going to see you again." He sighed mournfully. "I'm already lonely."

Angel and Miss Gabby exchanged a mystifyingly significant glance. Parker frowned, then shrugged. He'd find out eventually what they were cooking up. "Now—may I join you for tea?" he asked.

"Of course!" Miss Gabby gestured to a waitress nearby. "Sylvie," she said imperiously, "another pot of tea and a dessert platter, please. And Parker will need a place setting."

"Look what Gran-Gabby gave me as a going-away gift, Dad." Angel gathered the books that lay between her and the elderly woman and set them down in front of him. "The *Gabby* books, all ten of them. *Autographed!*"

Parker lifted the top book from the stack. "Miss Gabby, these are collector's items! Are you sure you want to give them away?"

"It's not as if I can't get more."

Parker nodded, stroking the colorful jacket of the award-winning children's book and tracing the author-illustrator's name with his forefinger: *Lettie Weatherspoon:* Gabrielle Weatherspoon's great-niece, as Angel had been thrilled to discover on meeting Miss Gabby—Weatherspoon being a difficult name to escape notice.

In the six years he'd been in the used-book business, Parker had never come across a second-hand *Gabby* in hardcover. The imaginative books, with their lilting rhythm and bright colored-pencil illustrations—detailed drawings framed by the artist's exquisite signature borders—were "keepers" or else were lovingly passed down from family member to family member and friend to friend. Even Angel's paperback copies, worn and bedraggled from much use, still stood on the shelf next to her bed at her mother's house.

Opening the book in his hands, Parker smoothed back the

title page: *Gabby and the Magic Teapot*. Below the title was printed Lettie Weatherspoon's well-known personal symbol, an image she included in every drawing: a Victorian teaspoon with "Lettie" incorporated into the design of the handle and one or another weather sign drawn in the bowl of the spoon—in this case, a radiant sun. An autograph in a hand that managed somehow to be both bold and feminine angled across the bottom right hand corner of the page.

"That's the one that started it all," Miss Gabby said proudly as Sylvie set a fresh pot of tea on the table.

Parker nodded again. He'd heard the story: Lettie Weatherspoon had written the first *Gabby* tale just for fun, for her great-aunt's seventieth birthday. Her original illustration—a gleeful girl in overalls clinging to the spout of a giant winged teapot—still hung on the wall of the children's tea room at Gabrielle's.

"Started it all for us, too," Parker said, stroking with affection the blonde curly hair cascading down his daughter's back. "I gave it to Angel for her fifth birthday. She made me read it over and over and over again! Fortunately, I was as delighted with it as she was."

"The writer will delight you, too," Miss Gabby said positively. "Lettie's as enchanting as her books."

Parker turned the page, once again smoothing it carefully. "Is she coming to visit, Miss Gabby? Let me know beforehand so I can make sure Angel's here."

Clearing his throat, he lifted the book and began to read: "In a house on a hilltop there lived a girl-child. Her name was Miss Gabby. Miss Gabby was wild!"

He raised his shaggy eyebrows sternly at Angel as he wet his thumb and turned the page. She giggled, encouraging him to continue Lettie Weatherspoon's famous and familiar story.

Gabby was a rebellious and headstrong girl who discovered,

to her astonishment, that her great-great-grandfather's teapot could carry her off to wonderful adventures while the grown-ups sat around the table and gossiped, unaware even that she was gone. In fact, when she arrived back home from a wild ride around the world, the grown-ups all complimented her on how quietly she'd sat during tea! The experience made Gabby rethink her rebellion; after all, if she'd run off to play instead of sitting at tea as her mother insisted, she'd have missed out on all the excitement.

Angel joined her father in reciting the last few lines of the rhyming story, which she'd memorized long ago without even trying.

"Bravo!" Miss Gabby clapped her hands. "A wonderful reading, Sir Parker McPhee!"

Parker groaned. "Enough of the anapestic tetrameter, already!"

"Spoil-sport," she said peevishly. "Lettie and I can have entire conversations in rhyming anapestic tetrameter!"

Frowning in puzzlement, Angel asked, "Anna *who?*"

Parker explained: "The rhythm Lettie Weatherspoon uses in all the Gabby books. You know—ba-ba-BAA ba-ba-BAA ba-ba-BAA ba-ba-BAA."

"You sound like a stuttering sheep, Daddy!" Angel giggled.

Quirking his mouth in a comical expression, he teased, "Well, I feel pretty *sheep*-ish that I've never bought you a hardcover set of the *Gabby* books myself."

Angel rolled her eyes as Sylvie set a platter of tea desserts on the table. Parker reached for a petit four but stopped when he saw that Angel and Miss Gabby were both watching him. They wore identical smiles. Secret smiles.

He frowned. "What?"

They shook their heads in unison. Then Angel leaned over and kissed him on the forehead. "I love you, Dad."

His heart swelled as he tugged at the brim of her hat. "Love you too, pun'kin." He tried to swallow the lump in his throat. "I'm sorry you have to go."

"Angela!" a woman's voice intruded.

Parker took a moment to compose himself before he raised his eyes. Even then, his vision blurred; Marci and William looked watery and insubstantial, as if existing on a different plane, on the other side of an invisible wall impossible to breach from either direction.

Somehow, though, Angel managed to do it.

Thanksgiving

I 've really done it now, Mr. Tibbs," Nicolette Weatherspoon said forlornly. She lifted the brightly-feathered bird to eye level and gently rubbed his breast with a knuckle.

Mr. Tibbs cocked his head and looked at her with black beady eyes. "Itsakay, itsakay," he whistled.

Nicolette smiled wanly. "Not this time, Baby Bird." She carried the parakeet into the bathroom and tossed a hand towel over her silk blouse, then let him hop from her finger to his favorite roost on her shoulder. He danced on one foot and then on the other, chortling, "Baby-bird, baby-bird."

Twisting the cold water tap at the sink, Nick bent over the basin and held her hands beneath the stream. Mr. Tibbs circled around to the back of her neck as she upset his roost, his claws tickling across her shoulder blades. Nick splashed water on her face, then pressed her fists against her eyes for a moment before shaking her head and reaching blindly for a towel. Mr. Tibbs crabbed across her back to resettle on her shoulder as she stood upright.

She avoided looking in the mirror as she patted her face dry. How did women in the movies always look so *pretty* when they cried? Nick didn't need the glass to confirm she had no talent for glamorous tears; she knew her eyes were puffy slits and her skin was raw and blotchy—an altogether unattractive sight.

Maybe if she'd had more practice… But Nicolette Weatherspoon was practical, down-to-earth, and not given to fits of crying. Tonight was a definite aberration.

Burying her face in the towel, she sniffled, "It's Tom, Mr. Tibbs. I've lost him; I know I have." She hiccuped into the terry cloth. "What am I going to *do*? I'm thirty-six years old!"

Shoulders slumped, she sank to the rim of the bathtub. Rinsing her face hadn't done a lot of good; her eyes were still leaking like broken faucets, though finally without the accompanying noise. She dabbed at her face again. Really, this wasn't like her at all! No wonder Tom had been so taken aback.

She lifted a finger to her shoulder. Mr. Tibbs pecked at it once, then hopped on board. Nicolette shook her head sadly as she brought the colorful bird around and gazed at him. "You know all those relationship books you and I've been reading, Mr. Tibbs? The parts about 'Getting to Commitment'?"

Mr. Tibbs cocked his head and didn't reply.

"Then let me remind you: 'Never give an ultimatum unless you're willing to lose him.' I've gone and done it, Baby Bird, I've given Tom an ultimatum, and I *don't* want to lose him. I love him. And besides, who else *is* there now? I'm thirty-six years *old!*"

"Baby-bird, baby-bird," Mr. Tibbs repeated unhelpfully.

Nick could not console herself. She was certain, after her rash action, that her future was destined for single-serving cans of soup in the kitchen cupboards and a lone toothbrush in the bathroom cabinet. No warm Saturday morning snuggling with a dearly loved husband and a giggling child or two; no one to share the Sunday funnies with except for Mr. Tibbs, who hardly ever laughed at the same things she did.

"Not that you don't have your good points, Baby Bird," she sniffled.

"Tea-time, tea-time," he squawked.

She dabbed at her eyes one last time and sat up straighter. "Your good advice, for once," she told the parakeet. "You're right, of course. Tea is just the thing." It was from her great-aunt Gabrielle—Gran-Gabby—that Nicolette had learned how reviving the ritual of tea could be.

A strong, resourceful woman with seemingly boundless energy—at seventy-six Gran-Gabby still worked in the Victorian tea restaurant she'd owned for more than twenty-five years, although she'd finally hired a manager last summer—Nick's great-aunt was both her hero and her champion. She was also the inspiration for Nick's award-winning series of children's books, *Gabby and the Magic Teapot.*

Growing up, Nick had spent at least a couple of weeks every summer in California's gold country with her father's spinster aunt. Then, from the time she was fourteen until she graduated from college with her teaching degree seven years later, she'd lived above Gabrielle's Tea Garden with Gran-Gabby three months out of the year. All summer long, she had worked at the restaurant, helping out in the kitchen and waiting tables. Her tips from the tourists who flocked to Nevada City every year had helped pay her way through university.

Tea was a verb in Gran-Gabby's vocabulary. "To tea," she would say in her not-to-be-argued-with tone of voice, "is to stake out an island of calm in the chaotic ocean of life. Always make time to tea." If Nicolette had ever needed calming, it was now.

Tossing the damp towel over the shower rod, she plodded down the hallway and settled Mr. Tibbs on top of his large cage in the kitchen alcove, ignoring his injured squawks at being abandoned. She emptied the tea kettle and filled it with freshly

21

drawn cold water, the metallic rush of sound not quite drowning out the argument that still echoed in her head.

"Nick, for goodness' sake! Pull yourself together!"

In three years, Tom had never spoken to her in that tone of voice. Of course, she'd never burst into tears in front of him, either.

With the kettle warming on the stove, she carefully lifted her favorite teapot off the shelf over the sink, filled it with hot water from the tap, and set it on the counter to warm. The teapot was a childhood gift from Gran-Gabby—a grinning crocodile wearing roller skates and holding a pretty nosegay behind his back. Using it made her great-aunt seem near.

While the kettle boiled, she dug in the refrigerator and pulled out thinly sliced rye bread, cream cheese, celery, and walnuts. The familiar activities of preparing a "proper" tea were already beginning to ease her tension. The chop-chop of the knife as she diced the celery and walnuts, the thump of the wooden spoon against the bowl as she beat the cream cheese, the rhythmic flourish of her arm as she spread the mixture on the bread, all served to soothe and comfort her.

For Nicolette, the ritual of tea seemed always to create distance and objectivity, allowing her to analyze her situation instead of being swept away by her feelings. Leaning against the counter for a moment, she closed her eyes and took a deep breath, letting it out slowly as she thought back on the day.

It *shouldn't* have been difficult. Six months ago it would have been delightful. Babies and pregnant women *every*where! Why did something that once gave her such joy now make her ache so inside?

You know why, Nicolette, she told herself.

She glanced across the room at the photos on her bookshelf, her eyes stopping to focus on the most recent addition to the gallery. It was a school picture, the kind mothers groan about at the time they're taken ("Couldn't you have brushed your *hair?!*") but pull out of the closet years later to embarrass their children in front of dates.

Angela McPhee's fourth-grade picture was certainly nothing to be embarrassed about, Nicolette thought. Angela—Angel, her father called her—was a lovely little girl, with curly blonde hair, serious gray eyes, and a warm smile.

Nick wondered: how was it that someone she had never even met had come to feel so important in her life? Angel's first letter had come in September, completely out of the blue; since then, the articulate, precocious nine-year-old who was Nicolette's most attentive fan had written her from San Francisco every week.

Angel wanted only two things in life: to be a famous writer of children's books when she grew up—as famous as Lettie Weatherspoon, the name under which Nicolette published—and to be an older sister.

"I can't do much about that," Angel had written regretfully in her first letter. "Mom remarried a guy who doesn't like kids—although he says he's made an exception for me—and Dad's not even looking. So I'm just working on my stories for now." Rueful, but philosophical.

The story she'd sent with her letter, a first-person narrative about her father and his cat, had been quite good for a girl her age. She had a knack for humor. Nick told her so when she'd answered Angel's letter. She'd also encouraged the girl to continue writing about what she knew best. "Your family is your best resource," she'd written. "My great-aunt Gabrielle was the inspiration for my first *Gabby* book, and look where it's taken me!"

They'd corresponded ever since, Angel always including a story when she wrote. By now Nick felt as if she knew her, and her father as well; more often than not "Dad" was the hero of his daughter's chronicles. A bumbling hero, but a hero nonetheless, in his funny and likable way.

Though Nicolette was charmed and delighted by the little girl's tales, they also began to make her feel wistful, reminding her she was thirty-six years old and for all practical purposes alone. "Don't give up on that baby," Nick had written in her first reply. "I believe in miracles. Who knows what might happen?"

Somewhere along the way, she'd started saying the same words to herself. She loved the way Angel wrote about her father, with such sincere delight and affection, and began to realize how much she longed to have a child of her own to whom she might be so indulgent and so important.

But Tom always put her off when she suggested there must be more to life than work and golf and going to the ballet.

The kettle started to whistle, and Nick hurried to pick it up from the burner. "Never overboil your water," she could almost hear Gran-Gabby instruct. "Overboiling makes your tea taste flat." She poured the warm water out of the crocodile, measured three teaspoons of loose apricot tea into the pot, and added the boiling water.

As the tea steeped, she finished making her open-faced sandwich, carefully trimming the crusts and cutting the bread into four triangles. Placing the pieces on a dinner plate, she added a small bunch of red grapes and three coconut macaroons. After eyeing the plate for a moment, she dug in the refrigerator again, emerging with several sprigs of parsley. "Presentation is everything," Gran-Gabby would say.

The garnished plate, the crocodile teapot, and a Tweety Bird mug went onto a tray which Nick carried into her small living room and set on the coffee table. A few minutes later, with candles lit on her fireplace mantle, soft instrumental jazz playing in the background, and Mr. Tibbs once more nestled on her shoulder, she sighed and sank to the carpeted floor. Leaning against the sofa, she sipped her tea and nibbled at her sandwiches and marveled at the calm she felt despite her earlier distress. Gran-Gabby would be proud.

Once more her mind turned to thoughts of her argument with Tom. They'd made the family rounds earlier in the day, a sumptuous midday Thanksgiving feast at her parents' home and late afternoon dessert at his. She loved her family and for the most part enjoyed Tom's; it ought to have been a wonderful day. If she hadn't been the only husbandless, childless woman around, it might have been.

Dinner at her parents' Green Lake house had been a nightmare. Nick's youngest sister, Doretta, and tiny Mindy, only three weeks old, were the center of attention. Her brother Darby's wife, Ione, who already had a sweet-faced baby girl just starting to walk, was as big as a hippo with child. The worst blow by far was her older sister Roxie's announcement that nineteen-year-old Chloe was pregnant—Nick's *niece!*

Nick had mostly managed to hide her growing depression, although her mother had commented on her uncharacteristic quietness and Tom had asked her several times if she were feeling all right.

Things were equally unbearable at Tom's parents' Summerset home in Bellevue, where two little boys were whooping around the house like gleeful Indian braves. The boys' mother, Hortensia, Tom's brother's wife, was expecting not only her third but her fourth! Twins ran in her family, Hortensia explained, glowing with happiness as her husband proudly produced the telling sonogram and passed it around the room. Nick had barely touched her pecan pie.

After that family event, they'd still had one more function to attend, an evening social obligation important to Tom. After they said their goodbyes, Tom helped her into his luxury car, a brand new burnished gold Lexus he'd appeared with when he'd picked her up for the ride to her parents'. Nick hadn't even known he'd been looking for a new car. She sank into the cream-colored leather seat as Tom pulled away from his parents' house and switched on the quadraphonic surround-sound stereo system, of which he was inordinately proud. Suddenly Bonnie Raitt was belting out the blues as though she were sitting right there on the console between them.

If it hadn't been for Bonnie, Nick thought, she might have escaped with her dignity intact. She might not have made such a mess of things. But as it happened, the singer's heart-wrenching cry was the straw that broke the camel's back.

"Listen, it's your song, Nick!" Tom had said, turning up the volume. He reached across the front seat to massage the back of her neck. "Love in the *Nick* of Time!"

Nick turned her head and stared at him through the early evening dark. Didn't he *know* what the song was about? Didn't he know Bonnie was singing about *her,* Nicolette Weatherspoon? True, she didn't cry at night like the woman in the song. But she *did* get misty-eyed, seeing babies everywhere she went and wondering if she'd ever have one of her own. Tom couldn't have missed that.

Bonnie crooned, "She's waited long enough, she says, and still he can't decide.…"

Suddenly it seemed as clear as Hortensia's sonogram that Nicolette had waited far too long for a man who couldn't even decide if he wanted to marry her, let alone be the father of her children.

"She's scared," Bonnie sang. "Scared to run out of time."

Nicolette burst into tears.

"Nick?" Tom pulled his arm away from her shoulder abruptly. "Nick, what's wrong?" He sounded alarmed.

She couldn't say anything for a moment, and when she did,

26

her words had to make their way around hiccups and sniffles. "Don't you know? Don't you even *know*? Tom, time is running out for me! *I need to know what you want.* Because I *know* what I want."

He sighed. "Nicolette—" He rarely used her full name. "If this conversation is leading where I think it is, the time is *not* appropriate. *Grow up.* We have fifteen minutes before we have to be at the senator's house." When she'd responded only with a fresh burst of tears, he'd added in annoyance, "Nick, for goodness' sake! Pull yourself together! I can't afford to have you looking like a blubbering escapee from a psychiatrist's couch!"

Maybe it was the words. Maybe it was Tom's tone of disapproval. Maybe it was the backlog of feelings she'd stored away for months—a seething brew of emotions that finally could do nothing but boil over the rim of her self-control. Against the advice of every self-help book on relationships she'd ever read—and she'd been reading a lot lately—she'd given Tom an ultimatum. "I'm thirty-six years old," she told him. "My biological clock is ticking as loud as Captain Hook's crocodile in *Peter Pan.* I want a family. I want a baby. If you don't, I need to know. You have to decide."

Then she had told him her feelings were far more important than any old senator's party and to please take her home. The ride had been silent except for her sniffles. The air between them had been thick with tension.

Thank goodness Mr. Tibbs was waiting for her when she got home. He'd squawked in concern from the kitchen as she threw herself across her bed and had a good cry. When that hadn't worked, he'd changed his tune to cheerful whistling. Eventually he'd gotten Nick off her bed and moving. And finally encouraged her to tea.

Just finishing her second cup and feeling more relaxed than she had all day, Nick almost didn't answer the phone when it rang. Two rings, three… She didn't want to talk to Tom. He'd done enough damage for one day. Then again…

Maybe he was calling to apologize, to tell her he'd been rude and selfish and inconsiderate, to tell her he loved her and wanted to marry her and start a family and would she please, please say yes, even though he'd been a jerk?

She almost tripped over her feet on the way to the phone. Mr. Tibbs squawked and dug into her shoulder. "Sorry, Baby Bird," Nick told him. She grabbed for the phone just before the answering machine would have picked up.

"Hello?" she said breathlessly.

"Lettie?"

Only one person had ever called Nicolette Weatherspoon *Lettie*. "Gran-Gabby!" she cried. Her crying jag had left her voice sounding nasal and thick with phlegm.

"What's wrong, child?"

Nick took a deep, trembling breath to keep herself from crying all over again. Then, as she had so many times in her life, she poured out her heart to the gruff, no-nonsense great-aunt she knew had always loved her fiercely.

"And I've just been thinking of you, Gran-Gabby," she finished. "I fixed myself a proper tea to find my island of calm, and you were right here with me, looking over my shoulder to make sure I was doing it right."

"And did you? Do it right, and find your island of calm?"

Nicolette laughed. It wasn't much of a laugh, more of a hiccup really, but it was her first laugh of the day, and it felt very good. "Of course! Didn't you teach me?"

"Good. Because I need your help in the restaurant. Right away. Through Christmas. Can you come?"

"You want me to come work in the restaurant? What's going on? I thought you—"

A fit of coughing on the other end of the line interrupted

her. "Gran-Gabby?" she asked in alarm. "Are you all right?"

"Oh dear," her great-aunt gasped. "I'm afraid I've caught cold—I hope it's not a case of pneumonia coming on...."

"And here I've been blabbering like a selfish child! How long have you been coughing like that, Gran-Gabby?"

"Oh, I don't know," she answered vaguely. "Don't worry about me, Lettie, I'll be fine. Been working too hard, I guess...."

"I thought you'd cut back! Didn't you hire a manager? Gran-Gabby, you can't be on your feet all day anymore. You're getting too—you're not—" Nick stopped, not knowing quite how to say, without offending her, that her great-aunt was getting too old for the daily grind of running a restaurant.

The old woman sighed heavily. "You're quite right, dear. I'm getting old and frail and perhaps a bit feeble-minded, though I hate to think it could be true." She sighed again.

Nick was almost too stunned to speak. This didn't sound at all like Gran-Gabby, who resisted every suggestion that she was getting on in years and ought to slow down. Her great-aunt's resigned sigh alarmed her as much as the coughing.

"Can you come?" the old woman prompted. "I've got my three special teas scheduled for the Christmas season, plus Victorian Christmas and the usual parties...."

Nick hesitated. She'd mailed off the illustrations for her last *Gabby* book less than a week before and had decided to take a sabbatical from the hugely popular series to think about a new idea. It might be just the thing for her creative process to do some physical work for a month or so. She could always hide a tape recorder in her apron pocket, just in case inspiration hit in the middle of a lunch rush.

On the other hand...

There was Mr. Tibbs to think of and the house plants. And what if the weather got bad while she was gone and her pipes all froze and burst? She'd heard about people coming home

29

from winter vacations to find their entire house an indoor swimming pool. And then there was Tom… Things felt so fragile between them right now. It really wasn't the best time to be leaving.

"Isn't your new manager working out?" she hedged.

"Oh, she's fine…" Gran-Gabby's voice trailed off before she added, "It's just that nobody cares about Gabrielle's the way *we* do. You and me. Oh, excuse me—"

Nick heard a muffled sneeze. "All right," she said, in a tone more decisive than she felt. "Yes, Gran-Gabby, I'll come. As soon as I can arrange it." He might grumble about it, but there wasn't any reason Tom couldn't take care of Mr. Tibbs and watch the house for her while she was gone. Besides, she told herself, absence makes the heart grow fonder.

"Good!" Already her great-aunt sounded better. "I've made your reservations. Six o'clock on Sunday, Sea-Tac to Sacramento. I'll overnight your ticket. My friend Parker will be there to pick you up. Thank you, Lettie. Bye!"

Nick pulled the phone away from her ear and stared at it for a moment before she hung up, shaking her head in amazement. Impending pneumonia or not, Gran-Gabby was still in charge.

CHAPTER

Three

Sunday after Thanksgiving

Hitching her shoulder to keep her large handbag from slipping off, Nicolette jostled through the crush of disembarking passengers. In one hand she carried a small artist's portfolio and in the other a laptop computer, neither of which she'd been willing to risk to the airline's baggage handlers. It was already close to midnight; she hoped she wouldn't have to wait around for this Parker fellow who was supposed to pick her up.

She'd called Gran-Gabby before leaving Seattle earlier in the evening, realizing she had no idea how she was expected to connect with her ride. "How will I know him?"

"About your age and height," Gran-Gabby told her. "Dark curly hair. Beard and mustache. Teddy bear-ish. Don't worry, he knows what you look like."

"Oh?"

"Your book jackets, Lettie," Gran-Gabby explained with exaggerated patience. "You're not exactly anonymous."

Nick didn't have to stand on her tiptoes or crane her neck to see over the crowd milling about the gate. She'd been gazing over the tops of heads for years now. In grade school, not only had she been the tallest girl in class, she'd been taller than all

31

the boys. When her schoolmates called her "Stick" instead of Nick and giggled behind her back, Gran-Gabby—who'd been through the same kind of humiliation two generations earlier—told her to stand tall and be proud. Someday, she said, Lettie would be the envy of her tormentors.

Her prediction was correct—for about a month. When Alexander Pope Junior High School started a girls' interscholastic basketball team, Nicolette's height was the envy of every student athlete in the school, male and female alike. Her classmates looked up to her in more ways than one, and Nick basked in the attention.

Unfortunately, her height bore no relation to her minuscule athletic skill, and she once again found herself an object of ridicule. By the end of junior high, Coach Figanelli had finally given up trying to get her down the floor without tripping over her feet, and her nickname had changed from "Stick" to "Brick."

For her part, Nick was relieved to be left alone to curl up in the oversized swivel rocker at home with a novel or the notebook where she wrote her poems or to wander around the neighborhood with her sketchbook, stopping now and then to rough out a scene she would later embellish with her own imagination.

Increasingly, Nicolette's creative mind was somewhere other than the present. She walked about with her head in the clouds and a faraway look in her blue eyes. Although she was well-liked by the few classmates who took the time to know her, she was largely ignored by the rest, most of whom had grown accustomed to her height and her solitary habits.

Teaching Sunday school at the Peace and Goodwill Bible Baptist Church during the school year and working at Gabrielle's Tea Garden in the summers made up for Nick's anonymity at school. The five- and six-year-olds at church adored her, and practically everyone in Nevada City knew her. She did, after all, work at Gabrielle's, and she was Gabrielle Weatherspoon's great-niece.

Absorbed as she was in her varied activities, Nicolette didn't even notice when she outgrew her awkward adolescence and became a young woman of enviable and quite unconscious grace. She finally stopped growing at five feet eleven. By that time, her mother reported, the ladies in the Missionary Sewing Support Circle at church had determined that Nick was capital-lettered Something Special: "Your Nicolette is just the Cat's Pajamas," Mrs. Philpott would say, clicking her knitting needles for emphasis. "A Real Beauty, that one—inside and out," Mrs. Jenkins agreed. "Like the Queen of May," Mrs. Hughley declared.

"What do you *say*, Mom?" Nick asked, embarrassed.

"I'm modest. I tell them you're very special to us."

She was. Nicolette never had any doubts about that. But she hadn't been special to a *man* until Tom Robison. It was a nice feeling. Now that she'd had it, she didn't want to do without. Tom would come around, she told herself. He *had* to.

"Lettie Weatherspoon?"

She pulled herself from her reverie to focus on the man pushing toward her through the throng of travelers. He *did* look like a teddy bear, she thought with delight. Soft, furry, and comfortable. His dark hair was curly, his gray-streaked beard neatly trimmed, and his chocolate brown eyes, exactly at her level, bright with warmth and humor. He wore a bulky wool fisherman's sweater with baggy cotton Dockers and Birkenstocks with bulky socks.

"You must be Parker." She smiled in automatic response to his pleasant expression. "I'm Nicolette. Gran-Gabby calls me Lettie, but I go by Nick." Setting her laptop on the floor between her feet, she reached to shake his hand. His short, blunt fingers wrapped warmly around her long ones. A nice handshake, she thought—respectful and gentle.

He picked up the computer and took her portfolio in his other hand as they made their way down the concourse toward baggage claim. "You write under Lettie," he said.

"My professional persona. It seemed to fit. You must have children," she added. "Grown-ups don't usually know about my books otherwise."

He raised a shaggy eyebrow. "Are you being modest or do you really believe that?" Without waiting for an answer, he added, "But you're right, I have a daughter. She lives with her mother in San Francisco during the school year, except for the weekends I get her."

"It was awfully nice of you to come pick me up so late on a Sunday night. Thank you."

He shifted the portfolio under his arm. "My pleasure. Actually, I've been to the city today. I might have left a little sooner if Miss Gabby hadn't asked me to pick you up, but it was really no problem."

Parker talked Nick into stopping at a coffee shop before they left the airport. He needed a caffeine fix before the last leg of the trip, he told her. He'd already driven the three hours from Nevada City to San Francisco today, returning Angel to her mother, and then another two hours from there back to Sacramento.

What he *really* wanted was an opportunity to study Nicolette Weatherspoon in more detail. All in innocence, he told himself. He knew that Lettie—Nick—had a serious boyfriend in Seattle, though Miss Gabby had told him the relationship was "unsettled" right now. He couldn't be faulted for wanting to enjoy the company of a pretty woman, could he? It didn't mean he planned to muscle in on another man's territory.

Parker frowned and shook his head at the idea, wondering where it had come from. Normally he considered himself a sensitive, nineties kind of guy, with more than a reasonable measure of empathy for women's issues. If Nick were anything like her great-aunt, she'd spit fire at being referred to as someone's "territory." Primal instincts must die hard, he thought.

He was unquestionably taken with the lanky, loose-boned woman whose fringe of wispy bangs framed the most beautiful blue eyes he'd ever seen, as wide as a wondering child's and the color of cornflowers. The short, casual style of her shiny, brown-gold hair accentuated her prominent cheekbones and a nineteenth-century sort of mouth, the kind that used to be called a cupid's bow. She had an *interesting* face, lovely for its uniqueness rather than conformity to an artificial standard of beauty.

Sipping at his coffee, he watched her as she approached their table from the ladies' room. She was casually and unpretentiously elegant, with a fluid, graceful stride that moved him in ways he'd almost forgotten. She wore a tapestry vest over a deeply ruffled white blouse, which was tucked into comfortably faded blue jeans. Her shoes were classic cordovan penny loafers. Topping the outfit was a brown tweed blazer that might have been a man's. He wondered fleetingly if it had once belonged to the boyfriend Miss Gabby had told him about.

She sat down across from him, stretching her arms back and rolling her head. He silently sympathized, remembering the kinks his last plane trip had ironed in.

A puzzled frown appeared between the woman's brows. "What? Lipstick on my teeth?"

Parker laughed. "No. Sorry if I'm gawking. It's just that I've never seen such big blue eyes." After a moment's hesitation he added lightly, "I'm warning you, I could fall in love with those eyes." He held his breath, wondering if he'd been too forward. It had been a long time since he'd practiced flirting.

Nick took the compliment in stride, although her cheeks pinkened. "I wouldn't advise it," she teased. "I'm spoken for." She paused. "Well—sort of."

He wrapped his big hands around the ceramic coffee mug. "Yeah. I might as well tell you, your great-aunt told me the story. She doesn't think much of your suitor."

Nicolette sighed. "I know. It's my fault. She's never met him, and I only talk to her about him when things aren't going well. How could she possibly have a good opinion?" She sipped at her coffee. "How is Gran-Gabby, by the way?"

"Said her throat was ticklish this morning at breakfast." He stroked his gray-flecked beard and grinned. "But not so ticklish she couldn't tell me all about your troubles with your man."

"He's really very nice," Nick said quickly. "Just not sure he's ready for commitment. You know—that *man* thing."

Parker raised his eyebrows. "*Some* men. We're not all alike, you know." He motioned for a waitress to refill his coffee cup. "Besides," he said when she'd refreshed his coffee and moved away again, "there *are* women who have a hard time committing."

"You're probably right. To tell the truth, I don't have that much experience. Tom's my standard because he's the only boyfriend I've ever had."

He looked at her quizzically. "You mean *serious* boyfriend."

"I mean *boyfriend*. Period."

"And you've been dating him how long?"

"Three years."

Parker emptied a creamer into his coffee and added sugar from the glass shaker on the table. "I find it hard to believe you never had a boyfriend till three years ago," he said, clinking his spoon against the sides of the cup as he stirred.

She bristled. "Why? You don't think a woman can make it without a man?"

"Of course I do!" He was surprised at her quick, prickly response. "It's just that you're so—beautiful, and smart, and creative, and—*interesting*. You seem the type who'd have *lots* of boyfriends."

Nick's irritation dissolved. She smiled at him, a white, even smile that nearly took his breath away. "Parker, I'm warning you—I could fall in love with your flattery!"

He lifted one shaggy eyebrow and parroted her earlier teasing remark: "I wouldn't advise it!"

"Oh? Are *you* spoken for?"

He shook his head. "Not for six years now," he said. "*Not* a fear of commitment thing," he added quickly. "I had a hard time when my wife—Marci—left. Guess I haven't been ready to try again." His fingers began an unconscious tattoo against the side of his cup. He hadn't talked about his divorce in a long time and suddenly found himself wanting to, though he didn't quite know how. *How curious that I feel so comfortable with her,* he thought, *and at the same time so wonderfully* alive.

Nick finished the last of her coffee and placed her hand over the cup as the waitress walked by with a steaming pot.

"Finished?" Parker asked. "Let's hit the road." He drained his coffee cup and scooted out of the booth, reaching into his back pocket for his wallet and dropping three one-dollar bills on the table. Reaching down, he clasped Nick's hand and helped her out of her seat. Her fingers were long and slim and cool. Artist's fingers.

"How do you know my great-aunt?" Nick asked as he helped her into his vintage Jeep Wagoneer a few minutes later.

"She didn't tell you? That's a surprise, for Miss Gabby." He closed her door and hurried around to the driver's seat, answering her question as he pulled out of the parking space. "I

37

bought out Easychair Books nine months ago, across the courtyard from Gabrielle's Tea Garden." He pulled up to the toll booth and handed over the parking fee.

"Oh, the used-book store in the old carriage house! I've always loved that place. I hope you dust more often than Mr. Jepperson did. Paper dust makes me sneeze."

Parker changed lanes to follow the signs for Interstate 80 toward Reno. "Old books are pretty dusty," he hedged.

Nick laughed, a deep, robust chuckle that suited her exactly, Parker thought.

"In other words, no," she said. "Oh, well. I guess the thrill of discovery makes old-book dust bearable. Finding a first edition Arthur Rackham Peter Pan portfolio—the signed and numbered Hodder and Stoughton edition—would be well worth a sneeze or two." She sighed rapturously. "It's *historical* dust, after all."

Parker felt unaccountably pleased. "You really do know something about old books!"

"A little. I have my favorites," she answered modestly. "I'd like to know more. I'll probably be in your store every waking minute I'm not helping out Gran-Gabby."

His heart jumped unexpectedly at the thought. *Careful, Parker,* he told himself. *Don't even think about it. The woman already has a man in her life.* He glanced at her darkened profile across the cab. "You're welcome anytime," he said, keeping his voice neutral. Then, teasing, he added, "Feel free to bring your dust rag!"

"Right. Sounds like *my* idea of fun," she said dryly. In a more thoughtful tone of voice she added, "So Gran-Gabby's your landlord.... Has she told you more about me than vice versa?" she asked curiously.

"Talks about you all the time, Lettie—I'm sorry, *Nick.* Might take me some time to get used to that name, after hearing

'Lettie this' and 'Lettie that' for months." He grinned in the dark. "And I do mean she talks about you *all the time*. Little things, usually. If we're in the foyer at Gabrielle's it's, 'Lettie used to dust the banister by sliding down it every day.' If she invites me for tea it's, 'Lettie was always my best cookie baker.' If she visits me in the bookstore it's, 'Do you have any of Lettie's books in this week?'"

"We don't call her 'Gabby' for nothing," Nick said. Parker couldn't read her tone.

He shrugged. "Characters get away with things us ordinary people don't. And even *you* have to admit Miss Gabby's a top-drawer character."

"Just remember to take everything Gran-Gabby tells you with a grain of salt," Nick advised as Parker maneuvered the interchange from Interstate 80 to Highway 49 toward Grass Valley. He reached forward to close the center vent. The in-flowing air was getting cooler as the old wagon began to climb the foothills of the Sierra Nevadas.

"She does tend to exaggerate, doesn't she? She must have been a kick to live with as a kid," he said. "I know my daughter, Angel, adores her."

Nick jerked her head around. "Angel? Did you say Angel?"

He glanced over at her in surprise. "Yeah, Angel. Angela. Why?"

"And she lives in San Francisco?"

"Except when she's with me."

"Parker—" Nick sputtered. "What's your last name?"

"I never said? How rude of me! McPhee. Part of the McPherson clan."

Nick's voice sparkled with laughter. "Parker McPhee! I can't believe it! Parker McPhee—I *know* you!"

He blinked in confusion. "I think I missed something. You mean Miss Gabby's gabbed about me after all?"

"Gran-Gabby might have mentioned you a time or two, now that I think about it. But she's not how I *know* you, Parker."

She sounded absolutely delighted, he thought, his curiosity roused. "Just what is it you think you know about me, Miss Weatherspoon?"

"Well, let's see. You're thirty-nine years old, divorced six years. Nine-year-old daughter Angela, better known as Angel, who thinks you're the best dad in the whole wide world." She ticked off each detail on her fingers. "You like cats, old books, thrift store shopping, going for walks, and building stuff. All of which we have in common, by the way, except for building stuff. I write books instead."

"You know Angel!" Parker was grinning in the dark like the Cheshire cat. "How in the world did you meet?"

"We haven't. She's my biggest fan and my most faithful correspondent. She's sent me a letter every week since—hmm, mid-September, I think. I can't believe it! And she must know Gran-Gabby—I'm surprised she's never said."

"She knows Miss Gabby, all right. Tight as crossed fingers, the two of them are." Parker scratched his beard in puzzlement. "I can't believe she's never mentioned to me that she's been writing you. You're her favorite author, you know. She wants to be a writer, too, someday."

"She already is. She's sent me some of her stories."

"She has!" He felt a little hurt. "I just can't believe she hasn't told me. We don't have secrets—or at least I *thought* we didn't."

"It probably just never came up," Nick tried to console him. "You don't see her much during the school year, after all. The first letter was for a school assignment, I think she said—she had to write to an author. I sent off a dutiful reply and the next thing I knew, we were writing back and forth every week. Angel's quite precocious," she added. "I'm really sorry I missed her visit."

Parker's hurt fell away as pride colored his voice. "She's a special child," he agreed. "And if you're still around in about three weeks you'll get to meet her."

"Wonderful! Is she coming for the holidays?"

"Not for Christmas Day, unfortunately. Marci's turn." He knew his voice sounded sad. "I really miss her when she's not around."

"I can imagine," Nick responded sympathetically.

"I worried the divorce and the traveling between her mother's house and mine would make her insecure, but she's remarkably well-adjusted." He hesitated. "I'm curious to know what Angel's told you about the divorce, Nick. If you don't think it's breaking a confidence."

"Not at all. It's probably the only thing I *don't* know about you. You're the hero in most of her stories, you know. I even know you're very particular about your toast—wheat at breakfast, with real butter and whipped clover honey, and sourdough for snacks, with old-style chunky peanut butter, blackberry jam, and a glass of buttermilk to wash it down." She made a face.

Parker shook his head ruefully. "Some hero! I'm embarrassed, Nick. Does she write at all about her mother?"

"Only that she remarried a man who doesn't like kids all that much. Angel says he makes an exception for her, but he definitely doesn't want any other kids around. She wants a baby brother quite badly, you know."

"She *does?*"

"Oh dear. She hasn't told you that, either."

Parker was quiet for a moment. "I wanted her to have a baby brother," he finally said. "Always wanted a passel of kids. And I thought...actually...I mean..." He cleared his throat. "Marci wasn't happy in the marriage, and I thought another baby might...help things out. We had a horrible fight when I

41

suggested it—we couldn't afford it, she said, and we'd never be able to afford it because I didn't have enough *ambition*." He paused, as if remembering still hurt him. "You might have noticed I'm not exactly the dress-for-success type," he added.

"So what? I like the way you dress," Nick returned. "You're very—*approachable*."

"Yeah. Well." He paused. "I didn't know it then, but Marci was already seeing William."

"The William who doesn't like kids."

"That's the one. They were married the day after our divorce was final." He sighed. "William is definitely ambitious. A much better catch for Marci than I was. They're happy, I think." He paused again. "We're civil, mostly for Angel's sake, but I can't say as I like William a whole lot," he confessed.

"I should think not."

They were silent for a moment before Parker added, "The man does know how to attract money, though. I'll give him that. Sometimes I think I'm jealous." Once more he sighed. "If William had opened a bookstore, it'd be a chain called Mega-Books with outlets in every mall in the state. He'd have gone public, and the shares would've tripled in value by now."

"Is that what *you* want?" Nick asked.

"No. All I've ever wanted is a family, a little store of my own, and a house with a big shop to putter around in. With Angel, Easychair Books, and my garage at home in the woods, I have as much as a man could wish for." *Almost,* he added in his mind as he turned and caught Nick's approving expression. She really *did* have the most beautiful eyes....

"Well, then," Nick said with finality, as if that settled it.

CHAPTER

Four

Monday after Thanksgiving

In Nick's childhood memories, the trip from the airport in Sacramento to her great-aunt's house in the foothills of the Sierra Nevadas was very long, but the drive tonight seemed over almost before it had begun. Parker was good company— so *comfortable,* she thought.

They both fell silent as they passed Grass Valley, slumbering beside the highway at this early morning hour, and traveled the last wooded miles through Brunswick Basin and over the final hill before Nevada City's Broad Street exit.

The town, bathed in the silver glow of moonlight, looked like a village in a fairy tale or a child's dream. Parker slowed the Jeep through town as Nick counted off her favorite landmarks: first the historic National Hotel, an old brick building with classic revival ornamentation; Confectionately Yours, the candy store on the corner of Broad and Pine, located in another brick building with wrought iron rails on the veranda over the sidewalk; the domed tin roof of Bonanza Market just past City Hall, and the clapboard New York Hotel across the street, now housing high-rent retail stores; the Nevada Theatre, where Mark Twain, Jack

London, and Emma Nevada had all appeared during the city's heyday; the old brick firehouse, its white belltower glowing dimly against the dark sky; and finally, Gabrielle's Tea Garden, sitting on the ridge overlooking the town.

Nick sat motionless even after Parker had turned off the engine at the top of the hill, her breath caught in wonder at the sight of the big house that held so many vivid memories for her. The inky sky above it was bleached to indigo by the glow of thousands of twinkling lights delineating the wide porch and the windows and gables and braided around the trellis over the courtyard like a garland of tiny white flowers.

Warm, inviting light glinted through the shutters of one upstairs room and lit up the stained glass over the front doorway, the image of an angel in flowing robes of crimson and white trumpeting good will to all who chose to enter. A spotlight illuminated the familiar black-and-gold-lettered sign swinging from its post in front of the elegant house, the sign Nick had designed and painted for the restaurant's twenty-fifth anniversary in business: *Gabrielle's Tea Garden* in flowing script, arched over a gilt angel like the stained glass seraph guarding the doorway.

Parker helped her with her bags and waited with her quietly in the circle of the porch light as the doorbell rang through the old house. Nick pushed aside the beribboned cedar swag hanging over the window of the front door to peek into the foyer. Dark wood glowed in the yellow light. The mahogany banister of the grand staircase shone as if it had just been polished.

Gold embroidered slippers and the hem of an emerald silk dressing gown appeared on the stairs and descended.

In a moment Nick was smiling through the glass at Gran-Gabby's dear face. The old woman's eyes were as piercing as she remembered, her hair a cloud of blue-tinted gray around a handsome, patrician face that might have been described as haughty except for the hint of mischief that played around her mouth.

Nick felt as if she was home again.

She woke the next morning to a sharp rap and opened her eyes to see her great-aunt poking her head through the crack at the bedroom door, her dark eyes sparkling. "Lettie? You're not still *sleeping?*"

Groaning, Nick pulled herself up against the carved head-board as Gran-Gabby pushed the door open with her hip and carried a loaded tray across the room to the nightstand next to the four poster. Steam rose from the spout of a delicate china teapot decorated with sprigs of violets. Nick's mouth began to water at the sight of strawberry jam and Devonshire cream in crystal dishes; she knew the basket next to the teapot hid hot, flaky scones.

"Who, me?" she answered groggily. "Nothing a hot scone and a cuppa can't handle. Will you join me?"

"Dear me, no, I've got breakfast guests in the restaurant to take care of!" The old woman unfurled the napkin over the basket with a flourish. "Sweet lemon scones," she said. "Tea's Earl Grey." She leaned over to pat Nick's cheek. "Seems to me a girl I knew *loved* lemon scones and Earl Grey tea." She poured the steaming tea into a china cup patterned with yellow rosebuds as she continued to talk, barely stopping long enough to catch her breath. "Take your time, Lettie. Only morning you'll be getting breakfast in bed."

"But Gran-Gabby," Nick finally got a word in edgewise. "I thought you were sick!" She struggled with the blankets and swung her feet over the edge of the bed as her great-aunt added cream and sugar to her tea. The bed was so high off the ground that even her long legs failed to reach the floor. The sensation was disorienting, as if she had shrunk like Alice in Wonderland after she'd taken a bite of the magic mushroom. She slid to the floor and pulled the white chenille robe off the bedpost and over her shoulders. "You go lie down, Gran-Gabby—I'll be ready in no time—"

Her great-aunt waved a hand. "Oh, pshaw!" She was the only person Nick had ever known outside the comic strips who actually said 'pshaw.' "That was Thanksgiving, four days ago! Just a little sniffle. Healthy as a horse. Now *you're* the one needs taking care of, seems to me."

"Gran-Gabby!" Nick interrupted sternly. "Have you gotten me here under false pretenses?"

"And what if I have?" her great-aunt huffed. "Only way I thought you'd come. Not good for you, moping around up there in the rain while what's-his-name makes up his mind whether or not he wants to marry you."

"Tom," Nick supplied automatically.

"Tom," Gran-Gabby repeated scornfully. "*Tom!* Why, that's a name for a *turkey!*"

Nick hooted with laughter. She ought to have been insulted, at least for Tom's sake; she ought to have been irritated by her great-aunt's deception. But she couldn't bring herself to it. The truth was, she'd much rather be here in Nevada City, arguing cheerfully with her great-aunt, than "moping around" in Seattle. Gran-Gabby was right.

She threw back her head, still sputtering with laughter, and swept her hand across her brow in a dramatic gesture. "Go on then," she said. "See to your guests. Let me languish alone in my misery!"

Gran-Gabby stared at her suspiciously, arms akimbo as she rested her hands on her bony hips. "Laugh if you will! Seems to me if the man can't make up his mind, he doesn't deserve you, Lettie." She shook her head emphatically. "Not one little bit." She swept across the room and out the door, regal in dark, pleated slacks and a lace-trimmed blouse, with her smoke-blue hair perfectly coiffed. An instant later she popped her head back around the corner. "What do you think of Parker?"

Nick blinked. "Parker? He's very nice."

Gran-Gabby nodded in satisfaction. "Didn't I tell you?" Then she was gone.

Nick stared at the door as it closed, dazed by her great-aunt's brash energy and puzzled by her last comment. Flopping back on the bed and closing her eyes, she tried to recall what her great-aunt had told her about Parker. Something was niggling in her memory, something more than the teddy bear description, but she couldn't think what.

Thoughts of Parker disappeared as she slathered a flaky scone with jam and Devonshire cream and sipped at her tea. No one baked scones like Gran-Gabby.

Or had a tongue like Gran-Gabby. Her great-aunt's low opinion of Tom really was Nick's fault. How could she blame Gran-Gabby for verbalizing what Nick sometimes wondered herself? Maybe his inability to make a commitment to her *was* a sign he didn't love her as much as she thought he did....

She pulled a shade over the thought as soon as it entered her mind. Of course Tom loved her. Why else would he still be hanging around?

Nick hadn't dated much in high school or even college. By the time she'd outgrown her insecurities enough that she might actually have enjoyed it, she was teaching first grade. Elementary schools weren't exactly hopping with men, let alone interesting, available men. After ten years, she'd quit teaching to write full-time at home, where the odds of finding an agreeable companion were even worse.

Tom Robison owned, among other businesses, Rainbow Press, which published Nick's *Gabby and the Magic Teapot* series. The dashing young businessman who'd been on Seattle's "Most Eligible Bachelors" list since he was twenty-five—fifteen years—was the first man who'd openly pursued her, and she hadn't even tried to resist. He was almost too perfect, a big, blond, blue-eyed Scandinavian god of a man, a good six inches taller than Nick; eminently successful; a bit arrogant, with a slightly cynical sense of humor.

Tom owed much of his success in publishing to Nick's *Gabby* books, a point which he conceded with such winsome charm the first time they'd met she couldn't possibly say no when he asked her to be his date for a prestigious charity dinner. In Seattle society's eyes, they'd been a couple ever since—a "stunning couple," as they'd been called more than once.

They'd been dating off and on over the last three years—the "offs" being the times Nick had hinted a little too openly for Tom's comfort that she wanted more from him, and the "ons" when she'd backed off and resigned herself to having only the parts of him he was willing to give.

For better or worse, she'd put an end to that, she thought with resignation. With their Thanksgiving confrontation, she'd either feathered her nest or cooked her goose. At the moment, she hadn't the faintest notion which.

By the time Nick had finished her breakfast tea, showered and dressed for the day, and called to leave a message with Tom's secretary that she'd made it safely to Nevada City, it was after nine o'clock. She balanced the tray with the empty teapot and dishes as she descended the gracefully curving stairs, almost running over Parker as she reached the bottom. With his beard and curly hair and dressed in jeans and a plaid flannel shirt, he looked as if he were born to the mountains.

"Morning, Nick!" He hurriedly slipped his newspaper under his arm and reached for her tray. "Let me get that for you." Stepping around the cash register, he headed for the kitchen with Nick close behind. "How long did you say it's been since you've been back to Nevada City?" he asked over his shoulder.

"Four years." Parker was moving around the restaurant with the familiarity of an employee, Nick noticed with surprise. "Gran-Gabby lets you have the run of the place?" she asked as she followed him through the swinging doors.

"I've done some work for Miss Gabby over the last few months—minor repairs, building shelves—that sort of thing. She pays me in meals. I must say I think I get the better part of the deal." He emptied the tray in the dishwashing area and turned to lean against the stainless steel counter. "So, what are you up to today?"

"I'm not sure. I was on my way to find Gran-Gabby for instructions."

"Have you looked around the place yet?"

"Not yet."

"Good!" Parker grabbed her hand and pulled her toward the hallway. "Miss Gabby and Angel and I spent Thanksgiving weekend decorating for Christmas. Come see!"

Gran-Gabby had done an outstanding job remodeling the grand old family home when she'd first opened the restaurant more than twenty-five years ago. The entire rear third of the first floor had been gutted and redone as a roomy, industrial kitchen; its swinging doors opened onto a central hallway leading to a dining room on each side and the foyer and staircase in front. The rooms shared hardwood floors, white lace curtains at the windows, and coordinating color schemes, but each had a distinctive theme and character. The solarium, which could be reached either through the kitchen, the smaller of the dining rooms, or the courtyard, housed a third dining area.

Swags of cedar with deep red bows and gold garlands decorated the floral-papered walls of the hallway. It was so much fun to be here, Nick thought, in the rooms where she'd worked every summer from the time she was fourteen till she'd finished her teaching degree at twenty-one. In many ways, Gabrielle's Tea Garden had been the mise-en-scéne of her growing up. *If she could consider herself as grown-up*—which she usually did, Tom's recent characterization notwithstanding.

Parker led her first into the elegant Victorian Room. The most formal of the dining rooms featured paneled wainscoting, a large, marble-tiled fireplace with a carved mantel, and built-in china closets, all in a rich mahogany finish. A beveled mirror over the mantel reflected a row of white poinsettias in gold foil pots. Pine wreaths hung at intervals along the walls, which were painted a heathery green above the wainscoting.

Parker pointed to the shelf that ran around the room below the coved ceiling. "When Miss Gabby decided to add the retail business, she needed more display space. She remembered that when she was a girl, there were plate rails in most of the rooms. It seemed the logical way to add shelving without destroying the integrity of the architecture."

"Retail business?" Nick asked blankly. She looked around. The china closet and the high shelves were artfully arranged with beautiful bone china teapots and teacups.

"You didn't know? Last summer, after all these years, she realized that coming to Gabrielle's is an *event* for people, not just a meal, and that they might want to take home a souvenir or two. Expensive souvenirs, if you ask me, but she's done well with it."

Nick shook her head in amazement. At an age when most people would have been content to sit in a rocking chair on the front porch, Gran-Gabby wasn't even ready to slow down. At seventy-six, she was still thinking innovatively and moving forward with new ideas for the business.

"She's quite the woman, my Gran-Gabby," she said, a mixture of pride and wonder in her voice.

"D'you like the tree?" Parker asked. "All three of us worked on this one." A tall evergreen reaching nearly to the ceiling rose from a stand in a corner, filling the room with its fragrance. Burgundy and gold moiré bows, strands of gold beads, white candle-shaped lights, and angel ornaments adorned its branches. A Victorian angel with golden wings outspread hovered at its tip.

"It's so *elegant*. This house is perfect for Victorian Christmas," Nicolette responded, turning in a circle to take in the rest of the room. White lace cloths draped the round tables over solid-color linens in claret, navy, and forest green, colors derived from the rich Oriental rug underfoot. Tall white tapers rose from crystal candlesticks in the center of each table, surrounded by simple but attractive arrangements of evergreen boughs, strands of gold beads, and shiny red apples.

Grabbing Nick's shoulders from behind, Parker guided her across the hall to Gabby's Room, the preferred dining room for children's teas. The room was named after Great-Aunt Gabrielle herself, whose childhood stories had in turn inspired Nick's *Gabby and the Magic Teapot* books. Nick smiled to see that a framed and matted colored-pencil drawing of a little girl riding a teapot, her first illustration for her children's series, hung in a place of honor on the wall.

The tables were covered in a pink-and-white striped fabric, while a cotton rag rug in bright yellows, pinks, blues, and greens rippled across the floor like a field of grass and wildflowers. White woodwork contrasted with bright, cheerful wallpaper in a pattern of yellow and pink cabbage roses on robin's egg blue. A wide, pink-and-white striped border circled the room beneath the plate shelf, which was crowded with exquisite porcelain dolls, fuzzy teddy bears, and whimsical animal teapots.

"Angel decorated this tree all by herself," Parker said proudly, pointing to the small evergreen sitting on an old wooden tea cart in the corner of the room. Its branches were laden with fresh cranberry and popcorn garlands and antique children's toys. "I tried to help her string popcorn, but she shooed me off. Said I was eating too much."

Nicolette sighed in mock sympathy. "Ungrateful child! Only adds to the injury that she did such nice work without you, doesn't it?"

Parker scratched his beard, his eyes glinting with good humor. "You've got it. Sometimes I just *hate* how fast she's growing up!"

Nick nodded, her sympathy real this time. "I'll bet she's not too old to love this room, though. Gran-Gabby's done a great job giving it that Alice-in-Wonderland kind of feel."

"Miss Gabby had some special tea in this room last summer, just for little girls and their favorite dolls, no grown-ups allowed. Angel was delighted."

"Ah, yes, the 'Dolly and Me Summer Tea,'" Nick said, remembering the ones she'd served. "I wonder if Gran-Gabby still has her 'Teddy Bear Tea' in the summer. I always thought it was so weird, when I was a teenager, to see grown-ups get all dressed up and bring their teddy bears to tea!"

"She does. And it *is* weird! Who'd have thought grown-ups would be caught dead having a meal with a *teddy bear*? I can tell you no *man* would," Parker said with conviction.

Nicolette laughed. "Men have more expensive, grown-up toys," she said, thinking about the quadraphonic surround-sound stereo system in Tom's new Lexus.

Parker looked as though he meant to protest but thought better of it. "I'm not sure I can disagree," he answered noncommittally as he followed her into the sunny Garden Room in the solarium, the primary breakfast room in the restaurant. And a business conference room, it looked like this morning, Nick

52

thought as she glanced around. It seemed that every party had papers spread out on the table between the guests as they waited for their meals or finished up with a steaming cup of tea or a mug of strong coffee.

With its pleasant ambiance and a breakfast menu including conventional bacon and egg meals as well as cream teas with scones and exotic daily breakfast specials—asparagus-arugula fritatta today, the chalkboard indicated—Gabrielle's had developed a strong local breakfast clientele.

A jungle of houseplants, looking lush and healthy, hung from hooks in the sky-lighted ceiling or stood on the window ledges. The tables wore crisp white linen cloths over colorful flowered ones. Woven grass mats on the white-painted floor and narrow laths nailed against the dark green walls in a lattice pattern lent texture to the room.

French windows overlooked the trellis-shaded flagstone courtyard that provided additional seating during the summer, when the tourist trade regularly doubled the restaurant's winter guest count. The thick wisteria vines snaking through the lattice-work had been trimmed back in preparation for new spring growth when the weather warmed again.

The small Christmas tree on one of the tables was decorated entirely with gilded pine cones and fresh or dried fruit—pomegranates, sickle pears, orange slices, apple slices decorated with rosehips. "Let me guess," Nick said to Parker. "You painted the pine cones."

"Yep. What can I say? I'm a talented guy."

A retort was forming on her lips when a loud voice interrupted.

"There you are!"

Nick and Parker turned at the same time to see Gran-Gabby hurrying toward them.

Parker nodded politely. "Morning, Miss Gabby. Which one

of us you looking for?"

"The both of you together," she said tartly, a glint in her dark eyes.

CHAPTER

Five

❧

First Sunday of Advent

Gran-Gabby, Nick, and Parker had fallen into a pleasant daily routine of breakfast together at Gabrielle's Tea Garden before Parker left to open the bookstore at ten and Gran-Gabby put Nick to work.

Christmas inventory began arriving fast and furious. Although the retail business was new to Gabrielle's this year, Gran-Gabby was anticipating heavy gift sales, especially during the four days of Nevada City's Victorian Christmas celebration.

"Looks like you're optimistic," Nick had commented in a neutral tone as she surveyed the tower of boxes in the basement her first day. "Confident," Gran-Gabby replied shortly. Privately, Nick wondered if her great-aunt might have taken on more than she could handle with this retail enterprise.

Nick found herself buried in the basement most of that first week, carefully unpacking and checking the contents of the boxes delivered daily by the cheerful UPS delivery man: delicate china tea sets with Christmas designs; ceramic teapots shaped like Rudolph, his red-nosed muzzle the spout; brightly painted nutcrackers; beautifully detailed Victorian porcelain angels; exquisitely carved Father Christmas figures.

Each item had to be marked off on the packing list, checked for damage, cleaned, priced, and displayed somewhere on Parker's ever more crowded shelves in the dining rooms or on the temporary units Gran-Gabby had him install in the foyer. By Saturday, Nick had most of the Christmas stock out.

"Parker's taking us to church after breakfast," Gran-Gabby told her Sunday morning when she knocked to wake her. "Wear something suitable."

Nick felt her hackles rise—not that she didn't want to go to church or wear something Gran-Gabby would consider "suitable," for that matter. Weekly worship services were a regular part of Nick's life, refreshing her spirit as well as providing a chance to emerge from the solitude of her writing for a time of connection and community. She'd been cloistered in the basement or busy stocking shelves most of the week, and going to church with Parker and Gran-Gabby sounded—well, *appealing*.

No, it wasn't the idea of going to church that raised her hackles. It was her great-aunt's domineering manner. She didn't remember Gran-Gabby ever being quite so *bossy*. Several times this week already Nick had literally held her tongue between her teeth to keep from snapping at the old woman.

She did so once again, rejecting the "Says who?" at the tip of her tongue and asking instead, "What time is breakfast?"

Some things weren't worth arguing about.

Sunday morning dawned crisp and cold, and Parker woke exhilarated. After a brisk early morning walk along the irrigation flume behind his log cabin home off Red Dog Road, he joined Nick and Gran-Gabby at Gabrielle's for gingerbread waffles with peaches and whipped cream. He was undeniably enjoying this arrangement of being paid off in meals for his work around the restaurant. Especially now that Nick was here.

He helped Gran-Gabby into her coat at the end of the meal, watching Nick's graceful movements from the corner of an eye as she pulled her jacket over a narrow apricot-colored dress with an interesting textured trim on the yoke. The sapphire jacket made her eyes look even bluer, if such a thing were possible. Gold button earrings and low black pumps completed her elegant outfit.

A week of seeing Nick's face across the breakfast table every morning had made it quite clear to Parker how drawn he was to her cornflower eyes and to the buoyant spirit behind them, gazing out at the world with warmth and curiosity. Her eyes were like magnets, drawing him irresistibly, promising delights he dared not dwell on. She'd already given her heart to another man. Still, he didn't try to deny the pleasure he felt in her company.

To keep himself grounded, he made a point of asking her each time they met what she'd heard from Tom. Nick had told him that she e-mailed her boyfriend from Gran-Gabby's business computer every morning before breakfast. She said she'd realized that while "Absence makes the heart grow fonder," "Out of sight, out of mind," was another distinct possibility. Tom *always* checked his e-mail.

She purposely kept her messages to him light, she told Parker, relating one anecdote or another about her great-aunt— "Gabby-isms" she called them—and not asking much more than "How's business?" and "How are you and Mr. Tibbs getting on?" She was careful not to refer to her ultimatum. If there was anything Tom hated, she said, it was feeling pressured. She'd done enough of that.

From what Parker could deduce, Tom's e-mail responses were short and business-like. He, too, studiously avoided reference to their future together. "Mr. Tibbs is out of grace," he wrote instead. "Bit me when I tried to pick him up this morning. Don't know what's got into him."

"Tom will miss me this morning," Nick told Parker confidently as he led her and Miss Gabby across the street to the lot where he'd parked the Wagoneer. "We always go to church together on Sundays."

The wrench to Parker's gut was stronger than he expected; he wondered if the pang registered on his face. Miss Gabby's lips were pressed together in a grim line, as if she were afraid she might say more than she wanted to. Nick didn't seem to notice.

"I think you'll like New Hope, Nick," Parker said, for once purposely steering the conversation away from Tom. He helped Miss Gabby into the front passenger seat of the Jeep. "Unless you're used to church being a big production?" Parker's inflection made the comment a question.

She shook her head. *"Used* to it, maybe. Not really *comfortable*. I've been going to Tom's church the last couple of years—one of those places the size of a small city where the service is telecast on cable every Sunday morning." She climbed into the back seat as Parker held the door for her, then reached over to unlock the driver's door.

"You can't even sing if you're not a professional—they hold weekly auditions for the musical numbers," she went on as Parker climbed in and slid the key in the ignition. "And sometimes the sermons seem more like exhibitions of oratory skill than messages from God."

"Doesn't sound as if you like it all that much," Parker said, turning to look over the seat as he backed out of the parking space. Nick leaned out of his way. "Why do you go there?" he asked, curious.

"Oh, a lot of people important to Tom's business go there; it's a good place for him to network."

Something in Parker's expression must have communicated his astonishment, because she added quickly, "It's not so bad—the teaching's good, and I keep reminding myself God is just as much there as he is at the Peace and Goodwill Bible Baptist Church where I grew up. Mount Olivet just feels more like a television studio than a church sometimes. For all the warmth and fellowship, we might as well be curled up on the sofa at home watching the service on TV!"

"If it's warmth and fellowship you're missing, you'll *really* like New Hope," Parker said, relieved that Nick's motives for attending church weren't as mercenary as they'd first sounded, even if Tom's might be. He was really beginning to dislike this boyfriend of hers.

"And Pastor Foley," he added hurriedly, wanting to rid himself of the ungracious thought. "No performance with him— just practical, down-to-earth insights from his own walk with God. A regular kind of guy who doesn't pretend he's farther along his spiritual journey than he really is, and reminds his congregation all the time he's learning right along with the rest of us. He's starting a series today on 'The Miracles of Christmas.'" Parker slowed and switched on his turn signal as he approached an intersection.

Miss Gabby, who'd remained uncharacteristically quiet up till now, broke into the conversation with a loud snort. "Miracles! You young people don't know a miracle from a hole in the ground," she said crossly. "Always looking for the grand gesture and ignoring the little things! Can't you see every *day's* a miracle? Being able to get out of bed in the morning. Sunshine and rain. The *christollen* rising like it's supposed to. Babies are a miracle. *Love's* a miracle."

Parker raised his bushy eyebrows, startled by her sudden, seemingly irrelevant tirade. "Yes...," he said slowly. "I don't think Pastor Foley would argue with that...."

Nick leaned over the seat and put her arms around her great-aunt's neck. Parker glanced over to see an impish expression on her face. "I think I hear someone who's feeling quite crabby," she recited in a sing-song voice. "Don't tell the wide world, but I think it's Gran-Gabby."

The old woman sniffed. "Watch where you're steppin', you impudent urchin, or where you was walkin' you soon will be lurchin'!"

Parker groaned theatrically. "Help me! I'm locked in the car with two crazies!" He paused for a moment, thinking hard, while the women looked at him expectantly. "Unless I escape, I'll be pushing up daisies!"

Miss Gabby allowed herself a smile as Nick laughed, the deep sound rolling pleasantly through the wagon, and clapped in delight. "Not bad, McPhee. Not bad at all," she said gleefully. "Maybe the three of us should co-author Lettie Weatherspoon's next book."

Parker pulled into the church lot and found a space for the old Jeep. "Maybe so." He grinned at Miss Gabby, who was eyeing him with a replica of the impish expression he'd seen on Nick's face just a few minutes earlier. When their eyes met, she dropped hers to fiddle with her seatbelt release. "Don't think you need me in on it." She looked sideways at Parker. "Seems to me Lettie's met her match."

Pulling the key from the ignition, he turned around to smile at Nick in the back seat. He didn't know how she'd done it—so quickly flipped her great-aunt's ill humor on end—but she had.

Nick winked. His heart jumped, as if pulled by a string.

Parker had been right about New Hope Community Church, Nick thought. The people were warm and friendly, the atmosphere relaxed and comfortable. Pastor Foley was an older man with gray hair and glasses and a deep, dramatic voice that boomed through the small chapel.

One of the sopranos in the choir squeaked on a high note

during the call to worship, but later when the group sang "Come, Thou Long-Expected Jesus," the descant was perfect, the same soprano voice soaring effortlessly. The congregation sang loudly and joyously when it was their turn: *"Angels from the realms of glory, wing your flight o'er all the earth…"*

Nick always felt a bit timid about singing at Mount Olivet Bible Temple in Seattle. She wasn't sure if it was the maze of microphones and video cameras or Tom's cynical remarks about people who belted out the hymns "as if they thought they could sing." At any rate, she didn't feel at all shy about belting out the hymns herself this morning. *"Come adore on bended knee, Christ, the Lord, the newborn king,"* she sang, her heart stirring with unaccountable happiness. *"Gloria in excelsis Deo!"*

Pastor Foley's sermon—the miracle with which he was beginning his Advent series—was from the first chapter of Luke, the story of the birth of John the Baptist to the priest Zechariah and his wife Elizabeth.

"They had no children," the minister read from his Bible, "because Elizabeth was barren; and they were both well along in years…."

Nick shifted in her seat, her mind jumping ahead in the familiar story. When she'd started getting those letters from Parker's daughter in September—when Angel's longing for a baby sister or brother had fanned the flames of Nick's own desire for a child—a similar story had come to mind: Abraham and Sarah. Sometimes, defiantly, Nick had told her image in the bathroom mirror, "Sarah gave birth to Isaac when she was a hundred years old!" The crow's feet around the eyes gazing back at her hadn't discouraged her. But the resignation in the eyes themselves had.

Sarah had Abraham, the wide blue eyes reminded her. *You have Tom.* Tom Robison, who like Abraham was a leader of men, but who didn't seem particularly interested in becoming even a husband, let alone a father of nations....

"Do not be afraid, Zechariah," Pastor Foley was reading. "Your prayer has been heard."

Your prayer has been heard, Nick repeated to herself. Elizabeth would bear a son.

"So there's hope for me yet," Gran-Gabby whispered loudly. She leaned in front of Nick. "Parker McPhee, I'd be honored if you'd father my children. Will you marry me?"

Parker's face went instantly red.

"Gran-Gabby!" Nick whispered fiercely, embarrassed. "Behave!"

The old woman settled back into the pew with a satisfied smile. Nick leaned toward Parker. "Is Gran-Gabby acting a little strange, or is it just me?" she whispered.

"It's *not* just you," he whispered back, his brow creasing in concern. "Has she been to see her doctor lately?"

"Says she's healthy as a horse." Nick made a mental note to suggest, as gently as possible, that her great-aunt pay a visit to Dr. Middleton.

"He will be a joy and delight to you," the minister's words broke into her thoughts, "and many will rejoice because of his birth."

He will be a joy and delight to you, Nick repeated in her mind. A pang of intense longing unexpectedly gripped her heart and then released, leaving her weak.

Pastor Foley continued to read the passage, his resonant voice echoing in the sanctuary. Instructions to the parents. Predictions about the child. Zechariah's doubt: "I am an old man...." The asking for a sign.

"I am Gabriel," the minister thundered dramatically. "I stand in the presence of God, and I have been sent to speak to you and to tell you this good news. And now you will be silent and not able to speak until the day this happens, because you did not believe my words, which will come true at their proper time."

Nick chewed unconsciously at her lower lip. *My words will come true at their proper time,* she reflected. *Your prayer has been heard....*

For months she'd been praying. For this very thing. For this miracle God had performed for Elizabeth and for Sarah centuries earlier.

Your prayer has been heard, Nicolette Weatherspoon. My words will come true when the time is right.

Nick sat up straighter, startled, and glanced around. Gran-Gabby was watching Pastor Foley intently, as was Parker. She looked over her shoulder stealthily. Everyone's eyes were on the minister. No one was paying attention to her. She frowned. Was she going crazy?

"The Lord has done this for me," the pastor read, quoting Elizabeth. "In these days he has shown his favor...."

I will do this for you, Nicolette....

Once again Nick glanced at Parker and Gran-Gabby, but she knew this time no man or woman had spoken the words. She closed her eyes and listened to the steady beat of her heart and the slow, even rhythm of her breathing. She thought she could even hear the coursing of her blood through her veins. And then she heard the still, small voice again.

I will do this for you, Nicolette. I know your tenderness; I delight in your delight. I will give you the desire of your heart.

That was all then, except her heartbeat and her breathing and the rush of blood beneath her skin, peace like a river flooding through her veins.

For all her flights of fancy in her children's books, in her everyday life Nick was practical and down-to-earth, highly skeptical of "mystical" experience. But at this moment there was no doubt in her mind that God had spoken to her heart. She had never experienced anything like the absolute *knowing* that his word to her was true and that his promise would be realized.

Lost in wonder and silent thanksgiving, she heard only the last few words of Pastor Foley's sermon: "For nothing is impossible with God."

When Parker turned to help Nick into her jacket after the closing prayer, he stopped and stared, his breath caught in his throat. He had never seen anyone so beautiful in all his life. She was radiant, as if the sun had risen inside her, illuminating her face with its golden glow and scattering light across the blue waters of her eyes.

She smiled at him, a beatific Mona Lisa smile. "Parker." She turned toward her great-aunt and took her hand. "Gran-Gabby. I know it sounds crazy, but God told me during the service I'm going to be a mother. I'm going to have a family. He's promised to give me the desire of my heart."

Looking at her, Parker didn't have a doubt that Nick had heard God's voice. With very little convincing, he could even believe that God was speaking to him right now—telling him that he, too, would have his heart's desire. He knew what he wanted. He wanted to be married again. He wanted his family to be whole. He wanted Nick.

She released Miss Gabby's hand and interlaced her long, slender fingers in her lap. Contentment radiated from her skin, warming him as he sat quietly next to her, basking in her glow.

For a moment. Until she added, "I wonder if he's told Tom yet."

"It's funny—knowing I'm going to be a mom is making me feel so domestic," Nick told Gran-Gabby later that evening. She'd begged her great-aunt to let her help bake scones, the one task in the food prep part of the business which the old woman still insisted on doing herself.

Gran-Gabby had relented enough to allow Nick to sift together the dry ingredients and beat the milk and eggs, but refused help with the mixing, kneading, patting, and cutting. Nick watched from a tall stool she'd pulled near the wood-block baker's table in the restaurant kitchen, holding a bowl of egg yolk glaze to brush over the cranberry scones when they were ready.

"Lettie." Gran-Gabby's fingers expertly patted the ball of kneaded dough into a flat pancake on the floured surface of the table. "Did God say you were going to be a mother or you were going to marry Tom?"

"That I'm going to be a mother," Nick answered promptly. "But Gran-Gabby—" Dimples appeared on either side of her mouth. "I'm not expecting a virgin birth."

"Of course not!" Gran-Gabby answered irritably. "I'd just like to point out, as I've said before, that Tom is *not* the only fish in the sea."

"Maybe not. But he's *my* fish, Gran-Gabby," Nick answered patiently. "I've been with him for three years now. I'm not ready to give up. Unless—" Her throat felt suddenly constricted. "Unless *he* is." *And I'll know soon,* she added to herself.

New Year's Eve. Exactly four weeks.

"All right. All *right,* then." Gran-Gabby punched out a row of scones with a round biscuit cutter, using more force than necessary. "I won't say anything else but this: God's ways are unsearchable." She eyed her great-niece severely. "Don't limit him, Lettie."

Nick was silent for a moment. "I couldn't, Gran-Gabby," she finally said. "Even if I wanted to."

Six

St. Nicholas' Feast Day

The shop bell jangled as Nick stepped around a box of books on the porch and shoved open the front door to Easychair Books with her shoulder, her hands laden with a large platter of cookies covered in plastic wrap. The dusty, slightly mildewed odor peculiar to used bookstores tickled her nose. She looked around the store, seeing no one but a large, orange tabby draped over the back of an armchair near the window, snoozing in the sun.

"Parker!" she called. No response.

The longhaired tabby opened one round copper eye and then the other, an indolent stare his only acknowledgment of Nick's presence. His snub nose and the ruff of long, silky fur around his broad face gave him an air of unmistakable hauteur; his unflinching stare only added to the effect.

The sudden bang of a door at the back of the shop made Nick jump, but roused the cat only enough to stretch and yawn, like the king of the jungle in caricature.

Nick stopped in her tracks as a story idea sprang to life—a housecat with pretensions to lion-hood. A sniffy, snooty cat who thought he was king of the castle... Maybe Parker would let her hang around the bookstore to do some sketching later this week—if Gran-Gabby would give her a few hours off. She tucked away the idea and stepped across the room to the counter.

"You're not much of a watch-cat, Riley," she admonished as she set the plate of cookies next to the cash register. The clatter of glass on glass finally got the tabby's attention. He leaped down from the armchair and pattered toward her, the bushy tip of his short, thick tail waving behind him like a flag. With one leap he was on the counter.

"What—you think it's dinnertime? Dream on, cat!" She rubbed his head between the small, tufted ears and ran her fingers down his back. Riley slunk closer, burrowing his head into the cup of her hand and purring with raspy vigor. "Coddled and spoiled, is what you are!"

"You've got Riley's number," a deep voice agreed. Nick looked up to see Parker squeezing sideways between two rows of bookshelves toward the front of the store, a large cardboard box balanced in his arms. "Riley runs the place," he said to Nick, setting the heavy box of books on the floor. He stood up and clapped the dust off his hands. Nick's nose twitched.

Parker scratched the big cat under the chin, and when Riley dropped to the counter and rolled over on his back, rubbed his furry tummy affectionately. "Gets whatever he wants. Spoiled rotten." He grinned at Nick. "Can't imagine how he got that way."

"You named him well," Nick said. "He certainly does 'live the life of!'"

Parker looked pleased. "You know *The Life of Riley*, then! One of my hobbies, collecting old radio shows." He nodded at the plate of cookies, which the old cat was batting with a large paw. "Brought him a treat? I'm warning you, he's particular. Canned sardines in tomato sauce—yes. Broiled halibut—no.

French cut beans and asparagus tips—yes. Peas and carrots—no."

"Actually, they're not for him," Nick said, picking up the cat before he could do damage to the plate of cookies. "You feed him real people stuff?" she questioned.

Parker raised his shaggy eyebrows as he took Riley from Nick and settled him in the crook of his arms. The cat arched his back and purred loudly. "Are you kidding? He won't touch his canned food if he thinks there's a chance of getting some 'real people stuff!' Seems to believe that whatever *I'm* eating has to be better than what I've put in his dish."

Nick sympathized. "Guess I'm not surprised," she said, thinking of her parakeet's predilection for Melba toast and his refusal to eat Ritz crackers. "Mr. Tibbs is the same way." She indicated the platter on the counter. "Anyway, Gran-Gabby thought you might want treats to set out tonight."

It was the first evening of Nevada City's annual Victorian Christmas celebration. The old-fashioned street fair, held three Wednesday nights and one Sunday afternoon in December in the downtown historic district, attracted shoppers and revelers from throughout the Sierra gold country and as far away as the Bay Area. The local merchants and bed-and-breakfast operators who sponsored and promoted the event added immeasurably to the little town's appeal as a destination for the holidays.

For the hours of the celebration, city streets were closed to motorized traffic as the clip-clop of horses' hooves pulling carriages and hay wagons transported fair-goers a century back in time. More than two hundred vendors dressed in Victorian costume sold food and handcrafted gifts from booths set up down the center of the streets. The city kept a huge bonfire going in the Bank of America parking lot at the south end of town, where fair-goers could warm their hands, listen to Christmas music, drink hot cider, and roast chestnuts over an open fire.

Gran-Gabby always made the courtyard between Gabrielle's Tea Garden and Easychair Books available for a living nativity scene, complete with donkeys, chickens, and sheep, which was enacted several times each evening by local performers. Gabrielle's would be open for business as usual, and would also have a food booth on the street and gift tables set up on the porch. Parker, too, was in the middle of setting up business on the porch in front of his store in preparation for the evening.

"I helped Gran-Gabby bake this morning for the food booth," Nick explained. "These are the broken cookies."

"Oh, so *I* get the broken ones!" he teased.

"Be glad for that, complainer! We're selling the whole ones for a dollar and a half a piece."

"Hmm." He eyed the plate hungrily. "Shall we sample one or two?"

Nicolette patted her tummy. "I'm afraid I've been sampling all morning. Here, let me show you what's what." She lifted the plastic wrap off the platter and picked up a piece of broken cookie shaped like Santa's boot. "Dutch *speculaas*—spice cookies." Since Parker's hands were full of cat, she lifted the fragment to his lips. "Open up!"

When she popped the cookie in his mouth, a few crumbs fell from her fingers and caught in his beard. Nick automatically reached over to whisk them away. Their eyes caught and held briefly before she dropped her gaze to his chin and brushed her fingers across it. His beard was surprisingly soft; her hand lingered as if it had a mind of its own.

"Crumbs?" Parker asked, his voice husky, as if he'd just wakened and it was his first word of the day.

She jerked her hand away. "Yeah. I got them." She couldn't think of anything else to say, laughed shakily instead.

He cleared his throat. "So what else have you got?"

"Spritz cookies..." She picked up a fragment, hesitating for a moment as she met his eyes once more. There was something unmistakably male in his gaze. She could have looked away, could have set the piece of cookie back on the plate and said something bright and cheerful to break the sudden tension of physical awareness between them. But she didn't. The truth was, she liked the way his maleness made her feel so *female*.

What are you doing, Nicolette?

She tried to ignore the question in her mind as she fed him pieces of German *springerle* and Russian teacakes and Swedish *Luciapepperkakor*—holiday gingersnaps. Their names rolled tenderly off her tongue, like terms of endearment, as she lifted a sample of each to his mouth. She watched him chew, fully conscious of her fascination with the movement of his bearded jaw.

The voice in her mind refused to be ignored. *What are you doing, Nicolette?*

Just a little innocent flirting, she finally answered.

Why are you flirting with Parker when you're in love with Tom?

Riley, who'd been batting his paws at falling crumbs, finally twisted out of Parker's arms and leaped to the floor, slinking off between the bookshelves to find his own food dish. Parker wiped a hand over his mouth and down his chin.

Good question, she answered herself. *My mistake. Won't happen again.*

When she realized she was staring at the dark hair on the back of Parker's hand, she jerked her eyes away and turned to restretch the plastic wrap over the plate of cookies. "Gran-Gabby sends me a can of cookies every Christmas," she said deliberately. "Tom's favorites are the Russian teacakes."

Parker didn't answer. "Tell Miss Gabby thank you, Nick," he said after a moment. He hesitated. "Does she need you back right away, or could I talk you into helping me set up a couple of tables on the porch?"

Nick nodded, grateful for something to do. "She told me to

take my time. When I get back I won't have a break until it's all over tonight."

They worked together for a few minutes in silence, putting up tables on either side of the door and unpacking the books he'd chosen to display, several beautiful old Bibles, their illustrations embellished with gold-leaf and their pages parchment thin, but mostly old children's books: Edward Stratemeyer's Lakeport Series from the early 1900s, *Essays Every Child Should Know*, with a 1914 copyright, a set of George MacDonald Stories for Little Folks. Nick fingered the worn cover of a 1913 edition of *The Princess and the Goblin*, remembering the story from her childhood.

She felt herself relaxing as she handled the old books, their feel solid and comfortable. *Like Parker*, she reminded herself. No reason for disquietude with Parker.

"Did you know about Victorian Christmas before you bought the store?" she asked, reaching for a stack of books Parker had pulled from a cardboard box.

He nodded. "Victorian Christmas was one of the reasons I bought the store. Angel and I came up a year ago to do some shopping. We'd never been to Nevada City. It was cold, just right for Christmas, and we'd stopped for tea and cookies out in front of Gabrielle's. The living nativity scene was staging its final presentation, and just as they started to break up, it began to snow." Parker stopped his work for a moment, staring out into the courtyard where a stage crew was setting up the backdrop for tonight's nativity scene.

"I remember Angel was holding tightly to my hand," he continued, "not saying anything, but her eyes filled with wonder. Somewhere behind me carolers were singing "Silent Night." I looked over at the bookstore. The front door was open, and light was pouring out the windows. It was almost as if God said to me out loud, 'This is the place I've prepared for you, Parker.' Without even thinking, I walked in and asked old Mr. Jepperson if he was interested in selling his business. By the first of April, I was here." He grinned at Nick. "Angel was delighted. I'm afraid she thinks I'm a bit of a stick-in-the-mud at times."

Nick nodded, smiling as she remembered one of Angel's descriptive passages about her father. "It is a term she's used. She says she has hope for you, though."

Parker's face slipped into a sudden frown. "I can handle the rest of this, Nick," he said abruptly. "You'd better get back to Miss Gabby."

She jerked her head in surprise at his sharp tone and stared at him slapping books down on the table, then finally asked in a hurt voice, "Did I say something wrong?"

He sighed. "Sorry. It's just—well, all these things Angel's told you about me. And Miss Gabby talking about *you* so much. I've been thinking about it ever since your great-aunt's miraculous 'recovery.' Don't you think it's odd, Angel all of a sudden becoming your pen-pal after spending the summer here? And Miss Gabby getting you to Nevada City the way she did, and asking *me* to pick you up at the airport?"

Nick shook her head in denial. She didn't like where this was going. "You're the logical person to pick me up at the airport, Parker. Gran-Gabby depends on you for a lot of things."

He ran his fingers through his curly hair. "Yes, she does. That's just it. She never asked for any help until September, after Angel left. And that last day before Angel went back to the city, they had their heads together a good long time over your *Gabby* books."

"What are you suggesting?" she asked, her heart sinking.

Parker took a deep breath. "That it's more than coincidence. That your great-aunt is trying to play matchmaker. And using Angel in the plot."

"Matchmaker? You mean—me? And you? I'm *sure* not,

72

Parker!" Nick stared at him, suddenly aware of the smudge of dirt across his nose, the cobweb hanging from the cuff of his flannel shirt, the fine powdering of dust from his tasks earlier in the day dulling the shine of his dark hair and beard.

And then she remembered. Gran-Gabby *had* mentioned Parker before, though not by name. Over the phone, on her thirty-sixth birthday last June. Tom had given her a bottle of Chanel, very expensive, very nice. Except she'd thought he might give her a ring.

She'd swallowed her disappointment and called Gran-Gabby. "Forget Tom!" her great-aunt had said even back then. "Plenty of other fish in the sea. New man next door in the bookstore's a better match than Tom. Dusty sort of fellow, but has potential. Too bad you're so far away."

"A dusty sort of fellow?" She'd laughed half-heartedly. "No thanks, Gran-Gabby. Tom will come around."

"Nick?" Parker's voice interrupted her musings.

She shook her head emphatically. Her great-aunt might be a bit overbearing at times, even manipulative when it served her, but matchmaking was not her style. "You're wrong, Parker. Gran-Gabby knows I'd never let someone interfere in my romantic life, any more than *she* did when she was a girl."

"What d'you mean?

"Gran-Gabby refused the marriage her father had arranged."

"An arranged marriage? I thought those went out a century ago!"

"Not arranged in the formal sense, but planned without her input, nonetheless. Her father made it clear he expected Gran-Gabby to marry his business partner's son."

"She told him no?"

"Told him no. And then the fellow she was in love with, who claimed he loved her too, married the girl *his* parents had matched him up with." Nick fingered the leather cover of the old family Bible in her hands. "Broke her heart," she said, swallowing a lump in her throat.

She set the Bible on the table. "On the other hand," she added thoughtfully, "it made her what she is today. She never thought she could depend on a man after that, so she set her mind to make a success without one. Taught school for twenty-five years before she retired and turned the old family home into a restaurant. As you can see, she's still going strong."

Parker remembered Nick's quick irritation in the coffee shop at the airport, when he'd registered surprise that Tom had been her only boyfriend. Now he understood her caustic question about "making it without a man."

"Well, good for Miss Gabby!" he said. "She's made it on her own, all right."

Nick felt suddenly deflated. "Yes, she has. But at a price. I know sometimes she wished she'd had a family of her own, a husband and children to love her and need her."

"At least she had the kids she taught."

"Not the same." Nick knew from experience. "When you teach, you've got a classroom of kids for nine months. That's it. They move on, you get a new group for another nine months. Everyone keeps moving on." She stopped, unable to speak for a moment as a wave of melancholy swept through her.

Parker, too, was silent for a moment. "No wonder she talks about you so much, Nick! You're like the daughter she never had."

She nodded. "I am," she finally said. "That's why you can't be right. Don't you see? No matter what she says about him, Gran-Gabby wouldn't interfere when she knows I've chosen Tom."

Parker had been looking forward to his first night of Victorian Christmas on the merchant's side of the counter for almost a year now, but somehow, after his conversation with Nick, the day had lost its luster.

Cosmo's arrival at four cheered him a little; his teenaged clerk was dressed in black jeans, cowboy boots, and a fringed leather vest over a sleeveless T-shirt. "Outlaw," he drawled in answer to Parker's raised eyebrows, flexing his arm so the animals in his tattoo jumped. The gold ring in his ear gleamed, and a few strands of purple hair poked from the rim of his black cowboy hat. He pulled the hat low on his forehead and added, "Hear there's a stage comin' through to pick up a shipment of gold."

Despite his low spirits, Parker had to laugh. "Now why does it not surprise me you'd come to the party as an outlaw and not a respectable Victorian gentleman?"

Cosmo served the customers while Parker donned his own Victorian finery in the tiny bathroom at the back of the store. He buttoned up his silk waistcoat and knotted his string tie absently as he gazed in the mirror at his solemn expression.

"So what's it all about, Parker?" he asked the sober-faced gentleman reflected in the glass.

It's about the way you feel about Nick, the bearded image seemed to answer. He closed his eyes as he pulled a black coat over his starched white shirt, as if the disappearance of his reflection could wipe away the thought as well. It didn't work. He knew what he knew.

And he knew Nick was right about Angel and Miss Gabby. Only his fear of admitting his feelings had made him imagine intrigue where none existed. Only his failure to acknowledge the truth required his conspiracy theory.

From that first moment in the airport when he'd seen her standing head and shoulders above the crowd, her inquisitive cornflower eyes taking in the world as much as searching for him, he'd been lost.

Her blue gaze hit him like a runaway train speeding toward destiny. He hadn't even known he was ready for love until he'd seen her. Neither Angel nor Miss Gabby could possibly have known how he'd react to her.

Face it, Parker, he told himself as he set his top hat at an angle much more jaunty than he felt. *You didn't need any help to fall in love with Nicolette Weatherspoon. You did it all on your own.*

It was true. He'd never felt for anyone the way he felt about the playful, intelligent, curious, creative woman who'd stolen his heart without even trying. The loveliest woman in all the world. A woman who was in love with another man.

"Maybe she only *thinks* she's in love with Tom," he said to his reflection. "After all, he's there and she's here. And *I'm* here. Right next door."

What are you suggesting, Parker McPhee? his frowning image returned. *Love isn't something you can force someone to feel!* He could do a lot of things, but making Nicolette love him wasn't one of them. Either those feelings were in her heart or they weren't.

He bent his head and closed his eyes as a wave of grief washed over him. How could he feel so sad about losing something he'd never had? "God—what do you want me to do? Why would you let me feel this way about someone I can't have?"

I wondered when you'd get around to talking to me about it, Parker.

He took a deep breath, holding it in and listening to the silence. "God—is that you? Where'd you come from?"

I've been here all along. Waiting patiently. Watching you fall in love with Nicolette Weatherspoon. Where'd you ever get the idea you can't have her?

Parker felt a sudden surge of energy. Lifting his head, he stared at his counterpart in the mirror. Was God giving him the go-ahead to interfere in Nick's life—to muddle her mind, displace her dreams, unhinge her heart?

You've never been known as a man of action, his image seemed to say doubtfully.

He nodded in embarrassed agreement. Action wasn't his strong suit, especially when it came to women. Sometimes he wondered if he'd ever have married at all if Marci hadn't talked him into it—if Marci hadn't, in fact, started the whole thing by asking him to the Sadie Hawkins Dance his senior year of high school. Saying yes to her proposal eight years later seemed the reasonable thing to do.

What had surprised him about Nick didn't seem the least bit irregular for Parker himself: like Tom for Nick, Marci had been his only romance. He hadn't had to *do* anything to make it happen, which at the time had been fine with him—but after a few years not so fine after all, for him *or* Marci.

And definitely not for the marriage. Marci got tired of always being the one in charge. By the time he figured it out, she was gone, irretrievably.

"But I *can* take charge when I need to," he argued with himself, thinking back over the last six years.

After the divorce, hurt and anger had galvanized him to action where regard and affection had not. He'd quit the stuffy job in banking that Marci's connections had gotten him and found work managing a bookstore, where he learned the ins and outs of the retail trade. He hadn't known until he'd walked into Easychair Books last Christmas that he wanted to be in business for himself. *Like you didn't know you wanted to be married again until you met Nick,* his reflection reminded him.

It was almost as if the used bookstore and Gran-Gabby and Nevada City itself had been waiting for him to grow up and make up his mind and settle down where he was meant to be. God had been preparing *him* as well as his future, and when he was finally ready, it only took the right moment for him to know. *This is the place I've prepared for you, Parker McPhee,* God had told him about Easychair Books. *Do what you need to do.*

Only the distance from Angel had given him pause; but Marci had been surprisingly supportive of his move and more flexible than he would have imagined about scheduling their daughter's stays with him. Getting together the financing so quickly had taken some doing, but he'd figured it out; he'd done it.

And so Parker had finally grasped one of the most important truths he would ever learn: that when he was being the person he was meant to be and learning the things he was meant to learn, God would lead him. God would go before him and prepare the way. The place. The people.

This is the woman I've prepared for you, Parker McPhee, God seemed to say in the stillness of his heart.

"But does *she* know it?" Parker asked aloud.

Leave that part to me, came the answer. *Just do what you need to do.*

Seven

Third Sunday of Advent

W hen Tom called from Seattle on the Sunday morning exactly three weeks after Nick's arrival in Nevada City, she was curled up on the window seat in her bedroom, wrapped in her white chenille robe, watching the sky lighten over the wooded slopes in the distance. Broad Street stretched quietly down the hill from Gabrielle's front door, like a royal carpet rolled out between the retinue of village stores on either side, the tiny white lights twinkling along their gables as if in silent applause for the grand lady on the ridge above them.

A thin braid of steam rose from the teacup on the windowsill. Gunpowder tea: the delicate, fragrant green tea had seemed a better choice this morning than her usual Earl Grey. Her stomach was unsettled, and she hadn't slept well.

Gran-Gabby tapped lightly at the door and seemed almost disappointed when her great-niece called, "Come in." Nick looked at her disheveled hair and naked face in surprise; she'd rarely seen Gran-Gabby looking less than perfectly put together. The hour, however, was early; perhaps that explained her great-aunt's unkempt appearance and peevish expression. She handed Nick the cordless phone without comment and turned on her heel, letting the door slam behind her.

"Nick? How are you?" Tom's voice sounded tinny and far away. "I tried to call last night, but no one answered. Your aunt isn't working you too hard, is she?"

"Hi, Tom. No, we actually took an evening off together. If anyone's working too hard, it's Gran-Gabby." She hesitated. "I'm worried about her. Even with a manager, she can't seem to let go of responsibility at the restaurant. She insists she's 'healthy as a horse,' but it's taking its toll on her."

"Well, I'm sure you've been a big help."

"I have. She needs me, Tom. I've decided I'm not coming back till New Year's Eve."

"But you were coming home next weekend! I made special plans for Christmas!"

"I'm sorry, Tom, I just can't leave. The week after Christmas is going to be too much for Gran-Gabby. She needs me here."

She waited for Tom to say, "I need you, too, Nick. Please come home." If he had, she might have done it. Instead, he said with a longsuffering sigh as a preface, "I wish you'd have let me know sooner."

The tea in her cup was cold by the time she hung up the phone. She got up to empty it into the water glass next to her bed and poured herself a fresh cup, kept warm by the quilted cosy over the teapot. Settling back onto the window seat with her hands wrapped around the china teacup, she gazed out the window without seeing.

Even beyond Tom's annoyance that she'd spoiled his plans for Christmas, their conversation had been unsatisfying. He felt so far away. God's promise felt impossible. Could she have been wrong after all?

She'd listened patiently to the details of Tom's newest business venture and the latest gossip from their social circle, but she couldn't seem to get him interested in how she was spending *her* time—almost as if he didn't believe anything important could be going on in her life if he wasn't there.

The fact was, there *were* important things going on in her life, things she wanted Tom to care about. For one, Gran-Gabby had arranged her schedule so she could spend an hour or two every day at Easychair Books to observe and draw. Her sketchbook was rapidly filling up with studies not only of Riley, but of Parker, his colorful clerk Cosmo, and of Easychair Books itself. Spending time in the bookstore had triggered an idea for a new children's series she was very excited about.

Tom had listened to her plan with only half an ear and interrupted in mid-sentence to tell her to call Faye Bryant, her editor at Rainbow Press, in the morning. Nick knew his interest in the business was in running the financial end of things and not in the details of publishing; still, she thought he'd be at least attentive for her sake.

She tried to tell Tom how much fun she was having working in the restaurant again, but he changed the subject before she could give him any specifics. The holiday season at Gabrielle's Tea Garden had been in full swing since the first night of Victorian Christmas ten days ago. Once again this afternoon, Nevada City would be transformed into a Victorian era village for the afternoon version of the festive street fair, and Nick would be busy in the food booth selling Cornish pasties, English cheese tarts, and bangers-on-a-bun.

Last Saturday had been Gabrielle's annual Dickens Tea, yesterday the Nutcracker Tea; the Victorian White Christmas Tea was still to come, next weekend. Thanks to an article in *Sunset* magazine five years ago and word-of-mouth since then, Gran-Gabby's special Christmas teas were known up and down the West Coast, and reservations were filled six months in advance. Yesterday, to Tchaikovsky's stirring score for the ballet, Nick, costumed as the Nutcracker himself, had helped serve a five course tea to a full house of guests—among them, to her great delight, a very grown-up looking Angela McPhee.

Because Marci was scheduled to have Angel on the twenty-fourth and twenty-fifth, this weekend was Parker's Christmas with his daughter. Nick had tried to protest when Angel asked her and Gran-Gabby to help them celebrate last night, thinking Parker would want some time alone with her, but he insisted he'd be honored if the two women would join them. They'd all gone to Parker's house, a log cabin on a beautiful wooded site outside Nevada City, to watch a video of the Nutcracker Ballet.

"Dad's taken me to see the Nutcracker every year since I was five," Angel explained earnestly, "but now that he has the bookstore to take care of, I'm going to have to bring the ballet to him."

Angel was every bit as delightful and precocious in person as she was in her letters and adored her father every bit as much as her stories about him implied. Nick watched them together thoughtfully; their relationship was obviously warm, close, and mutually respectful. And they had so much *fun* together! Seeing Parker's interactions with his daughter, Nick was sorry his dream of a "passel of kids" with Marci hadn't worked out; he really needed to have more children.

But Tom hadn't been interested in hearing about Angel or her father.

And Nick was no closer to knowing how he felt about marriage and family than she had been three weeks ago.

Parker took his last bite of blueberry crepes and wiped the syrup off his mouth, then sat back in his chair, taking a quiet moment to listen to Nick and Angel in animated conversation over the breakfast table. He noticed that Miss Gabby, too, was leaning away from the table, studying her great-niece and his daughter.

Nick was giving Angel the gift of her undivided attention—something Parker had found grown-ups usually had a hard time doing with other people's children. Her thoughtful responses to his daughter's questions and comments indicated respect and acknowledged her importance.

Somehow he wasn't surprised at their comfort with each other, their easy conversation and spontaneous laughter. Yesterday he'd asked Angel about her missives to Nick over the last few months, and she'd shared some of her stories with him, complete with Nick's comments written in the margins in a bold hand—glowing words of praise as well as thoughtful suggestions.

"I didn't mean for you to feel left out, Dad," Angel had told him, her gray eyes intent and serious. "I just didn't know you'd be interested."

Yeah, Parker thought. *I didn't know I'd be interested either.*

For Parker, Nick and Angel's ease with each other only added to his growing conviction that Nick was the woman for him. *God, prepare her heart for me,* he prayed in the mornings when he woke and at night before he fell asleep. *Prepare her heart for me, and make me worthy of her love.*

He noisily scraped his chair back from the table and stood. "We'd better get going if we're going to make the early service," he said.

The church service promised to be his only further contact with Nick today; they'd all have to hurry home afterward to set up for Victorian Christmas, and when it was over, he had a three-hour trip to get Angel back to her mother's.

Despite a forecast of rain, it turned out to be a perfect day, clear and crisp without being too cold. The fine weather brought out the crowds for the holiday celebration, and Parker kept busy with waves of customers moving through the store—busy enough that for a few hours he managed to stop thinking about Nick.

Until Angel squealed her name, late in the afternoon. Parker, kneeling to pull a box of books from under one of the tables on the porch, lost his balance and barely caught himself on one arm. He looked up at his daughter. Dressed in a makeshift costume Nick and Miss Gabby had helped her come up with last night so she'd feel more a part of Victorian Christmas, she had temporarily abandoned her task of straightening books and was leaning over the porch railing, waving across the courtyard.

Parker's breath caught in his throat as he turned and saw Nick sailing toward the bookstore, the layers of crinolines under her full skirt swishing around her legs.

The cow in the living nativity scene stretched her neck and mooed just as Nick passed by. Without a break in her stride, she turned her head and mooed back. Parker shook his head, his mouth quirked in amusement. Only Nick!

Standing, he unabashedly watched her as she made her way through the crowd like a ship cutting through the swells. The high-necked bodice of her dress, a cornflower blue that exactly matched her eyes, was stitched in rows of tiny vertical tucks, the only ornamentation on the simply-styled Victorian gown. A riding jacket of black velvet protected her from the chill December air. She had her hair fixed differently, tucked behind her ears with her bangs brushed away from her fresh, open face. Gold-trimmed cameo earrings and a matching necklace completed her period costume.

"Does Miss Gabby know you've deserted your post?" he teased as she lifted her skirts to climb the stairs to the porch.

"And hello to you, too, McPhee!" Her cheeks were flushed and her blue eyes sparkled. Parker wondered fleetingly if it was only the brisk mountain air that made her look so vibrant and alive. "Actually, Gran-Gabby sent me," she said. She turned to his daughter. "Having fun, Angel?"

"Lots! I'm going to write a story about it," the girl said decisively.

"Perfect! I came to relieve your dad so he can take you for a turn through town. Got your notebook? There's great stuff out there to help you establish your setting."

"You've come to relieve me?" Parker interrupted in surprise.

"A couple of college kids who waited tables for Gran-Gabby last summer showed up yesterday, home for the holidays and short on Christmas cash. She couldn't say no."

Nick picked up a tattered orange book from the table and read the cover aloud: *"Lee's Priceless Recipes. The Standard. 3000 Secrets for the Home, Farm, Laboratory, Workshop and Every Department of Human Endeavor. A Gold Mine.* Wow!" She looked up. "Now *here's* a book no one should be without." When she set it back on the table, Angel reached over to straighten it. Nick laughed and slung an arm casually across the girl's shoulder. "You've got a great helper here, Parker. What kind of saleswoman is she?"

He raised his bushy eyebrows and stroked his beard. "She's about sold out my stock of picture books, Nick. Seems all she has to do is smile and flutter her eyelashes."

"Oh, Dad," Angel groaned.

"You'll have to be watching out for her pretty soon," Nick warned.

"I know. Scary times ahead!"

Angel rolled her eyes.

"You serious about relieving me?" Parker asked Nick.

She nodded. "Gabrielle's is over-staffed. Gran-Gabby and I thought you might want to show Angel around town before everything closes up for the day."

The girl clapped her hands. "Let's, Dad!"

Parker nodded, pleased at the chance to share the fun with his daughter. "Any way you could come, too?" he asked Nick, trying not to sound too eager.

"Not unless you're willing to close up shop on one of your busiest days of the year!"

He sighed with melodramatic disappointment. Angel giggled. "You're right. It's great of you to watch the store for a while, Nick. Cosmo's inside if you need help with anything. We'll try not to be long." He gave her a few instructions, then grabbed Angel around the waist and swung her off the porch to the sidewalk.

"Da-ad!" she squealed breathlessly.

"An-n-gel!" he mimicked. He gave her a hug, then let her go. "How about some hot cider, daughter mine?"

"Nick's really nice, isn't she, Dad?" Angel asked a few minutes later as they strolled down the hill, hands warming around steaming styrofoam cups of spiced cider.

"*Very* nice," he answered without hesitation.

"Do you like her?"

"Well, of course I do! What's not to like?"

"You know what I mean. Do you *like*-like her? Like boyfriend and girlfriend?"

Parker stroked his beard nervously. "Aren't you getting a little personal?"

"Dad! You *are* my father!"

He was silent for a moment, not sure what to tell her. "Even fathers have private lives," he finally said. "But I think you should know Nick has a boyfriend in Seattle. She's only going to be here another week." Not that God couldn't perform a miracle in a week, but Parker wasn't clear about the timeline on this thing and he didn't want to set his daughter up for disappointment. She was obviously as taken with Nick as he was.

He'd stopped asking Nick about Tom, but to his disappointment, it hadn't made her stop talking about him. In fact, every time Parker thought he was making headway with her—inch-

86

ing his way into her heart—Nick unexpectedly brought her boyfriend into the conversation, throwing a pall over their camaraderie.

Nick and Parker had been spending a lot of time together—taking meals at Gabrielle's and hanging out at the bookstore while he priced and stocked inventory and she worked on sketches for a new story idea. She'd even agreed to see a movie with him one evening, Jane Austen's *Sense and Sensibility*, which he'd hoped she might apply to their own situation. He didn't mean to imply that Tom was necessarily anything like the young cad Willoughby, merely that he identified wholeheartedly with the besotted colonel. Nick hadn't seemed to have made the connection.

"Gran-Gabby says Tom's not right for Nick, Dad," Angel interrupted his thoughts.

"I'm afraid Gran-Gabby's going to have to leave that up to Nick and Tom, Angel," he told his daughter gently. "Love isn't a choice you can make for someone else."

"But you're always telling me if you want something bad enough, you'll do whatever it takes to get it," she insisted.

"Who said anything about wanting anyone—any*thing?*" His voice rose in unconscious frustration. "Besides, it's not as if I'm sitting on my hands, Angel!" Then, worried he'd said too much, he added with finality, "And that is *all* I'm going to say."

His daughter had to have the last word. "Well, I'm not giving up, even if you are. I'm going to pray. Gran-Gabby says the angels are always listening."

Thankfully, when he didn't respond, Angel dropped the subject. For the next hour, to the background of church bells ringing through the crisp mountain air, father and daughter wandered around Nevada City, poking through the booths crammed full of every hand-crafted item imaginable: handmade wool sweaters, tie-dyed T-shirts, velvet hats and handbags, jewelry of every kind, stained glass, basketwork, hand-painted pottery and hand-turned wooden bowls, quilts, bird houses—even dulcimers.

The streets were crowded not only with shoppers and sightseers, but also with strolling entertainers: a kilted bagpiper and snare drummer, a local juggler and magician with the unlikely but appropriate name 'Izzy Tooinsky,' carolers dressed in Dickens' costumes. In front of the New York Hotel two schoolgirls not much older than Angel played flute and clarinet duets for change thrown in their cases, while at the Freeman Building a recorder band performed. On the veranda of the historic National Hotel at the bottom of Broad Street the celebrated Grass Valley Cornish Choir sang. The Sierra Brass Choir, which had earlier performed two concerts in front of Easychair Books, had moved to a location outside the Miner's Foundry on Spring Street.

Food booths were scattered throughout the town, adding to the heady aroma of roasting chestnuts that permeated the air. Angel talked Parker into a hot dog, a giant pretzel, popcorn, hot chocolate, and a brownie before he finally told her enough was enough. The warm glow of gaslight spilled across the pavement as evening began to shadow the streets and they made their way up the hill and back to the bookstore. Nick, looking as if she belonged there on his porch, smiled a greeting as they climbed the stairs.

"Well, what did you think, Angel?" Nick asked later in the evening as she walked Parker's daughter across the empty courtyard from Gabrielle's to Easychair Books. Angel's Christmas with Parker was over, and she'd gone to tell Nick and Gran-Gabby goodbye before her father drove her back to the city. "As good as last year?"

"Better," Parker's daughter answered. "Because Dad's part of it."

"He's a good dad, isn't he, Angel? You're lucky to have him." Nick gave her young friend a hug. "And he's lucky to have you."

"Nick—"

"Hmm?"

"Are you going to marry Tom?"

Nick stopped short, dropping her arm from Angel's shoulder and staring at her. "How do you know about Tom?"

"Gran-Gabby."

Should have figured, Nick told herself, feeling a surge of anger toward her great-aunt. With Gran-Gabby, nothing—except perhaps afternoon tea—was sacred.

But talking about her personal life with a nine-year-old girl was going too far. "Tell your father I'll see him tomorrow," she said shortly, spinning away. She wasn't going to let this happen anymore. She was going to have it out with Gran-Gabby.

"Well, are you?" Angel called after her. "Because if you're not, I just want to say my dad likes you a lot."

Nick stopped short once again and turned around. "He *told* you this?" Anger and disbelief colored her voice. Was she the only one who didn't think telling a little girl one's private business was inappropriate?

She softened at Angel's surprised expression. "I'm sorry, Angel, it's not you I'm angry with. But did your father really tell you that?"

Angel looked at her feet. "No," she admitted, her voice small. She looked up, her solemn gray eyes meeting Nick's snapping blue ones. "But I *know* he does," she said adamantly. "I can tell."

Eight

⤸❧

Fourth Sunday of Advent: Christmas Eve

Gran-Gabby, having had a lifetime to think about it after her own ill-fated love affair, was of the opinion that a great match in marriage was extremely rare. The convocation of factors required to secure such a match, she'd decided, was nothing short of miraculous.

And so, when she'd reached the conclusion a match between her great-niece and Parker McPhee might just be one of those rare, great ones, she felt no compunction at all about stepping in—not "meddling," as Lettie had called it last Sunday when she'd come storming into Gabrielle's at the end of the evening; simply helping to smooth the way.

There were several factors to consider in the way of a match coming to be. The compatibility factor, of course, was dependent entirely on the backgrounds, personalities, and dreams of the principals, matters in which one wouldn't want to intervene even if one could. Gran-Gabby's responsibility to Lettie and Parker lay only in her *recognition* of their suitability for each other, and doing whatever she could to get *them* to recognize it as well.

And so she had contrived her plan.

The proximity factor was the easiest to manipulate and absolutely essential to the process. Falling in love was entirely impossible without the principals being in the same place at the same time. If, for example, one resided in Seattle, Washington, and the other in Nevada City, California, and never the twain did meet, the match would certainly not eventuate.

And so she had persuaded Lettie to spend a month with her.

The readiness factor was more difficult to control. One could do only so much, and only in the way of helping the principals recognize and name their hopes and hungers, to influence their preparedness for love. The rest of being ready depended on maturity, a domain simply out of her hands.

And so she had given Angel instructions about writing her great-niece and begun her own pro-Lettie campaign with Parker.

Over the chemistry factor, she realized she had no authority at all.

. And so she prayed. *God, I see no reason why Lettie Weatherspoon and Parker McPhee shouldn't be together as man and wife. If you concur, I'd be much obliged if you'd let them fall in love. Just a little thing, and it would make this old woman so happy.*

She was surprised and a bit put out that her great-niece hadn't seen things her way. "I can't believe that after the way your father tried to arrange *your* marriage, you'd *meddle* so in my romantic life!" Lettie had lit into her.

Gran-Gabby had insisted that was a different matter entirely. "My father had his own agenda in arranging that marriage, and it didn't have a thing to do with me! He had a selfish streak, Lettie—you just don't know." She drew herself up to her full height and looked down her patrician nose. "And if you can't see the difference, if you can't see the reason I've tried to smooth the way with Parker McPhee is because *I love you—*

well, I suppose there's nothing I can do to convince you any differently. I only want you to be happy, Lettie," she declared. "Your contentment is my sole motivation."

"Do I look happy to you?" Lettie had fumed. "Gran-Gabby, I'm frustrated, confused, overwhelmed, and just plain angry! Choosing a life partner is a serious thing!"

"My point exactly," Gran-Gabby sniffed.

"And a *very personal thing*. Gran-Gabby, give it up!"

"All I ask is that you think about it, Lettie. Think about it before you go off half-cocked and marry someone who's just a habit. Listen to your heart!"

Lettie hadn't let it drop. "Your interference is completely unfair to everyone concerned," she said. "It shows no respect for me, it's building false hopes in Angel, it completely disregards both Tom's and Parker's feelings. You haven't even given Tom a chance, and Parker certainly doesn't deserve to be my second choice, waiting in the wings just in case Tom decides he doesn't want me. Parker doesn't deserve to be *anybody's* second choice!"

Then she'd stormed upstairs, Gran-Gabby's words following her up the staircase: "He certainly doesn't. Think about it, Lettie!"

It was true Gran-Gabby hadn't given Tom a chance; she'd never seen her great-niece with Tom. But she *had* seen her with Parker. If all the pieces weren't in place, including the chemistry factor—though Lettie would probably deny it—she'd be very surprised indeed. How could the girl be so stubborn and so *blind?*

The next day Lettie had apologized for flying off the handle but not for what she'd said. "Can't you just let things *be*, Gran-Gabby?"

Gran-Gabby had pressed her lips together, not promising anything. She had a trick or two still up her sleeve. Mistletoe, for one—there wasn't a doorway in the restaurant that didn't have a sprig of mistletoe hanging over it by now. It wasn't much, but at least it provided *opportunity*.

And then there was the Urn of Fate.

The Spanish Urn of Fate was a light-hearted custom Gran-Gabby had introduced at her annual New Hope Golden Agers Christmas Open House several years before, when a widowed friend had expressed a wish to get to know a particular gentleman, but having been out of the dating loop for fifty years, wasn't sure how to go about it.

"I know just the thing," Gran-Gabby told her friend. "We'll choose our seatmates at the party with the Urn of Fate!" She explained the Spanish tradition she'd come across while doing research for her Christmas teas: cards with names printed on them were thrown in a jar, shuffled, and drawn out two at a time, the resulting pairs supposedly destined to have a special friendship in the coming year.

Not that "fate" had the slightest thing to do with it, of course. In fact, her source informed her, cheating was accepted and even *expected,* in order to maneuver certain promising couples together.

This Christmas, Gran-Gabby couldn't think of a more promising couple than Nick and Parker. And by now, of course, she had the cheating down to an art.

Miss Gabby had recruited a half-dozen junior highers from the youth group to serve the tea and pastries at her Christmas open house. Parker made his way through the group of shuffling, giggling kids in the hallway outside the door of the Victorian Room. A freckle-faced redhead gave him an odd look, as if to ask, "What are *you* doing here?"

Nevada County was home to a growing number of retirees from all over California, many of whom seemed to have found their way to New Hope Community Church. Parker enjoyed the special kind of wisdom and second-childhood energy they brought to the congregation, but he'd been puzzled himself when Miss Gabby had invited him to the Golden Ager's party. "I don't have *that* much gray in my beard!" he'd protested.

"Of course you don't," she'd answered crisply. "I merely thought you might help move furniture around between the tea and the program."

He'd grinned and flexed his biceps. "Well, then! If it's my *muscles* you want..."

The dining room looked especially inviting this afternoon. A fire roared in the mahogany and marble fireplace and the white lights draping the tall evergreen in the corner twinkled brightly. Candlelight cast soft shadows across the eclectic but elegant mix of silver and china place settings at the tables, and soft instrumental Christmas music in the background added to the ambiance.

It took only a moment for Parker to locate Nick over the sea of gray heads. She stood across the room deep in conversation with Pastor Foley and his wife, looking wonderful, her green silk dress like a fresh spray of pine against the snowy lace curtains at the window. He'd been worried about her; she hadn't been coming down for breakfast in the mornings and he'd barely seen her all week. Her great-aunt had told him Nicolette wasn't ill, just feeling "out of sorts." Still, it was a relief to see her looking so healthy.

Miss Gabby clapped her hands to quiet the merry buzz of conversation in the room. "The time has come," she announced, holding up a large pottery jar, "to discover your seatmate for the evening." She shook the jar, into which each person had earlier dropped a card with his or her name printed on it. "I do not pretend to be a prophet," she stated gravely, "but I wish to remind you the drawing of names from the Urn of Fate in Spain each Christmas is said to determine who will be especially significant in your life in the coming year."

Within ten minutes everyone was seated at a table next to his or her potential "special friend." Amazing, Parker thought, that out of all the people there, his and Nick's names should be drawn together! Parker took it as a sign from God until Nick said in a low voice, "I think you should know I didn't sign my name to a card."

He stared at her until she turned her blue eyes to meet his gaze. "What d'you mean, Nick?"

Her eyes flickered away again immediately, as if there were something reflected in them she didn't want him to see. "I didn't put my name in the 'Urn of Fate,' Parker," she said. After a moment of silence she sighed and continued, still not meeting his eyes. "Look, Gran-Gabby isn't going to apologize for her meddling, so I'll do it for her. Your suspicions were right. She's been trying to play matchmaker with us. I confronted her about it last weekend and she confessed. Not that she's a bit contrite."

"Oh." Parker carefully unfolded his linen napkin and smoothed it over his lap. "That's why I haven't seen much of you this week." It was a statement, not a question. He tried to keep the hurt out of his voice, but Nick's response told him he hadn't succeeded.

"I'm sorry, Parker. It isn't that I've been avoiding you, exactly. I've been feeling a little—I don't know. *Overwhelmed,* I guess. I didn't see how being around you was going to help me figure things out."

"What things, exactly?"

She hesitated, started to say something, then shook her head and fell silent, her eyes downcast.

Parker knew suddenly, in one of those moments of insight that come when one is truly tuned in to someone he or she loves, that *he* was part of Nick's confusion and discomfort. The thought was both exhilarating and frightening. He took a deep breath and said gently, "Never mind. Nick, forget about Miss Gabby. It's Christmas Eve. I don't care how we ended up sitting together—I'm just glad we did."

A young teen, looking uncomfortable in his dress shirt and necktie, interrupted. "Tea, anybody?" By the time the boy had filled their cups and moved on, the elderly woman on Parker's left was nudging him with the platter of sweets. He held the tray for Nick as she placed a cranberry scone and a couple of gingerbread cookies on her plate, then helped himself to several items. Even when she took the platter from him to pass it on, she didn't meet his eyes.

Parker sliced his scone in two and reached for the Devonshire cream. "Now—I want to hear all about your new story idea," he said to Nick, determined to lighten her mood. "Is Riley going to be the hero of Lettie Weatherspoon's new series? A cat with pretensions to lion-hood?"

He was rewarded with a smile and a look of genuine relief in Nick's eyes as she finally lifted them to meet his gaze. "Actually, I'm thinking about Cosmo. Don't you think he'd make a great character?"

"Cosmo's a character, all right! Tell me more," Parker prompted.

Nicolette's tension appeared to dissolve as she told him about her story idea, her voice growing more animated as she responded to his interested questions. Once again he thoroughly enjoyed her company.

So how was it, he wondered later that evening as he sat between Nick and her great-aunt at the candlelight service at church, that now *he* was so tense and distracted?

He couldn't seem to concentrate with Nick sitting next to him, close enough that her arm brushed against him when she reached for the hymnal, close enough that he could smell her subtle, musky perfume. He couldn't focus on anything else, though he did everything he could think of—turning his body away from her, sharing a hymn book with Miss Gabby instead of her, focusing his eyes on the flickering candles of the advent wreath at the front of the church as if he could hypnotize himself into forgetting her existence.

Nothing worked. Oblivious to the music and the readings and the message, he found himself trying to carry on a conversation with Nick in his mind: *Just because your great-aunt got carried away doesn't mean we shouldn't think about it,* he argued with her. *I know you're angry with Miss Gabby, but don't let your frustration with her come between us!* No, that focused too much on Miss Gabby and not enough on the two of them.

I don't know what it is you've got with Tom, he tried again, *but how could it possibly be better than what we have? I'd never keep you waiting like he's done, Nick. You just say the word and I'm here.* No—he still wasn't getting to the point.

I love you, Nick. I don't want to spend another hour without knowing you'll be there next to me the rest of my days.

Yes. That was it. That was what he needed to say. It was all he could do—just tell her how he felt about her. The rest was up to God and Nicolette Weatherspoon.

Miss Gabby did him one last favor—unwitting or not, he didn't know—when she asked him in, after he'd driven them home from church, for a final cup of tea and cookies. They'd fixed the tea tray together, the three of them strangely subdued in the bright stainless steel kitchen of Gabrielle's Tea Garden as they worked side by side. Miss Gabby led them into the Garden Room, turning the lights to their lowest setting as she entered. "Clear night," she said. "Ought to be able to see the stars from here."

She was right. The skylights framed glorious rectangles of

sky, brilliant lights twinkling against the black velvet night. *Same stars that looked down on the shepherds in their fields Christmas night,* Parker thought. *Same stars that heard a multitude of angels, praising God and saying, Glory to God in the highest, and on earth peace, goodwill toward men.*

Gran-Gabby excused herself halfway through her cup of tea. "I'm tired. You two finish up and rinse the pot when you're through. Parker, don't forget Christmas dinner at two tomorrow. I'll wish you a 'Merry Christmas' then."

She started to leave, but stopped in the doorway and looked up at the mistletoe over her head.

"Changed my mind. Come give me a Christmas kiss, Parker, and I'll wish you a 'Merry Christmas' now."

He jumped up from his chair and met her in the doorway. "Miss Gabby, I can't believe you haven't caught me under the mistletoe before now!" He leaned forward and planted a loud, smacking kiss on her cheek. Her lips on his own cheek a moment later were cool and dry, just an angel's touch before she pulled away and looked at him. "Merry Christmas, Parker," she told him in a voice softer than he'd ever heard her use. "May your every Christmas wish come true." Then she turned, making her way through the tables in the children's dining room and disappearing around the corner of the doorway.

He stayed where he was a moment longer, staring through the dim room and across the brightly lit hallway into the other darkened dining room, where he could see the Victorian angel at the top of the Christmas tree, arms outstretched. He could almost hear the words of the angel in the shepherd's field so long ago: *"Fear not; for behold, I bring you good tidings of great joy...."*

The front stairs creaked as Miss Gabby ascended the staircase to the second floor. Turning, Parker saw that Nick was watching him over the rim of her teacup. She set the cup down as their eyes met.

He raised his dark eyebrows and quirked his mouth into a grin, pretending his heart wasn't beating in double time. *Fear not....*

"How about it, Nick?" he asked, gesturing with a nod toward the gray-green foliage hanging from the doorway. "Miss Gabby would be disappointed if we didn't share a kiss under the mistletoe."

Nick hesitated, then returned his quirky grin. "You're right," she said, scooting her chair back and walking toward the door. "It's the least we can do for Gran-Gabby."

She stopped in front of him, smiling, her head at a saucy angle. Parker reached for her arms.

He only meant to brush his lips against hers, make the kiss a light and playful one, so as not to scare her away before he told her what he had to say. But when their lips touched, he couldn't help himself. The longings he'd been reigning in for weeks now clamored for release. He tightened his grip on her arms as the kiss lengthened and, miracle of miracles, she didn't pull away.

When he finally came up for air, he saw that her cornflower eyes were round, her pupils wide with surprise and wonder. They stared at each other for a long moment, their eyes only inches apart. *I love you, Nick,* Parker thought. He took a deep breath, but the words that came out were only, "I think we'd better try that one more time."

As he bent to kiss her again the front doorbell chimed melodically. Nick jumped, pushing against his chest, and he saw that her eyes were glazed and startled, as if the sound of the chime had wakened her from a dream.

"Let...let me get that," she stammered. "So Gran-Gabby doesn't have to come down."

Reluctantly he let go of her arms and stepped back as Nick hurried through the dining room and disappeared beyond the corner Miss Gabby had rounded minutes earlier. He started to follow her, but stopped short at Nick's startled exclamation.

"Tom!"

He heard the chain slide out of its slot, the deadbolt click, the door swing open on creaky hinges as he stood frozen. *Need to oil those hinges for Miss Gabby,* he told himself inanely.

"Tom!" he heard her say once more. "What are you *doing* here?"

A deep, breathless laugh answered her. Parker closed his eyes, as if the wall wasn't enough to shut out the sight of Nick's reunion with her boyfriend, and discovered neither the wall nor his closed eyes did the trick. In his mind he saw Tom's arms go around her, saw him lift her face to look at him, saw him lower his mouth to kiss the lips Parker had kissed only moments before. A lifetime before.

Tom's words reached Parker with the same clarity as the unwished-for image. "I've made up my mind, Nick. I wanted to tell you in person. I've missed you. I don't want to lose you. If you want to get married, I'll do it. If you want kids, let's have kids."

Parker heard the *whoosh* as Tom let out his breath. "There, I've said it. Nicolette Weatherspoon, will you marry me?"

"Tom!" Nick said again, as if every other word in her vocabulary had been erased from her mind.

Epilogue

Christmas Day, One Year Later

Nick carefully shifted the bundle in her arms and grinned at the man in the Santa Claus hat who sat in the chair next to her hospital bed. He looked as exhausted as she felt. And as happy.

She wondered if her smile was as goofy as his. He looked positively loony with delight, she thought, as if at any moment he might jump up on his chair and dance a jig. A bit the way *she* felt—although, a sudden pang reminded her, a jig was probably out of the question for at least a week or two.

"Penny for your thoughts," she said.

"A penny! Wouldn't give these thoughts away for less than a hundred thou'."

"Even to me?"

Reaching across the space between them, he gently stroked her cheek. She turned her face into his palm, kissing its center, knowing how it made him melt.

He sighed in contentment. "From you I wouldn't accept a penny, Love o' my Life. In fact, every thought I *have* is yours," he teased. "Even my million-dollar thoughts are yours for the asking."

Nick rolled her eyes. "I *knew* I'd married a generous man!" She laughed, waking the baby in her arms, who squirmed and started to squawl. Pulling the newborn closer, she rocked him softly and cooed, in a way she'd sworn she'd never do if she ever had a child of her own: "Nuffin wong wif your 'ittle lungs, is dere, baby? Uh-uh, 'ittle sweet one, uh-uh." She lifted her head again, raising her voice over the increasing volume of the infant's cries. "We're quite a team, you and I," she said with satisfaction.

"Nick, do you realize it was only a *year* ago I asked you to marry me?" he asked.

"We worked fast," she agreed. "Once we both knew what we wanted."

He nodded. "*That* was the part that took some getting to. Both of us knowing what we wanted and being brave enough to ask. *I* think it was a miracle."

How could she disagree? Here she was on Christmas Day, a thirty-seven-year-old first-time mother smiling down in utter but contented exhaustion at the red-faced baby caterwauling in her arms, as the dearest man in the world looked on with infinite tenderness.

A year and a month ago, at Thanksgiving, she'd despaired that her house would ever ring with a child's laughter. A year and a week ago, when she'd felt so distant from Tom after their disappointing phone conversation, she feared she'd completely deceived herself, that the promise she believed she'd heard from God was only a delusional expression of her longings. A year and a day ago, before Tom had shown up on her doorstep—who would even have dreamed she'd be here now?

"Well, Christmas is a good day for a miracle," she said. "Especially a *baby* kind of miracle." She paused. "You really don't mind that I want to call him Gabe? It's really okay not to have your first-born son be a 'Junior'?"

"It's really okay, Nick." He reached to smooth the golden

102

fuzz of the infant's hair, a motion which seemed to lessen the volume of his crying. "His name will always remind me that the angels were watching out for us," he said.

Nick snorted. "You're not referring to Gran-Gabby as an angel, are you?"

"You have to admit she had *something* to do with our getting together. To think I almost lost you for want of asking!"

"You! To think *I* almost let Gran-Gabby's scheming come between us!"

"A miracle certain, the way things happened," he answered, shaking his head in wonder. "Christmas Eve last year, I thought I'd lost you."

"Never. My heart had already made up my mind."

They'd been married less than two months later, in a Valentine's Day wedding at the Peace and Goodwill Bible Baptist Church in Seattle, with the Rev. Carl Jarlsberg, Nick's childhood pastor, officiating. Her mother's old Missionary Sewing Support Circle chums, Mrs. Philpott, Mrs. Jenkins, and Mrs. Hughley, who'd been waiting for the day their capital-letter Something Special Nicolette Weatherspoon would marry, organized the reception in the basement of the church. Nick insisted she didn't want it anywhere else.

She smiled again at the rumpled man sitting next to her, cooing improbably at the child of their love—the dear, dusty, rumpled man who'd held her hand and helped her survive eight hours of hard labor.

He returned her smile. "I love you, Nick."

"Love you, too." At that, the baby interrupted his squalling with a wide yawn, fluttered his eyelids, and, finally relaxing, snuggled deeper into Nick's arms with his eyes closed. Nick sighed in contentment.

"Thank you, God," she murmured as her own eyes drifted shut.

"And what about *me?*"

She smiled without opening her eyes at the pretended injury in the gruff, velvet-edged voice of the man she loved. "Thank you, Parker. You're my very best angel," she told him drowsily and drifted off to sleep with his kiss lingering on her lips.

Just outside the door, Angela McPhee and Gabrielle Weatherspoon looked at each other, eyes bright, smiling secret smiles. "Didn't I tell you?" Gran-Gabby crowed triumphantly.

"I never doubted for a minute," Angel said.

FELIZ NAVIDAD

LORENA McCOURTNEY

CHAPTER

One

❧

C arolyn McAndrews dropped to the sofa, hot, tired, and frustrated.

You'll love Playa Luna de la Creciente, Helen had said from her hospital bed. *Gorgeous blue sea, miles of beach, endless sunshine, wonderful seashells. No ringing telephones, no hustle and bustle, nothing but peace and quiet.*

From the sofa, gazing at the beach through the wall of windows in the room attached to the small travel trailer, Carolyn couldn't tell about the "wonderful seashells," but surely everything else was true.

Playa Luna de la Creciente...Crescent Moon Beach! Her pulse quickened in spite of all her problems.

The blue of the sea was a shade only the Lord's paintbrush could achieve, a blend of sapphire and mystery and flickering silver. The long curve of sandy beach framed seagulls and pelicans dotting the glassy surface like hand-placed decorations, and the sky was so clear and sun so warm that it was difficult to believe the snow and cold she'd left behind in Colorado. At the point of the crescent, a lone figure jogged in splendid solitude.

There were, however, Carolyn thought with a return to frustration, a few points Helen had skimmed a bit lightly. "Oh, you're so competent and resourceful," Helen had said airily. "You won't have any problems."

No?

Sure, she'd managed to turn on the propane, and the kitchen stove worked, but the propane refrigerator, after repeated pleas and even a threatening whack, just sat there, no more effective at cooling than a hatbox. She'd gotten the water from the rooftop storage tank turned on...and found it too awful tasting to drink. As for starting the generator to provide electricity because there was no public power supply here—just what did a generator look like?

To top everything off, when she went out to turn the minivan around so she could unload her luggage and supplies from the rear doors, she'd gotten it stuck in the loose sand, the tires sinking as if they were grimly digging their way to the center of the earth.

She couldn't even soothe herself with music. The battery radio took "D" batteries and sulked silently on the "C" size Carolyn offered it.

Of course you may be disappointed if you're looking for romance, Helen had warned. It was couples and families from the States who came to these vacation and winter homes on the Sea of Cortez coastline of Baja, Mexico, not eligible single men of an appropriate age.

Romance? Romance was not on Carolyn's agenda either at home or here. All she wanted was rest and relaxation, a quiet time to recharge her seriously depleted batteries. And at this point, with the realization that she was shortly going to be sitting in the dark in silence, dehydrating from lack of drinkable water, with nothing but a rapidly souring carton of milk for company, the total irrelevance of *romance* gave her a peculiar desire to giggle.

What, oh what, she wondered as she balanced on that pre-carious pinpoint between laughter and panic at her ignominious situation, had she been thinking, making this trip across the border alone? Ignorant optimism, foolish recklessness, sheer madness!

She shouldn't even be here, chasing blue sea and Christmas sunshine. She should be at home, making plans for a big Christmas dinner, baking cookies for the grandkids, using her vacation time to catch up on house cleaning. She was, after all, a middle-aged widow with duties and responsibilities, not some carefree college girl on holiday break! And so many things could go wrong while she was away—

She jumped up and stared out the window at the cluster of a dozen houses and trailers ranged along the beach and hillside. Except for that lone jogger, she hadn't seen a soul anywhere. Where *was* everyone?

Perhaps she should go back to San Felipe, rent a room for the night, and then simply head home. The thought reminded her that the van was as stuck as the dead lizard her five-year-old grandson Mike had once glued to his bedroom wall. She *couldn't* leave.

She also reminded herself that she need not worry about problems at home. The grandkids were crazy about their fun Uncle Scott, and he was perfectly capable of handling any emergency that might arise while he took over for her in caring for them. He might, to Carolyn's fond motherly eyes, still show traces of the dirty-kneed little boy he had once been, but at twenty-six, he hadn't gotten his Ph.D. in economics on his curly-haired good looks alone. He had convinced her she needed these two weeks to herself, although she wouldn't have chosen to be away from her grandchildren at the Christmas holidays if he could have come at any other time.

A shower, that was what she needed! Even if the water tasted as if it had been filtered through old shoes, surely it was good enough for bathing, and everything would look less overwhelming after a refreshing shower. Perhaps by then the refrigerator would start working. She'd never admitted it to anyone, but the competent and resourceful Carolyn McAndrews sometimes operated on the hopeful theory that mechanical things "got well" if you ignored them for a while.

There was no hot water, of course, so she simply heated a saucepan of water on the stove. She opened the louvered, frosted-glass window in the bathroom for fresh air and laid out clean clothes. She hummed a cheerful tune the grandkids had learned in Sunday school, feeling some of her tension dissipate as she lathered herself with delightful suds from neck to toe. By the time she was ready to rinse off, the water in the pan was also filled with suds. She reached for the faucet knob so she could wash herself off with cold water—

And saw the handle fall like a rock into her hand.

Frantically she reached for the other faucet. It didn't fall off. No. For all she could tell from the strength of its stubborn resistance to her two-handed clutch, it could have been welded in place.

And just at that most inappropriate moment, while she stood there cocooned in rapidly drying, soapy lather, a knock sounded on the door. In spite of her awkward predicament, she leaned toward the narrow opening in the louvered window to investigate.

She couldn't see much, just the lean midsection of a man standing at the door of the room that had been built onto the small trailer. He knocked again, then, apparently deciding no one was inside, turned to leave. She still couldn't see his face, but she had a better view of him.

Crisp silver hair, a trim build clad in cutoff jeans, blue T-shirt, and jogging shoes. Something metallic dangled from one hand, and a small, oblong object bulged in his back pocket, surprising her as she realized what it was.

Watching his departing back, Carolyn felt the strangest little prickle across her own back. A man with silver hair, a New Testament in his hip pocket, and a wrench in his right hand…

She discarded the unfamiliar prickle instantly. *Of course you feel prickly,* she muttered to herself. *You're standing here covered with drying soapsuds.*

She also realized that her only source of help was about to walk off and disappear.

"Wait!" she called through the crack. "Don't go!"

#

H e turned, peering uncertainly toward the sound of the dis-embodied voice.

"Hi," she said, feeling a little foolish speaking through the screened crack. She knew he couldn't see her, but she scrunched down so only her eyes were at window level. "I can't come to the door for a minute, but if you don't mind waiting—?"

"I'll take a look at the van. Looks as if you may have a little problem there." The voice was nice, with a hint of cheerful good humor in the understatement about her half-buried van.

"Okay, I'll be right out." Carolyn hastily cranked the window shut, sloshed what remained of the soapy water in the pan over her body and hurriedly dressed in khaki shorts and pale yellow cotton blouse.

She opened the door and walked out to where he was kneeling in the sand to peer under the van. "I'm sorry to keep you waiting. I was…tied up with something."

He stood and brushed sand off his tanned legs. He was medium height, as trim and fit as her first peephole impression had suggested. Friendly blue eyes—more the color of sunlit sky than mysterious sea, with sun-crinkles at the corners—greeted her. A good-humored quirk to his mouth matched his voice. The contrast between tanned skin and thick silver eyebrows and hair was most attractive, and maturity only emphasized his bone-deep good looks. She realized she was staring and hastily stuck out a hand. "I'm Carolyn McAndrews."

He transferred the wrench to his left hand and shook her hand with comfortable self-assurance. "Ward Setlow."

"I wish I could blame this on someone else." She motioned ruefully toward the van. "But I did it all by myself."

"No problem. I can pull it out with my motorhome." He nodded toward the home-on-wheels parked by a house tucked into the steep hillside.

She instantly noted that the phrase was "my motorhome," not "our motorhome," and just as instantly gave herself a mental thumping. She was *not* a woman whose radar went into a check-marital-status mode every time a good-looking guy got within range. "I don't want to put you to all that trouble. I understood that the Mexican family that owns the land lives here year-round—?"

"There was a death in Emelio's family, so they're all in Mexicali. Several families from the States are supposed to be here over the holidays, but Ray and Ruth Milton are the only ones here now, and they went to San Felipe for the day. I'll go get the motorhome and a tow chain—" Then, as if recognizing she might feel uncomfortable alone here with a strange man, he added, "Unless you'd rather I came back later?"

Carolyn appreciated the sensitive insight but still hesitated. "That's your place, there on the hill?"

"No. It belongs to some friends. I'm just parking the motorhome there for a while."

"Was that you I saw jogging on the beach earlier?"

"I try to put in a few miles every day." His in-shape physique said he had the will power not to skip many days.

113

She hesitated briefly, then plunged ahead. "Actually, at the moment, the stuck van is the least of my problems."

He lifted the wrench in a small salute and grinned. "The wrench may not be mightier than the pen or sword, but at times it comes in a lot more handy. What can I do?"

Carolyn mentally hopscotched through her list of problems. Which was the most pressing? "I can't get the propane refrigerator to work, and the fresh food I bought in San Felipe won't last long without it."

"I'll take a look."

He went through the same unsuccessful procedure she had. But, where failure at that point had left her stumped, he went outside, opened the back of the refrigerator and within minutes had a proper flame burning. "Anything else?"

"Well…" Carolyn glanced toward the motorhome. "Won't your wife wonder what's taking you so long down here?"

He grinned again, the blue eyes echoing the amusement of the smile. He'd acquired a smudge of grease on his cheek, and the silver hair was rumpled now. "I hope that question really means you're checking to see if I'm married," he said candidly.

Carolyn blushed, guilty and embarrassed. Then she was further embarrassed *because* she was blushing, which was practically an admission of guilt, and a little put out because *he* seemed to be so thoroughly enjoying her reaction.

"I just meant—" She hadn't *consciously* planned the question to snoop into his marital status, but she wasn't so certain what her sneaky subconscious might be up to.

He gracefully let her off the hook. "My wife passed away about six years ago, so I'm alone now." His quiet tone gave his wife's memory respect, but Carolyn also sensed acceptance, that he'd worked his way through the grieving stage. As she also had.

"I'm sorry. I lost my husband nine years ago."

Unexpectedly he looked confused. "But the Miltons said he'd died just two years ago, and you hadn't been here since then."

"Oh, that's my friend, Helen Cavanaugh. This is her place. We planned to spend the holidays here together, but at the last minute she slipped on some icy steps, broke her leg, and wound up in the hospital."

"And you decided to come alone?" He sounded both surprised and impressed. "You're very adventurous."

"What's that old saying? Fools rush in where angels fear to tread?"

"Ah-ha, you're holding out on me, aren't you? There *are* more problems."

"I hate to bother you—"

He held up the wrench again. "This isn't just for decoration," he reprimanded with mock severity. "Lead me to your loose bolts, your leaking faucets, your stopped-up sinks, and stuck windows—"

She did. And one by one he efficiently took care of her problems. He repaired the fallen faucet in the shower and loosened the stuck one. He explained that there was no public water supply, and the water Emelio hauled in from a well several miles away to fill the individual storage tanks was safe enough, but everyone used the better-tasting bottled water from a plant in San Felipe for drinking. He also supplied her with a five-gallon bottle to use until she had a chance to fill the three empty ones she now saw lined up beside the sofa. He even went up to his motorhome and returned with batteries of the proper size to fit the radio.

Maybe, she thought as she lifted a glass of water to her mouth for another sip, the nineties knight came in cutoff jeans rather than shining armor. With a New Testament in his pocket, a wrench in his hand, and a wonderfully warm, male, fresh sunshine-and-sand scent.

Impulsively she asked, "Do you always show up with a wrench and all your expertise when someone new arrives?"

"I try to be helpful. Although in this instance, I'd heard this place belonged to a beautiful widow, so when I got back from my run and saw the van, I thought I'd check it out." His smile and mischievous blue eyes suggested he was teasing about this ulterior motive, and she suspected he'd have come to offer his help even if he'd heard the owner of this trailer was some crotchety old bachelor.

But those eyes also held an open male interest that flustered her. She managed to murmur, "I'm sure my friend Helen will be pleased to know how she's described here."

He just smiled and went on to diagnose another problem before she even mentioned it. "Most of the houses here are set up with individual solar systems for electricity, but I don't see any solar panels on this place. So there must be a generator. Do you have a key to the garage?"

Somehow she wasn't surprised that the green piece of equipment he dragged out of the garage didn't work when he pulled the starter rope. She felt frustrated with yet another problem, but Ward, after asking her to hold a flashlight for him in the gathering dusk, merely whistled softly as he patiently cleaned a spark plug, tinkered with various wires, gave the rope several more strong-muscled pulls and...lights!

She clapped her hands delightedly. "Thank you, thank you so much for everything." She almost had to shout over the noisy roar of the generator until he muted the noise with a piece of plywood from the garage. She also felt rather awkward. He had done so much for her, but she knew instinctively that he'd never accept payment. "Would you like a cup of coffee or tea?" It was the only way she could think to show her gratitude.

"Another time. You look beat." It wasn't a critical statement that made her feel unattractive, merely a sympathetic insight. "Get some rest, and tomorrow we'll pull your van out of the sand."

He gave her a little wave and started off toward his motorhome, then turned and grinned again. "By the way, that description still fits."

Description? Carolyn tilted her head, puzzled, but then as he started up the hill she realized what he meant and felt the not-unpleasant warmth of another blush. *Beautiful widow.*

At home, Carolyn never had the luxury of sleeping late and fully intended to do so here. Instead, after going to bed early the night before, she found herself awake and standing at the wall of windows just as a fireball of sun appeared to be rising out of the sea.

An intriguing thought struck her. God could have made a serviceable enough world in black and white. Instead he'd created this glorious palette of pink and peach and coral sky, pale blue sea, and red-gold blaze of sun. The tide was out now, exposing a wide, almost flat area of dark rocks, and a flock of seagulls squawked and squabbled at the shoreline.

She raised her arms and stood on tiptoe to stretch, unexpectedly flooded with a delicious, something-wonderful-is-going-to-happen-today feeling. A feeling so unfamiliar that it took her a moment to recognize it. Not that she was *unhappy* with her life. The Lord had given her much joy in the unexpected responsibility of raising her daughter's three children. It was just that she seldom felt this sweet, exciting sense of anticipation.

And what was she anticipating? She listed the delightful possibilities. Go back to bed. Cook an outrageously spicy omelet for breakfast, the kind of thing that would make the kids melodramatically clutch their throats and act as if they were strangling. She could take a walk, read a book, write a poem!

Yet she had the sneaky suspicion the wonderful feeling of anticipation came from another source entirely.

Ward Setlow.

Ridiculous, she scoffed. She barely knew the man. He was nice, obviously. Attractive. That wonderful grin, with a hint of mischievous tease. A lean, fit build and physical strength that would put many a younger man to shame. She'd seen generosity and good humor and solid, practical competence in the way he'd helped her, patience as he tinkered with balky equipment, sensitivity in his recognition of how tired she was last night. She broke off as she suddenly realized she was *looking* at the object of her thoughts. He was sitting on one of the exposed rocks at the edge of the water, his back to her, head bowed, so motionless she hadn't noticed him at first.

Spotting binoculars on the coffee table, she impulsively lifted them to her eyes. He looked so at peace, she thought. Then he stood and slipped something into his hip pocket, and she realized she now knew something else about Ward Setlow: he read his Bible at sunrise beside the sea, a simple gesture of worship that deeply touched her.

She also realized with dismay that he was waving. He'd caught her spying on him through the binoculars! She momentarily thought about pretending she was bird watching but decided it was too late for that. Instead she opened the window and called, "Would you like that cup of coffee you turned down last night?"

"Love it."

She scurried around getting dressed, swishing a washcloth over her face and combing her short, curly hair with her fingers while he walked up from the beach. She still thought of herself as brown haired and now, as often, was a little startled to see the mirror reflect a silvery frost rapidly overtaking the brown. He was, she thought ruefully, going to see the basic, no-frills Carolyn McAndrews this morning.

But the warmth in his smile and eyes when she opened the door told her he liked what he saw.

"Do you always get up this early?" she asked. He looked wonderful: fresh-shaven, clear-eyed, distinguished even, in spite of the old green sweatshirt and jeans.

"I always read a few verses of Scripture when I first get up. I like to think it's a resurgence of youthful energy that gets me up early here." He laughed. "But it may simply be that without any time-wasting TV to keep me up at night, I go to bed earlier."

"There's no TV reception here?"

"Not much, unless you have a satellite dish. Which most of the people with solar setups for electricity do."

Carolyn tilted her head reflectively. Back home, she was usually too busy for much television watching, although, like electricity, it was always *there* if she wanted it. It was also an occasional source of friction with the kids, who had friends whose parents didn't monitor their television watching as closely as she did. "I won't miss it," she declared firmly, and he smiled approval.

Helen had said the cupboards were well stocked with canned goods and basic supplies, and that was true. But Helen's tastes were a little different from Carolyn's, and all she could find was instant coffee.

"Fine with me," Ward said cheerfully. "How about if I go get some rolls I bought at the *panaderia* and we'll make breakfast of it?"

"Wonderful."

"I also make a mean scrambled egg, if you're interested."

"Is there no end to your talents?" she teased lightly.

"After I was alone, it was learn to cook or spend the rest of my life eating out. So I learned to cook. Although it's pretty basic stuff—no veal cordon bleu or pheasant under glass. I do have a breadmaking machine back home that sometimes fools people into thinking I'm more expert than I am."

"And where is 'back home'?"

"Atlanta, Georgia. You?"

"Steele, Colorado. It's a few miles out of Denver."

"And a long drive from Baja," he observed. Again she heard admiration and interest in his voice.

Steele was also, she thought for no particular reason, a *long* way from Atlanta, Georgia.

He returned to his motorhome for the rolls, bringing back two oranges as well. While she made instant coffee and warmed the rolls, he scrambled the eggs. The trailer's tiny kitchen had them constantly bumping into each other, apologizing, and laughing. He decorated the plates with quartered sections of orange, then they carried their breakfasts to the round metal table in the attached room. Now the sea was almost turquoise, but the waves were still no more than white riffles at the shoreline.

"It's so peaceful here," Carolyn said a little dreamily. She had never spent more than a few weeks in her entire life beside the sea, and the power of its moving tides and changing colors fascinated her. "You can almost forget the problems of the world exist."

"Much different from Atlanta," he agreed.

"Have you lived there long?"

"Most of my life. Although I put the house up for sale a few months ago, when I started traveling."

"You're retired, then?" Actually, he looked too young to be retired, not past her own mid-fifties.

"I guess retired is what I have to say I am." He leaned back in the chair and took a sip of coffee. He drank it black, as she did. "Although I don't really feel retired. I feel more…in between phases of my life." His quick grin as his eyes met hers held a touch of embarrassment. "That sounds like some catch phrase spouted by a pop psychologist, doesn't it?"

"Not necessarily." There *were* phases of life. Although raising a young family was not the one she had anticipated for this time of her own. The rolls from the Mexican bakery were cream-filled, sticky, and delicious, and abandoning the good-manners example she always tried to set for the kids, she luxuriously licked a gooey drop from her fingertips. "What were you in the previous phase?"

"Husband, father, manufacturer of plumbing fixtures." A fleeting expression she couldn't quite identify crossed his tanned face. Not dissatisfaction, but…something.

"And where did you learn to do everything and fix everything?"

The brief, unsettled expression vanished, and he laughed, and she was for a moment achingly aware of how long it had been since she had heard a man's cheerful laughter in the morning.

"That's a bit of overstatement, but thank you for the vote of confidence. I started out in a two-man construction business with my father, and he taught me how to do a little of everything. But even after I started my own plumbing manufacturing business and was enveloped in all the paperwork that goes with management, I still liked tinkering with my hands. My sons and I rebuilt a couple of cars, and my daughter brought me dolls and bicycles to fix when she was little and hair dryers and tape decks when she was older. I managed to fix most things, except her frequent broken hearts." His voice held a fond note of affectionate reminiscence.

"You're out of the manufacturing business now?"

"About a year ago a much larger company offered to buy me out. I turned the offer down, and they raised it. I decided then that I'd better grab it quick before they came to their senses and backed out."

"Are you sorry you did it?" Carolyn asked impulsively, remembering that earlier, fleeting expression.

"No. For a while I thought I was. But not now." The answer was decisive, but he did not sound like a man who had decided to settle into a lazy retirement, even though he was apparently financially secure. Instead, this was the statement of a man with a purpose, and she wondered what it was. But he deftly changed the subject, apparently not inclined to elaborate at the moment. "And what do you do back in Colorado?"

"I'm an escrow officer with a title company. I handle real estate transfers, check the validity of titles, do title insurance, that kind of thing." She smiled. "And I'm a grandmother."

"Family?"

"A son and three grandchildren." She purposely did not go into further painful family details about her daughter Terry's death, which were basically irrelevant to a casual conversation. "And you?"

"Two sons, one daughter, five grandchildren." He set his coffee cup on the metal table and smiled. "There, I think that takes care of everything, doesn't it?"

"Everything?" She was a little taken back by how final that sounded. She had no big romance designs on Ward Setlow, of course, but he was pleasant company and she definitely liked him.

He smiled, and there was nothing "final" about the smile. "Single people always do this little dance of information exchange when they meet, and we've just done ours."

True, Carolyn agreed. Although she'd stayed off the "dance floor" ever since the unhappy surprise ending to the only serious relationship she'd had since Carl's death.

"We've covered home towns, occupations, and families." He ticked off the items on his strong hands. "Let's see, I could also add that I like Mexican food and pizza, Disneyland, and the color blue. I can't carry a tune, but I sing in church anyway. I'm a sucker for sob-story animal movies, and I don't think growing older is nearly the bummer, as my grandchildren would say, that some people do. And the most important thing, of course, is—"

Carolyn smiled, liking his list. "You're a Christian."

He didn't ask how she knew, just nodded. "Since I was barely tall enough to see over the pew in front of me at church."

"I can't claim my personal relationship with the Lord is anywhere near that long. Carl and I were in our thirties before we accepted Christ." Would her life be different now if they had found him sooner? Could Terry's tragedy have been avoided? But the past couldn't be changed now, and all she could do was concentrate on the future. And the moment. "Look!"

She pointed to a long line of pelicans flying barely above the calm surface of the sea as if they were playing a graceful game of follow the leader. The leader flapped his wings, and almost as if he'd muttered, *Pass the word along,* one by one, each of the pelicans in line behind him also flapped its wings. The line also rose and dipped in perfect follow-the-leader choreography, undulating gracefully until they were out of sight.

Carolyn and Ward looked at each other and smiled, the shared moment like a small, special bond between them.

"How long will you be here?" Ward asked.

"Two weeks. I have to start home on New Year's Day." A little awkwardly, she asked, "You?"

"Oh…I think I'll be here for a couple of weeks yet too." He stood up. "Now, let's get that van unstuck, okay?"

Three

෴

With Ward's expertise and the motorhome's powerful engine, getting the van back on solid ground didn't take long.

"Well, thanks again." Carolyn was in the van, and he leaned his forearms against the frame of the open window. He'd changed to shorts and added sunglasses and a straw hat with three dark feathers jauntily stuck in the band.

"Did you know there's a sandrail in the garage?" he asked.

"No!" Carolyn had immediate visions of some huge, unknown sand bug lurking out there, ready to pounce on her in an unguarded moment. "I think there's some ant spray in the trailer—"

He blinked, momentarily baffled at her response, then laughed and opened the door of the van. "Come. We'll face the dangerous beast together."

It seemed natural when he took her hand to lead her to the garage. There, the sandrail turned out to be not a lurking menace but an odd-looking vehicle. It was apparently homemade, with metal pipes forming an open cage around a single seat just wide enough for two people, engine in back, extra-wide tires, and a flat plywood top decorated with a frivolous pink fringe.

"What's it for?" Carolyn asked.

"For running up and down the beach. Almost everyone here has a sandrail or dune buggy or four-wheeler or something to use in the sand. Regular vehicles just get stuck. Would your friend mind if we used it?"

"She said to enjoy the place just as if it were my own. But somehow I doubt this thing is going to run."

He let go of her hand—giving her an unexpected little sense of loss when the warm, firm grip left hers—and went to check out the strange vehicle. He didn't have it running instantly, but within two minutes he knew *why* it wasn't running.

"No battery," he announced. "But it takes a common kind, and we can probably get one in San Felipe later. Right now, how about a walk on the beach instead?"

She thought about unpacked luggage, dust, dirty dishes from breakfast, van that should be swept…and impulsively discarded the entire list. Tasks such as these would always be with her, but how often did she have the chance to walk on the beach with a handsome, silver-haired man who read his Bible at sunrise beside the sea?

"I'd love a walk on the beach."

"I'll move the motorhome back to where it was and be back in a few minutes."

Inside the trailer, Carolyn hurriedly slathered on sunscreen and changed from sandals to walking shoes, because the sand here was a bit coarse for comfortable barefoot walking. After adding sunglasses and a stylish straw hat that granddaughter Kelsey, already fashion conscious at age eleven, had helped her choose, she tucked a plastic bag in her pocket for carrying beach treasures home. When he returned, Ward apologized for taking so long.

"Ray Milton needed help unloading this monstrous statue of a matador-and-bull that Ruth bought yesterday." Ward shook

125

his head. "I think the storekeepers were cheering and congratulating each other after that sale."

"I once fell for a palm tree lamp that looked great in Hawaii," Carolyn admitted. "I had to hide it in the attic when we got home."

"The Miltons also invited us up for dinner tonight," he added. "Some friends down at Puertecitos gave them a couple of big sea bass. I think that's a problem with being an avid fisherman here: you wind up with more fish than you can eat and have to pawn them off on friends before you can go catch more."

Carolyn heard what he was saying about the fish, but her attention jumped back to the first statement. "Invited *us?*" she repeated.

"I think I phrased that wrong." He rumpled his hair with one hand, his grin one of embarrassment. "What I mean is, they invited me and told me to invite you, too. Invitations here are often of an informal, 'y'all-come' variety. I didn't mean to suggest that we were locked into instant couplehood."

Carolyn smiled, not letting on how she felt about "instant couplehood." Actually, she wasn't certain herself. Her next thought was hardly an original one, but it was true: she felt as if she'd known Ward much longer than the less than twenty-four hours that had actually elapsed since she'd met him.

"I'd be delighted to have dinner with the Miltons," she said firmly. *And with you.*

He jogged up to let the Miltons know and returned to tell Carolyn that they were to be at the house about six o'clock. Then they started walking north on the beach. Carolyn dashed eagerly from a bit of broken shell that looked like part of a miniature shield to clam-shaped shells decorated with geometric designs in pink and red—from a spiky white shell with delicate pink throat to a narrow, pointed shell with only a tiny opening at the top—greeting each find with a cry of delight.

Ward, who was being much more selective in what he picked up, laughed. "You'll get more fussy after a while. The tide will go farther out during the full moon next week, and out there you can find shells that haven't been broken and weathered from coming in over the rocks."

But Carolyn didn't care. Each find was a wonderful new treasure to her, and within minutes her plastic bag was so heavy that Ward took it and handed her his own nearly-empty bag in exchange. A few minutes later they both spotted a colorful tangle of fabric caught on a rock. Carolyn dashed to it.

"Look! It's a...what is it?" she asked, puzzled, as she stretched the snarl of silky fabric between her hands.

"Looks like a windsock. Must have blown away from someone's place farther north. But I think it's too tangled to salvage."

"I'm going to give it a try," Carolyn declared.

Right there she sat cross-legged in the sand and started trying to unsnarl the knots and tangles in fabric and cord. Ward sat beside her, occasionally reaching in a hand to help.

"I look so pale next to you," she said, noting the contrast between the deep tan of his hands and her own winter-pale skin. And a bit chagrined by her plain, short-cut nails. She was always intending to get a professional manicure with some fashionable shade of polish, but taking Kelsey to a ballet class or tomboy Erin to soccer or cutting little Mike's hair, because barbers scared him, always took higher priority.

Or perhaps, Carolyn realized, she was thinking about tans and manicures because she didn't want to acknowledge the little electric tingle that passed between her hand and Ward's each time they touched. Or maybe she was the only one feeling it—?

No. She sneaked a peek at Ward and found him studying her with a bemused expression when that strange little tingle passed between them again. *Get a grip,* she told herself, a bit aghast at both herself and Ward. *This is adolescent stuff, and you're both grandparents.* Hastily she started a diverting discussion about the border crossing at Mexicali and then the relative merits of spending American dollars in Baja versus changing them into pesos.

They worked well together, her hands quick and agile in the tight places, his adding a touch of strength where needed, and finally the tangled fabric turned into an identifiable shape. Carolyn spread it on the sand and laughed in delight.

"It's a fish! A big, silly fish."

The wildly flamboyant fish had one green side and one orange, black and yellow fins, red stripes, and frivolous purple eyes. The mouth was the round opening where the cords attached, giving the fish a permanent expression of surprise.

"You're a very determined woman when you set your mind to something, aren't you? I really thought you were working on a lost cause when you started this." Ward squinted at the unlikely nylon creature. "You know what he looks like?"

"What?" Carolyn asked, expecting the formal name of some exotic fish of the sea.

"An Edgar."

Carolyn lifted the colorful windsock, letting the breeze flow through the opening and swelling the fish's sides to chubby plumpness. "Why I do believe you're right. He *is* an Edgar. Edgar, the Flying Fish."

They took Edgar home, where Ward found a wooden pole to stick in the ground, and a metal swivel with which to fasten him to the pole. Edgar danced cheerfully in the breeze, and they exchanged pleased glances at their shared accomplishment.

Carolyn fixed lunch: canned-ham sandwiches and green salad served on paper plates because she'd decided she had better things to do here than wash piles of dishes. Afterward, Ward went back to his motorhome, saying he might take a nap, although Carolyn suspected he could be trying to reassure her he wasn't pushing "instant couplehood" on her. This feeling was reinforced a little later when she saw him working on the roof of the house belonging to the friends where he was staying. No lazy napping for Ward Setlow!

Carolyn decided she *would* take an afternoon nap. How often at home did she think, *If I just had a few minutes of time out!* Yet after no more than ten minutes on the sofa she was up, sorting through her beach treasures, deciding which ones to take home to the kids, and looking through her limited supply of clothes to choose something suitable for the Miltons' dinner.

Late that afternoon she showered in cold water, not at all bad once she got past the first shock. She didn't dress any differently than she would have if the dinner were not going to involve Ward, choosing a tea-length full skirt in a flowery print and a soft, shirred blouse. But she found herself taking extra care to give her hair a flattering lift at the sides and experimented with layering one shade of lipstick over another, as she'd read in some fashion magazine recently while waiting to get Mike in to see the pediatrician, the only place she managed to grab a few minutes for such light reading. And at the last moment, finding a long-unused bottle of nail polish in her makeup box, she painted her toenails a frivolous pink.

She knew the efforts were not wasted when Ward showed up a few minutes before six. He took her hands in his and smiled, that wonderful grin that threw off more heart-stopping megapower than any generator could ever produce.

"Are wolf whistles considered unacceptably anti-feminist or politically incorrect these days?"

He wasn't dressed up—just tan cotton slacks and open-throated sports shirt—but if any single woman her age were asked to describe her ideal man, Carolyn suspected Ward

Setlow would be it. His hair had a fresh-washed silvery gleam and a bit of rebellious curl at the neckline, and a faint scent of some woodsy masculine soap drifted around him.

"I don't know. Are they?" she asked and, turning the tables on him, managed an expressive if somewhat shaky wolf whistle of her own as she let her gaze roam over him.

He laughed appreciatively, and they started up the hill toward the Miltons' hand in hand. "Perhaps I should give you a bit of warning about the Miltons," he said. "They're good-hearted, generous people, but Ray is totally outspoken on any subject, and because he hates his hearing aid, he doesn't wear it and then thinks you can't hear him unless he almost shouts everything. Just take whatever he says with the proverbial grain of salt because he isn't nearly the curmudgeon he tries to make himself out to be. And Ruth is a non-stop chatterer. She cheerfully says don't tell her any secrets because she can't keep them."

Carolyn quickly learned the accuracy of what Ward had said. The Miltons were in their late sixties, and their house was one of the nicest at *Luna*, the shortened version of *Playa Luna de la Creciente* that Ward had said everyone here used. A semicircular wall of windows gave a spectacular view up and down the shoreline. The centerpiece of that view at the moment was a not-quite-full golden moon shimmering a pathway across the dark sea. The matador and bull statue was indeed rather overwhelming, but it was almost lost among Ruth's other statues, colorful blankets, seashell wall hangings, and extravagant Christmas decorations.

Warm, sweet Ruth welcomed Carolyn with a hug and immediately lived up to her reputation as a chatterer. "It's so nice to have you here. Are you staying long? Oh, do tell me about Helen. I couldn't believe it when I heard about Frank. You're a widow, too, aren't you? Isn't this weather fantastic? Our son and family are coming this weekend."

Carolyn mostly just smiled and nodded. She and Ward were seated at the breakfast bar looking into the kitchen, where Ruth was making salad and Ray was preparing the huge fish steaks, dipping them in egg batter and cornflake crumbs, at the same time carrying on a booming conversation with Ward about the incompetence of a mechanic who'd worked on his pickup. When Ward mentioned the missing battery in the sandrail, Ray said there was no point in buying one and insisted Ward immediately look in his garage and see if one there would fit. With Ward temporarily out of range, Ray's attention focused on Carolyn.

"How come you drive that big ol' van anyway? Pretty little lady like you oughta have one of those snappy little sports cars."

The van was neither old nor big, as vans went, but Carolyn didn't argue the point. Nor did she say she sometimes did eye those sporty little two seaters with a certain wistfulness. She merely said, "I'm always hauling the grandchildren and their friends around—"

Ray rolled his eyes melodramatically. "Don't get me started on *grandchildren*," and then instantly proceeded to start on them. "Can you believe what kids expect these days? Gotta be driven everywhere, like they never heard of walking. And they expect their own TVs too, and all that other electronic stuff. How many grandchildren you got?" he demanded of Carolyn.

"Three—"

"Came down here to escape the little curtain-climbers over the holidays, right?" He didn't give her time to deny that before booming on about how some of his younger grandchildren had torn half their presents open before the adults were even awake last Christmas. "Why, if I'd behaved like that when I was a kid, I'd have been sent to the woodshed for a week."

Ruth smiled tolerantly. "Ray talks like an old grump, but if you want to see a grandpa who spoils his grandchildren, just look at this one."

Ray grinned, unconcerned at being caught. "Well, sure, that's what grandchildren are for—for grandparents to enjoy and then hand back to their parents. I can tell you one thing for certain though: I wouldn't want to be trying to raise a family myself these days. Some friends are stuck with their grandchildren, and I tell you, what with all the drugs and gangs kids are mixed up in these days, weapons at school, that awful screeching music, ridiculous clothes at ridiculous prices, and that weird internet stuff— Well, I wouldn't want to be in their shoes, that's for sure."

"It's true there are lots of problems raising grandchildren," Carolyn said. Sometimes she worried about the internet. One of Kelsey's friends had a computer hooked into it, and Carolyn wasn't certain how much attention the friend's parents paid to where the kids went on it. And she was often appalled at the price of children's clothes. "But there are so many joys and rewards doing it that are so much more important—"

"Ought to make these lazy young parents live up to their responsibilities, that's what I say," Ray grumbled, and Carolyn wasn't sure her comments had even penetrated. "They brought these kids into the world, let them take care of 'em."

"But if—"

"And if they won't do it, just kick 'em off the planet, that's what."

Carolyn swallowed and reminded herself of what Ward had said, that Ray wasn't nearly the curmudgeon he pretended to be, but the carelessly hard-hearted words shocked and hurt her anyway. Because, if one wanted to use Ray's terminology, Terry *had* been "kicked off the planet." She was just formulating a terse response about her own raising-grandchildren situation when Ward reappeared and set a battery just outside the open patio door.

"Course Ward, here, may have a different opinion on all this," Ray said, now sounding a little sly. "He just might have to get used to having a young family around."

Ward, just coming in on the end of the conversation, asked, "*What?*"

"Why, sure. You might up and marry some beautiful young thing and start a whole new family."

"Not me." Ward shook his head emphatically. "I don't know how you got on *this* subject, but I'm well beyond the raising-a-young-family age. I'll leave the 'young things' to the young guys, thank you."

"Including that good-looking one up at *La Roca*?"

"Ray Milton, why don't you just serve the fish and mind your own business," Ruth snapped in exasperation.

Within a few minutes they were all settled around the table, nicely set with real dishes. As Ray proceeded to tell a funny fishing-experience story on himself, Carolyn calmed her ruffled feelings. Running down the younger generations was practically a national pastime, nothing for her to get worked up about personally. After that, dinner proceeded pleasantly. It wasn't until Carolyn and Ward were ready to leave that Ray made another remark that rather startled Carolyn.

"Let's see, you're leaving us on Sunday, aren't you?" he said to Ward.

Ward didn't look at Carolyn. He'd told her he'd be here another couple of weeks. "Well, uh…"

"Didn't you say you were heading up to the L.A. area then?"

"Actually, I've decided to stay here a while longer."

"Good idea. We did have some miserable wind there for a while, but it's looking good now."

Ruth, for once pausing for a thoughtful moment before

speaking, shot Carolyn a shrewd look. "Oh, I don't think it's the weather that has changed Ward's plans."

Four

"W ell, that was an experience, wasn't it?" Ward muttered as they walked back to Carolyn's trailer together. He'd left the battery on the Milton's patio, saying he'd pick it up the following morning.

The moon had turned from golden to silver as it climbed the night sky. Carolyn's gaze followed the guiding line of the Big Dipper to the North Star, something Carl had shown her a long time ago. A half-dozen lights dotted the dark surface of the sea, shrimp boats, Ward had earlier said they were. The faint sounds of their chugging diesel engines drifted on the sea-scented air.

"I suppose you're...uh...curious about the 'young thing' at *La Roca?*" Ward suggested awkwardly.

Carolyn automatically started to give the stock answer to a question such as that, *No, it's really none of my business,* but instead she just smiled and detoured the subject. "Actually, I'm more curious about why I can never find all those constellations of warriors and animals that are supposed to be up there in the stars."

"I never can either," he admitted. "But I would like to explain—"

Then she couldn't avoid the cliché answer. "Really, it isn't any of my business."

"It's just that I'd like you to know I'm not some...rabid chaser of women half my age. Actually—" He broke off, moonlight revealing the lines of a small frown on his usually good-natured face.

With quick intuition and already a fair knowledge of Ward's character, Carolyn knew why he was frowning. "She was chasing you, not the other way around."

"I really feel ridiculous about the whole thing," he muttered, still too much of a gentleman to say such a thing about a woman.

They walked on, changing to the less personal subject of the good dinner, Ward's strong arm steadying her when her sandal slipped on a loose rock. At her door, he turned her to face him. She thought he was going to kiss her, and looking into his shadowed eyes, knew he wanted to. But all he did was touch her jaw lightly with a fingertip, and Carolyn was glad that in this day of instant intimacy they both had an old-fashioned set of standards that gave a first kiss real importance.

"Ruth Milton got one thing right, anyway," he said softly. "The weather didn't have anything to do with my change in plans."

"You don't have to be in Los Angeles next week?"

"I don't have to be anywhere until the Lord points me where he wants me, and right now I want to be here. See you tomorrow?"

She started to say simply *okay*, but with a little catch of breath at her own boldness, instead asked, "Would breakfast be too soon?"

He smiled. "I make a pretty decent hotcake, too."

"I'll have the frying pan ready."

It wasn't until she was in bed that the thought occurred to

her that the full facts about her own situation had not gotten into the conversation about raising grandchildren, and Ward had missed most of that conversation anyway. And then an unexpected twinge of uneasiness struck her. She hadn't really thought about it until now, but Ward undoubtedly saw her as an unencumbered widow. She was, after all, here alone at this most important family time of year. And when they earlier exchanged basic information, he had no doubt interpreted from the way she'd phrased it that her son and grandchildren were a family unit. How would he react to the information that she was definitely *not* unencumbered?

Yet the opportunity to tell him didn't arise as they shared a cheerful breakfast together or afterward, when he retrieved the battery from the Miltons' patio and soon had the sandrail zooming up and down the beach in a test run. When he was certain it wasn't going to conk out on them miles from home, he took her for a long ride up the beach.

The coastline was more populated than it had appeared from the road, many of the clusters of houses and trailers much larger than *Luna*. Ward stopped the sandrail frequently to let her look for shells, and in places the sand was so soft and tempting that she just had to take off her shoes and wiggle her bare toes in it. Ward smiled when he saw her frivolous pink toenails peeking through the sand. They planned a wiener roast for that evening, but by midafternoon Edgar was whirling in a strong wind, and Ward suggested hamburgers at the motorhome instead.

"And if you like working jigsaw puzzles I have this humongous one started—?"

Carolyn hesitated. "Ward, don't feel you're obligated to...entertain me just because I'm a lone woman here."

His expression turned solemn. "Don't feel you're obligated to accept my invitation just because I'm a lone man here." But there was teasing in his blue eyes.

"Has fate thrown us together to entertain each other, here in the land of that terrible menace of beach and desert, the sandrail?" she asked with theatrical melodrama and reference to her earlier misconception about what a sandrail was.

"I don't believe in fate," he said thoughtfully. "But I do believe in God. And his mysterious ways of working."

"So do I."

"Which gives us something to think about, doesn't it?"

Yes. Helen had warned of the lack of eligible men and romance here. Carolyn's friendly relationship with Ward could hardly be called a *romance*, but he was certainly the most attractive and interesting man she'd met in a long time. And apparently the interest was mutual.

Carolyn accepted the invitation and took a salad to accompany the hamburgers that evening. Ward's home-on-wheels wasn't one of the huge behemoths she often saw back home, but it had an airy feel, with big windows, light oak woodwork, and a cheerful blue-and-cream color scheme. There were big bucket seats for the driver and a passenger up front, two blue swivel chairs with a small, round table between them next to the door, and a blue-plaid sofa opposite it. Beyond the compact kitchen she could see the corner of a cream-colored bedspread and the door to a bathroom.

"Male housekeeping," he said, with an apologetic gesture around his clean but definitely lived-in looking abode. There were tools piled by the door, books on the sofa, and seashells everywhere.

Carolyn sniffed the fragrance of sizzling hamburgers appreciatively. "Smells wonderful." She set the salad on the small table.

His hands lingered a moment as he took the jacket she'd worn as protection against the chilly wind. He smiled. "So do

138

you." And she was glad she'd bothered with the dab of cologne on her throat.

Their conversation while they ate wandered into various byways. Ward was by no means uncomfortably nosy, but he was interested in everything about her. She told him about growing up in the midwest, dropping out of college to marry, helping with the bookwork in Carl's real estate business, the shock of Carl's abrupt death from a heart attack.

Carolyn kept thinking, *Now's the time to tell him that other most important fact. This isn't some momentous revelation, just another fact about me and my life.* But the moment never seemed quite right. By the time they were lingering over coffee, she had to wonder if she was *afraid* to tell him, afraid he'd react as had Ted, the man with whom she'd had that lone serious relationship since Carl's death. Ted had pulled back as if she'd suddenly developed barbs and thorns.

After dinner, Ward brought out the jigsaw puzzle on a square of plywood and set it on the table. He turned on the radio, roaming the dial with blaring and fading snatches of music and words in English or Spanish. He finally found a solid Arizona station broadcasting a mixture of sentimental oldies and Christmas carols. His only Christmas decoration was a silver-white, three-dimensional star hung in one window, but somehow it seemed more meaningful than all Ruth's gaudy decorations.

"What's the picture supposed to be after the puzzle is completed?" Carolyn asked as she studied the scattered pieces. At this point, only sky at the top and green foliage at the bottom were identifiable.

"Good question," he admitted. "One of the grandkids did something with the top of the box, so I haven't anything to go on."

She tilted a quick glance at him, wondering if that had

annoyed him, but getting no clues. She picked a piece out of the box at random and surprisingly found an immediate fit for it.

"Hey, you're *good!*"

It was, however, one of only a half-dozen connecting pieces either of them found during the next half hour. Finally, when Carolyn picked up a red piece that appeared totally unrelated to anything else in the box, she had to ask doubtfully, "Are you sure these pieces are all from the same puzzle?"

"Well, no. I hadn't thought of that, but the kids could have dumped several puzzles together. Sometimes they 'help' me clean house. Once they decided I had too many old bottles of aftershave lotion, so they dumped them all together, along with some old perfume of Doris's. Something about the blend created a fragrance that might be described as Eau de Skunk in a Fertilizer Factory."

He laughed, obviously amused, not angry, with what they'd done, and Carolyn said, "Mine surprised me by scrubbing the interior of the van for this trip. With bubble bath."

Ward laughed again. "They're great, aren't they? Such fresh, uncynical outlooks on life. I love doing things with them. I got as big a thrill out of seeing the youngest one catch his first fish as I did out of catching my own first fish. And Kaitlyn, she's my daughter's oldest, made the decision to be baptized last year, and I sat there with tears running down my face the whole time." Even now his blue eyes had a quick moment of suspicious brightness.

Oh, yes, Carolyn thought with relief, she could tell him. He wouldn't see grandchildren as some awful burden as Ted had.

"But—" He hesitated as if not quite certain how to go on. "I love my children and grandchildren. I enjoy being with them, and I'd give my right arm or anything else I have if they needed it. But they aren't…my entire life." He hesitated again before asking ruefully, "Does that make me a despicable person?"

"I don't think you could be a despicable person if you tried,"

Carolyn said honestly even as she hesitated again to tell him about her grandchildren.

"This really is a more difficult time in which to raise a family than when yours and mine were born."

"Some things never change. Children still need love and security and a decent home and clothing and food. And spiritual guidance."

He nodded. "And so many children in the world today have none of that. Neither do their parents, for that matter. I've been doing a lot of thinking about such things since I...retired, or whatever it was I did."

"Thinking in what direction?"

"After my company was sold, I thought, wow, this is the life. I can just kick back and enjoy myself. Golf. Fish. Throw away my razor and grow a beard."

Carolyn tilted her head to study him. She smiled. "I think you'd look very good with a beard. The Kenny Rogers look."

"I had a few compliments," he admitted. "But I also quickly learned I wasn't a full-time golf-fish-and-grow-a-beard kind of guy. It was so...aimless. Boring. And I was always wondering if something was caught in the beard, if I had a piece of lettuce or something dangling." He shook his head when she laughed. "So I shaved, bought the motorhome, and decided my goal was to see every state. *That* took about six weeks."

"Somehow I thought the point in traveling was to spend time at each place and really learn about it, not see how fast you can make a cross-country run."

He laughed ruefully. "True. But I've always been a get-things-done kind of person, and I got that done. About then was when I wondered if I'd made a big mistake selling the company. I had all this life left, and what was I going to do with it?"

"And now you don't think you made a mistake, but you're still traveling?"

"Only temporarily. What I'm actually doing is waiting."

"Waiting?"

"Carolyn, I've spent most of my life in the plumbing business. I see others who have devoted their lives to spreading the Lord's Word or helping the sick or homeless or hungry, something truly meaningful, but most of my life has been spent making plumbing fixtures." He spoke the words with a kind of amused exasperation and repeated them with even more emphasis. "Making *plumbing fixtures*. It's not that I feel that I've *wasted* my life—"

"It shouldn't be! Where would we be without dependable plumbing fixtures?" Without thinking she reached across the jigsaw puzzle and squeezed his wrist lightly.

He turned his hand over and squeezed back, although his gaze was focused on something unseen beyond the dark window. "But then I finally saw that what I had now was *opportunity*, that there was a reason and purpose for my early retirement."

Carolyn could easily guess what that opportunity and purpose was. "To serve the Lord?"

Ward nodded. "In a larger and more meaningful way than I ever could before. Don't get me wrong. I know that works don't earn salvation. Salvation is our free gift from God, and I'm right with God." His voice suddenly took on a youthful fire and eagerness. "But now, before I go to meet him, I have the time and opportunity to do something really worthwhile to show my love and gratitude to him."

"Do you have something specific in mind?"

"You don't hear much about the Peace Corps anymore, but it's still in existence, and I have an application in. I've also applied to a Christian organization that rescues unwanted street kids in several Latin American countries. Our church helps support an orphanage in Korea, a place that needs water and plumbing desperately, and I might be able to help there. And

I've applied several other places where I think I could be useful."

Carolyn swallowed. "All so...far away."

He nodded. "Maybe because, when I was a boy, I had dreams of being a missionary in the foreign field." He hesitated, and then all in a rush asked, "Carolyn, does all this sound completely ridiculous to you? My sister says it is. She's a good Christian, but she says I'm too old to think about, as she puts it, 'dashing off to grub around in some primitive country.' She says I should leave it to a younger generation. But I think I still have a lot to offer...my faith, my heart, my hands." He spread those strong, capable hands, with a glint of masculine silver on the forearms. He smiled lightly. "And my wrench."

"I don't think it's ridiculous. I think it's a glorious idea and plan. Something I'd think about doing too, if—" She broke off suddenly, her intention of telling him why she couldn't even consider doing such a thing halted in mid-sentence. "Have you any idea when you'll be doing this?"

"No. At this point I'm just waiting to see what path the Lord opens for me. And for the house to sell."

"You won't see much of your family if you're on the other side of the world."

"I know. And that concerns me. But I figure I can get home every six months or so. Money won't be a problem." He tapped his palms against his legs and smiled. "I'll still have my rocking-chair years to spend with the family. When I was young, *this* looked like old age. But I've discovered that old age recedes, always being somewhere well beyond where I am at the moment. I don't think it's too late to have dreams and ambitions at our age. Don't you still have them?"

Carolyn nodded slowly.

"Tell me about them," he prompted lightly when she didn't carry the response further than the nod.

"Years ago, I wrote a few Christian stories for children, and I'd like to do more of that. Our town of Steele desperately needs a shelter for abused women, and I'd like to help get one started and serve in it. I'd always hoped that sometime I could finish my college degree." For now, of course, all that had to take second place to the children's needs. It was the perfect time to tell him she was raising her three grandchildren, yet troubling undercurrents in her own mind, things she had to *think* about, made her simply smile and say lightly, "Maybe I'll get around to all that one of these days."

She abruptly stood and retrieved her jacket from the sofa. "Could you excuse me? I know it's still early, but I seem to be more tired than I'd realized. The hamburgers were terrific—"

He jumped up too. "I've bored you, haven't I? Talking about all my wild ideas—"

"No, no, you have not. And your ideas aren't wild. I applaud and admire them, and…envy them a bit, too." Impulsively she reached up and kissed him on the cheek. "But I really am much more tired than I realized."

"I'll walk you home—"

"No, please. I'll be fine. It's almost as light as day out there in the moonlight."

He was scowling, and she could see he was torn between wanting to see her safely home and not wanting to push himself on her. "I'll see you tomorrow?" he asked finally.

"I don't think you can miss me," she said lightly. "I'm practically in your front yard."

"Well…okay, then."

She was aware of his gaze following her all the way down the hill. The north wind was blowing even harder now, and she had to brace herself against its push. At the door she turned and gave him a reassuring wave, and his answering wave was a dark silhouette against the brightly-lit window of the motorhome.

Inside, Carolyn lit a lamp rather than turn on the noisy generator. She undressed, put on her nightgown, and blew out the lamp. But instead of going to bed, she curled up on the sofa with a blanket tucked around her for warmth and watched the slowly moving lights of the shrimp boats and jitterbugging Edgar. And let those undercurrents rise to the top of her mind.

She liked Ward. She knew he liked her. She was almost certain, if time and circumstances were different, that the feelings could grow and deepen into something much larger than *liking*. But time and circumstances were not different.

By morning she'd made a decision.

Five

❧

Carolyn tapped lightly on the motorhome, the warm pan balanced in her other hand. Ward opened the door, fully dressed in jeans and sweatshirt but with his hair still rumpled and a faint, but definitely not unattractive, shadow of silver whiskers on his jaw.

"Did I wake you?"

"No! Of course not. Come in, quick, before you blow away. I'm so glad to see you!" He spoke as eagerly as if it had been days instead of hours since he'd last seen her, and offered his hand to help her navigate the steep steps into the motorhome. "I was just sitting here reading some Scripture in Luke. Too windy for the beach this morning."

True. The day was sunny and cloudless, but Edgar stood straight out from his anchoring pole, whirling and bouncing in a dancing frenzy. A tumbleweed, incongruous against the background of white-capped sea, rolled along the beach. A pair of seagulls appeared to be standing still in the sky as they tried to fly against the wind.

"That's why I brought breakfast up to you." Carolyn smiled as she tossed back the hood of her jacket. "If you like hot biscuits—?"

"Carolyn, I'd be delighted to have breakfast with you even if it were spinach and grits, which are two of my least favorite foods," he declared with husky sincerity. "I was afraid, when you left so abruptly last night, that something was wrong—"

"Would I be dashing up here bearing biscuits at the crack of dawn if anything were wrong?" she asked in playful exaggeration.

"You do look bright-eyed and rested this morning." His blue eyes added even more expressive compliments as they appraised her carefully.

Carolyn did not *feel* rested after a night wrestling with her problem, so perhaps the peach-pink lipstick and the light makeup she'd used to cover the shadows under her eyes were doing their job. She'd taken her problem to the Lord, of course, although she knew she wasn't immune to the error of making a decision and then rationalizing the Lord's will to fit it.

Ward added eggs, orange juice, strawberry jam, and coffee to the menu, and while they ate, Carolyn purposely kept the conversation fast-moving and light.

"Isn't this homemade strawberry jam?" she asked after a bite of biscuit spread with the thick, fruit-filled jam.

"My daughter made it. She and Kaitlyn started right from the bottom, with picking the berries." He laughed. "She grumbled that if they'd been getting paid minimum wage, this jam would have to sell for fifty dollars a jar just to break even."

"Worth every penny. It's delicious," Carolyn declared, going on to tell him about her own first jam-making experience years ago, when the pot boiled over and jam flowed everywhere. "I kept seeing lurid tabloid headlines: *Jam Monster Escapes and Swallows Colorado Village.*" She did not add that her jam and jelly came from the store these days.

Yet beneath her chatter, she went over her decision once more. She and Ward were very much attracted to each other. She could feel that attraction even now as they sat at the small table with knees bumping, Ward laughing and reaching across the table to wipe away a drip of jam on her chin, she returning the favor and encountering the unexpectedly delightful feel of whiskery stubble on his jaw. It was an attraction that was mental and physical and emotional, an attraction that made the sunshine brighter and jam sweeter and coffee richer, an attraction that lent sweet magic to a simple brush of hands as they reached for another biscuit at the same time.

But she and Ward were not, she reminded herself, going to fall into a lifetime-commitment kind of love in two weeks. They were both too mature, too sensible, too cautious for that wild leap of youth. Perhaps, if they had longer to let their relationship develop...

They didn't have longer. He had his plans and ambitions, and wonderfully worthy dreams and ambitions of serving the Lord they were. She had her duties and responsibilities, and they, too, were worthy and commendable. But there was an uncrossable canyon between the two, and their relationship came with a built-in termination point at the end of two weeks. It *couldn't* go anywhere.

But not every relationship had to be happily-ever-after to be worthwhile, she'd concluded in those long hours watching the stars wheel silently across the sky. She would enjoy this brief time with Ward simply for what it was, for all it could be, a temporary holiday romance. And she would not clutter or burden it with the intrusion of complicating details that were, basically, irrelevant to these two weeks. If she told Ward that she was actually doing what both he and Ray had indicated they would *not* want to be doing at this time of life—raising a young family—walls and barriers would arise between them. Instead of enjoying what little time they had together, the *Problem* would become the focus of the relationship and drain all the joy from it.

She wasn't going to do that, she again decided almost fiercely. She was simply going to make the most of this unexpected "summer romance," enjoy it for what it was, not mourn what it couldn't be.

"Carolyn, is everything okay? You had such a faraway look...."

"I was just thinking, with the wind blowing so hard, perhaps this would be a good day to drive up to San Felipe."

"Good idea. I need to call home and see if there's been any action on the house. A nephew and his wife are living in it and taking care of things for me until it sells. We can have lunch on the *malecón*."

"*Malecón?*" Carolyn repeated, stumbling over the unfamiliar Spanish word.

"You'll see."

In San Felipe, they took care of practical matters first, filling the propane bottle, five-gallon water jugs, and gas tank in the van. Then Ward directed her to a public telephone he'd used before.

Carolyn tried her home number first but got a busy signal. She wandered down the unpaved street, circling a snoozing dog that didn't bother to move out of her way, while Ward made his call. The wind was less fierce here than at *Luna*, the sun warm on her legs, and she was glad she'd worn shorts and sandals. Even in just these few days, the north-of-the-border paleness of her skin was changing to a honey tan. By now she'd received several pesos in change for her purchases with American dollars, and she tucked away several of the attractive coins of silvery metal encircling a gold-colored center to give to the kids.

"No action on selling the house yet. And nothing about any of my applications, either," Ward reported, sounding frustrated, after he hung up. "I keep reminding myself that the Lord works at his own pace, but sometimes I do get impatient."

"Why, I'd never have guessed you were an impatient man," she teased, pretending wide-eyed wonder. "You, who took such a leisurely jaunt across the States..."

He grinned and then moved away to give her privacy for her call. This time Scott answered.

"Everything's fine here, just great," he said cheerfully. "Of course there was that minor incident with the spaghetti, but the carpenter repaired the ceiling and the stain in the bathtub is barely noticeable."

Ceiling repair and bathtub stain...in connection with *spaghetti*? After considering this unlikely situation for a moment, Carolyn said, "I don't think I'll even ask for details."

"Good idea," Scott agreed.

"Are the kids there?"

"Right beside me. Jumping up and down wanting to talk to you."

Carolyn talked to each one in turn, hearing about roller skating afternoons, sledding, washing machine overflow— another incident about which she decided not to ask for details—and the birthday party for Jesus that Uncle Scott said they were going to have on Christmas Day. When Scott came back on the phone she said, "Sounds as if there isn't a dull minute."

"Right. Actually, this has been such a terrific experience that I've made up my mind about something. I can handle the possibility of fatherhood! I'm going to ask Heather to marry me."

"Scott, that's wonderful!" Heather was the lovely, patient girl Scott had been going with for two years, although until now he'd been dragging his feet on a commitment to marriage. "I'm delighted. I think she'll say yes, and I'll be praying that she does."

"What about you, Mom, you knocking all the single guys

150

down there right out of their socks?"

"Don't be ridiculous." If he noticed she evaded rather than answered his question, he didn't comment. He and Carl had shared a close father/son relationship, but Scott's attitude had never been that she should spend the rest of her life alone. He'd been friendly with Ted, and she'd never told Scott, or anyone, what had ended that relationship, although Scott was an observant young man and probably knew. "I'll see you a few days into the new year, then," she said.

"Okay, and don't worry about a thing. Oh, by the way, you do have a cat now. Her name is Henrietta," he added and then hung up before she could respond to that news.

She was shaking her head and smiling when she rejoined Ward.

"Everything okay at home?" he asked.

"Yes, fine. My son—" She broke off abruptly. She'd started to say, *My son has decided to ask his girlfriend to marry him.* But that would require explanations that would reveal everything she'd decided not to reveal. Instead she said brightly, "He says the grandchildren are fine, and they have a new cat."

"I don't think you've ever mentioned what your son does."

Carolyn hesitated. If she told Ward that Scott was assistant professor at a university, he might ask where. Ward already knew the kids lived in Colorado, so Scott's residence elsewhere would raise further questions. She had not realized her decision would require such a careful verbal balancing act, and she was not at all comfortable with it. Feeling a little guilty she sidestepped a direct answer to the question with a vague, generic statement. "He's in…education."

Ward said he wanted to show her something, and he took her to an area near the entrance to town where a large, almost life-sized nativity scene had been set up.

"How lovely!" Carolyn said, delighted with the wonderful

wooden manger, lifelike sheep, and the feeling of gentle faith that it all portrayed. The old figures showed evidence of loving care, and apparently there were no arguments here about putting symbols of religious faith and the true meaning of Christmas on public ground.

"I thought you'd like it."

They went down to San Felipe's main street next, where all the little shops that catered to tourists were located. The shops held everything from clothes to colorful Indian-design blankets, curios, and a tourist favorite: big, inexpensive bottles of real vanilla. Some sellers had their wares spread on the sidewalk: seashell lamps and wind chimes, figures of eagles and dolphins carved from dark, glossy ironwood. Strolling vendors carried open cases of inexpensive jewelry, using a favorite enticement of, "Almost free," with a flash of smile to promote their rings and necklaces and bracelets. Bargaining was expected.

Carolyn and Ward wandered the busy street hand in hand to keep from getting separated by the crowds of shorts-and-sunglasses clad Americans here for the holidays. Or perhaps the crowds were just the excuse they used, because Ward didn't seem inclined to let go even when they weren't surrounded. And she didn't want him to.

There were no sidewalk Santas or gaudy street ornaments, no blaring Christmas music. But reindeer and Santa *piñatas,* red paper bells, and iridescent garlands adorned the store windows, and brightly colored decorations wished shoppers a cheerful *Feliz Navidad.* There was a definite holiday feel in the air.

For Mike, Carolyn bought a kite shaped like a parachute with the dangling figure of a little man attached. For Kelsey, a turquoise bracelet; and for Erin, who loved animals, a T-shirt with a trio of leaping dolphins. For Scott, she found a big seashell with tiny wooden legs and plastic glasses attached, which made it look like a pompous little man. It was the kind of thing anyone with good taste would instantly hide, but she knew that Scott, whose tastes ran toward the funky, would love it.

By then it was time for lunch, and Ward led her a block over to the *malecón,* which turned out to be a boardwalk street of open-air taco stands running parallel to the beach.

"I've eaten at several of these places, and they were all good, so you pick whichever one appeals to you." He was still holding her hand. He'd shaved before leaving *Luna* and added a fresh white feather to the straw hat. If there was a more handsome or attractive man anywhere in San Felipe, Carolyn certainly hadn't seen him.

They strolled past the crowded outdoor tables, tempted by scents of sizzling beef and warm tortillas and spicy beans, but Carolyn had to admit to a certain trepidation to eating anywhere. The warnings she'd always heard about the dangers of eating south of the border were loud in her mind. And the menus, painted in colorful letters above each stand, offered varieties of tacos unheard of back home. Beef and chicken were familiar, but—

"Shrimp tacos?" she asked doubtfully. "Fish tacos? *Stingray tacos?*"

She suspected Ward knew exactly why she was dragging her feet on choosing which place to eat and wouldn't push her if she begged off eating lunch here. But suddenly she decided to toss caution to the winds. She wasn't going home to Colorado with the regretful knowledge that she *could* have had a shrimp taco with the most handsome, silver-haired man in San Felipe, Mexico...and had been too scaredy-cat to do it!

"Here," she said decisively at a place run by a lovely, dark-haired woman with a younger version of herself serving as waitress. "Two shrimp tacos, please," she said, and Ward added an order for three more. The soft drinks were all familiar

American brands, and they asked for a Coke and a Pepsi.

A few minutes later the young woman handed them the freshly cooked, deep-fried shrimp wrapped in warm flour tortillas and motioned toward the counter where stone bowls were filled with various condiments. Carolyn heaped a bit of everything on her tacos: spoonfuls of guacamole, a mixture of cubed tomato, onions and cilantro, finely sliced cabbage. At the bowls of sauces, she hesitated.

"Risk the red one only if you like to eat with flames coming out of your mouth," Ward warned. With a toss of her head she chose it anyway, and laughing, so did he.

The tacos were delicious, the sauce fiery, the shrimp big and succulent, and the fish taco that she ordered for an encore, with the tender chunks of fish also deep-fried in an airy batter, was also marvelous.

"Stingray taco next? Or are you ready for a *pulpo* cocktail now?" Ward asked, motioning toward another painted menu listing seafood cocktails of everything from clams and oysters to this mysterious *pulpo*.

Something in his grin told her it might not be wise to order this particular seafood without investigating first.

"You are the adventurous type, aren't you?" he added by way of teasing encouragement. "Coming to Baja alone, eating the hottest sauce in town—"

"*Cautiously* adventurous." Motioning to the waitress she asked in her limited Spanish, *"Pulpo en Inglés?"*

The girl smiled and translated. "Octopus. Very good."

Ward's grin was more bland than guilty. "How about that? Octopus. Who'd have guessed?"

Carolyn just punched him companionably in the shoulder.

After eating, they went grocery shopping at a little *abarrote* and then to what was known locally as the "tortilla factory," which was actually half a dozen industrious women using a small moving press and a huge metal cooking surface to turn balls of dough into tortillas so hot and fragrant that Carolyn couldn't resist eating a fresh one right there.

"I'm going to have ten extra pounds to lose when I get home," she groaned. But when Ward stopped at a small open-air stand, she couldn't resist a chocolate ice-cream cone, especially when the girl gave it the wonderfully musical pronunciation of choc-o-la-tay. When she caught a falling drop on her fingertip but had no napkin, Ward laughingly took care of the sticky problem by lifting her hand to his lips.

She wanted to say something light and funny, but she couldn't say anything because of the peculiar flutter of her heartbeat.

By the time they returned to *Luna*, several families had arrived. The wind had died down, and a half-dozen children were playing at the water's edge. A smoky scent of something barbecuing drifted from a house on the hill. Carolyn let Ward off at the motorhome with his water jugs and groceries.

"I'll be down in a few minutes to unload your jugs and propane tank and hook it up for you," he said.

"No hurry—"

Unexpectedly, he reached through the open window of the van and curled his hand lightly around the back of her neck. "Yes, there is a hurry." His voice wasn't somber, but it held a seriousness that contrasted with the lighthearted day. "These two weeks are going fast. And I don't want to waste a minute of them."

Carolyn drove slowly down to her own trailer, the sweet warmth of his touch lingering on her skin, and her thoughts echoed his. Yes, the days were going much too fast.

The following morning they went to a Sunday worship service in a private home at one of the nearby *campos,* the general name given to these clusters of houses and trailers along the shoreline. The service started out rather disorganized because both the man who regularly led the meetings and the one who usually served as replacement were ill. But when it began to slip into little more than a social gathering, Ward, with quiet authority, stepped in to take over. He didn't preach but he deftly guided the group in a study appropriate to the day, the Christmas story in Luke.

Oh yes, Carolyn thought, feeling an odd little upswelling of pride as she watched and listened to him, Ward could surely serve the Lord well in whatever faraway place he went. His faith was so open and natural, as much a part of him as his quick grin and good-humored tease.

At the end someone suggested they sing some Christmas hymns, and for the first time Ward looked a bit dismayed. He glanced at Carolyn, and remembering his comment that he couldn't carry a tune, she found herself stepping up to lead the group in *a cappella* versions of "Hark the Herald Angels Sing" and "Silent Night." In the past she had occasionally soloed with the church choir, but in recent years she just hadn't been able to carve out the practice time for that.

Walking back to the van afterward, Ward squeezed an arm around her shoulders. "See how well we work together? How come you never told me you could sing?"

"I guess it just never came up."

His eyes, with his face only inches from hers, held a sudden hint of speculation. "Sometimes I wonder if there may be other things about you that have just 'never come up.'"

"Oh, dear." She touched her throat melodramatically and deliberately did not ask what prompted that comment. "I was afraid you'd discover my secret, that I'm really Glamma Glamorous, famous star of stage, screen, and television, hiding here under this going-gray wig."

If he still thought she might be holding something back, he didn't let on. He laughed with her, accepting the bit of frivolity. "I like your going-gray 'wig,'" he said and unexpectedly planted the whisper of a kiss on a silvering curl just above her ear.

That afternoon, with Edgar back to drooping lazily on his pole, they went for another long beach walk, Ward sometimes jogging on ahead while Carolyn lay on her stomach to sift through the sand for tiny shells, marveling at the care the Lord took in packaging intricate beauty where it was so often unnoticed. *Luna* was much busier now, someone backing a pickup and trailer down to put a boat in the water, a man and woman zipping around on four-wheeler all-terrain-vehicles, a noisy volleyball game going on around a net set up on the beach.

In the evening, after finding a recipe in a kitchen drawer, Carolyn tried making *chili rellanos*. Ward pronounced the eggs, canned green chilis, and cheese dish a success as they ate by lamplight. Carolyn was not fond of the noisy generator and much preferred the cozy flicker of the lamp's flame. After the meal Carolyn brought out a Chinese checkers game she'd found tucked away in the closet. The marbles to play it were missing, but they substituted small seashells, a dab of fingernail polish identifying Carolyn's set, and managed nicely, talking idly as they played. A window was open, letting in the gentle lap of small waves and muted sounds of gulls settling down at the water's edge for the night.

"Did you get to the Grand Canyon while you were dashing back and forth across the country in your travels?" Carolyn asked as she contemplated a strategic move. There was much more she'd like to know about him, but the more personal questions *she* asked, the more *he* would undoubtedly ask, so travel and geography were safer subjects.

"I rushed by there, with about a two minute look over the rim." Wryly he added, "I missed Old Faithful in Yellowstone because it was a few minutes late, and I just couldn't wait. Maybe that's why the Lord is being so slow in opening a pathway for me to serve him—to teach me a little more patience."

"Perhaps. Or perhaps you haven't made the right application yet, the one the Lord has in mind for you."

"Maybe." He paused with a fingertip poised on a tiny whorled shell substituting for a marble. "You know, I just thought of something. I also passed through Denver. I may even have driven through your town. Maybe we passed within a dozen feet of each other and never knew it."

Carolyn's immediate thought was that she'd probably have been surrounded by grandchildren and he'd never have given her a second glance. Ted had certainly bolted into reverse fast enough when the grandchildren appeared. But all she said was a teasingly tart, "Well, given your traveling speed, I'm probably lucky I didn't get in your way. I might have gotten tire tracks right up the middle of my back."

"Oh, no," he assured her. "I'd have braked for *you.*"

After they finished the last game and had a last cup of coffee, Ward finally murmured something about the time getting late. She knew he was reluctant to leave, but she also knew he wasn't a man to suggest sharing the intimacy reserved for marriage. At the door he turned to face her and ran his hands lightly up her arms.

"May I kiss you good night?" he asked softly, and she liked the old-fashioned gallantry of his asking.

"Yes," she whispered.

His hands slid up to clasp the sides of her throat, strong fingers meeting at her nape. With his thumbs he tipped her face to his and looked into her eyes for a long moment before tilting his mouth to hers. His kiss was warm and sweet, a hint of passion hovering in the background but only tender gentleness between them now. She lifted her arms to his neck, and he wrapped his arms around her, pulling her close without breaking the kiss.

When finally he did break it, he said huskily, "On that, I think I really had better go home. Breakfast?"

"After Scripture?"

"You'll join me?"

"I've only been waiting for an invitation."

"You've got it."

The sun was only a crescent edge of red-gold above the pale blue sea when he knocked on her door the next morning. He took her hand as they clambered over the rocks to get to the low-tide shoreline. There they held his small New Testament together, his other arm around her shoulders as they read in Psalms together, touching a verse that on this beautiful morning had special meaning for Carolyn: *This is the day the Lord has made; let us rejoice and be glad in it.*

Yes, their relationship had a built-in termination point, but she would rejoice and be glad in this day they had together.

After the sun was fully up, breakfast had to wait as Carolyn got sidetracked. Out here, where the wide area of shore rocks gave way to sand at these extra-low tides of the full moon, the shells were unbroken, their colors sharper. She dashed from one to another, not minding that her feet and pants legs were getting wet—big, curled shells with dramatic black and brown lines and spines; glossy, mottled shells that Ward said were called "olives" and felt like polished glass against her fingertips; and whole sand dollars that looked like miniature shields, with cutouts along the outer edge and an oval hole just above a design like flower petals!

"Oh, look at *this,*" Carolyn cried as she snatched up yet another shell. It was like many she'd found earlier, spiky white with a pink throat, but this pink was unlike any she'd seen before, almost a rose, deep and intense. "But there's something in it—"

"The owner and occupant." Ward touched the live, rubbery looking creature lightly, and it withdrew within the shell, trying to escape the touch.

Carolyn looked at the lovely shell a moment longer, then carefully, with a small twinge of regret because the color was more beautiful than any she had, tucked it into a sandy pool beside a rock.

"What are you doing?"

"Putting it back."

"Why?" He didn't sound critical, merely surprised and curious.

"Because I have lots of shells…and he has only one. I think I'll let him keep it."

She slanted a sideways glance at him, wondering if he'd laugh, because she already knew this sea creature was a favorite

160

edible delicacy of the locals, but he wasn't laughing. Instead he was looking at her with so much tenderness that her throat felt tight. He wrapped his arms around her almost fiercely.

"Carolyn, I—"

He broke off, blinked, and swallowed. She knew what he'd almost said. *I love you.* And also knew why he'd backed away from completing the words. He felt, as she did, that even though the emotion and words were there, right on his lips—as they were on hers!—that they couldn't really feel as deeply as *love* about each other so soon. The attraction was surely there, a powerful attraction physically, emotionally, and spiritually. But surely not *love*.

He swallowed again. "I think you're one of the most special people I've ever known," he finally said huskily. "Sweet and compassionate and wonderful."

"Thank you," she whispered. Then to lighten the emotional moment, she added, "Breakfast?"

"Breakfast," he agreed, smiling before he dropped a light kiss on her lips.

Over breakfast, they decided something else. They were going to have a wiener roast on Christmas Eve and invite everyone at *Luna.*

Together they visited all the occupied trailers and houses to issue invitations, then drove up to San Felipe for wieners and other supplies. The following morning, using the sandrail, they explored a nearby ravine and carried home several loads of prickly dead *ocotillo* for the campfire. At dark, Ward built up a big fire and soon it was surrounded by adults and children laughing and eating, dropping wieners in the fire, spilling soft drinks, and generally having a noisy good time. This was not a group of committed Christians, but they quieted and listened respectfully when Ward read the real story of Christmas to them from his Bible.

After everyone drifted home, Ward wrapped his arms around Carolyn as they stood by the fire. "That went pretty well, don't you think? Hot dogs, marshmallows, and the Lord." He smiled. "And you."

It wasn't Christmas Eve as Carolyn had always known it. Soft sea breeze instead of snow, dancing campfire instead of decorated tree, a blackened hot dog instead of overflowing dinner table. But the joy of Christ's birth shone through no matter what the surroundings were. And being with Ward... She swallowed, suddenly uneasy with the depth of her feelings for him, the *I love you* that churned to the surface even as she tried to hold it in check.

"Went great," she agreed lightly. "*You* were great. I had the feeling it may have been the first time some of those children have heard anything other than a Santa-Claus-and-reindeer version of Christmas."

He reached down and grabbed a broken chunk of *ocotillo* and held it over her head.

"What's this?" she asked, puzzled.

"I'm a little short on mistletoe. I hoped this would do."

"I guess you'll just have to try and see if it works," she offered with a smile.

It did.

He wrapped his arms around her again, and the kiss warmed her heart and tingled her toes, weakened her knees and soared her spirits. Yet at the same time she tasted the bittersweet reminder that it was all coming to an end. Soon.

"Ready to call it a night?" he asked. He rubbed his nose against hers in a small gesture of affection.

"Not necessarily. Are you?"

In answer he dropped down beside the campfire, pulling

162

her with him. He stretched out on his side, and she sat cross-legged. They watched the glowing embers in companionable silence until Ward turned and slid closer to her. His fingertip traced the faint shadow of a vein in her hand, lightly lingering on her bare ring finger. She'd worn Carl's ring for two years after his death, and then, not because she wanted to find someone new, but simply as a gentle closing on the past, she'd put it away.

"Do you ever think about marrying again, Carolyn?"

Carolyn felt a small shiver at the softly spoken question, vibrant with undercurrents. "When Carl first died, I couldn't imagine it." She hesitated, absentmindedly tracing a cord along the back of his strong hand now resting on hers. "But eventually I started dating occasionally. A thoroughly awkward situation after you've been married for years."

"Yes. Definitely awkward. I think it takes someone who has lost a mate to know that particular feeling. You had a good marriage, didn't you, Carolyn?"

"It was always a good marriage. We could work together and have fun together, although we sometimes got too wrapped up in acquiring material things, and Carl developed a gambling problem for a while. But after we both accepted Christ, it was an even better marriage. Carl conquered the gambling, and there was a spiritual depth between us that wasn't there before."

"But you never found anyone else you wanted to marry?"

A little reluctantly she said, "Actually, a few years ago, I almost did remarry."

"You did?" He sat up, as if that revelation startled him. "What happened?"

What happened? Catastrophe. Change. Grandchildren. But with a small shrug all she said was, "Oh, life, I guess. Life happens. It was for the best, of course, although it didn't seem so at the time."

"Did your son object?" She knew he was delicately fishing.

"Scott? Oh, no."

Ward was silent, apparently waiting for her to add more, but she simply poked the fire with a long stick, pretending absorption in the upward spiral of sparks. She wondered how he felt about remarriage, if he had ever come close, but she resolutely did not ask, because asking would keep this subject open for discussion, and she did not want discussion.

He was intuitive enough to sense that, but at the same time he said in a half-exasperated tone, "You're sometimes a rather mysterious lady, Ms. Carolyn McAndrews, you know that?"

"Me? Mysterious?" she scoffed. She turned to a diverting bit of foolishness again. "Of course, as Glamma Glamorous, I must remain incognito so my fans won't mob me—"

He wouldn't be diverted. "Every once in a while I feel we wander in the direction of some off-limits area. I don't even know what the area *is*, but sometimes I feel you leading me away from some...sensitive point. So I'm just going to ask straight-out about one thing. Are you involved with some guy back home *now*?"

That mistaken suspicion was so far off base that she tossed the stick in the fire and stared at him.

Yes, there was an off-limits area. And she was definitely "involved." But with her grandchildren, not some other man. Kelsey, Erin, and Mike were not, as he thought, part of her son's family. They were *her* family. In her home, in her care, in her legal custody. Child-raising was not, as it was for most women her age, behind her. It was part of her life every day, every hour, every minute. These two weeks were the first time she'd taken off since they'd come to live with her four years ago.

But even though she'd withheld that from him, it hurt that he suspected their relationship was a holiday fling for her while she was seriously involved with a man back home.

She didn't explain her hurt or anything else. She simply said, "No, I'm not involved with another man," in such a tight, closed voice that the discussion ended abruptly.

The following morning, a gloriously sunny Christmas Day, they exchanged gifts, each a little surprised that the other had a gift, each carefully skirting the tension lingering from the night before. Carolyn had homemade cookies for Ward, which delighted him, and for her he had a fitting little object he'd slipped away and bought in San Felipe.

Carolyn laughed when she saw the miniature sandrail, intricately constructed of shells glued together. Sitting in the sandrail were two shell figures, an appropriate wild-eyed look on their little seashell faces that leaned forward as if they were roaring down some invisible beach.

He laughed too. "Actually it's one of those tacky little souvenirs best hidden out of sight somewhere, but I thought the little seashell people looked so much like us that I couldn't resist."

She leaned over the breakfast table and kissed him on the cheek. "It's perfect. I'll always treasure it." Her voice unexpectedly broke as she spoke. It was a little tacky...and sweet, and she'd never, ever hide it.

"Everything forgiven?" he asked huskily.

She nodded. "You?"

He nodded too, and unspoken words passed between them: time was too short to waste being angry or aloof toward each other.

They spent the remainder of the week beachcombing, jogging, riding the sandrail on the beach and old roads back in the barren hills, driving down to explore the little village of Puertecitos, where they stuck bare feet in the surprising hot springs right at the edge of the sea. They talked more about the past, both marriage years and earlier, and also learned they were both interested in gardening, would both like to visit Israel, and that they had voted the same in the last election but could carry on a spirited disagreement about new candidates without getting hostile. They socialized some with other people at *Luna*, going to a barbecue and a fish fry, but by unspoken agreement most of their time was simply spent with each other. On Sunday they attended the worship service again, afterward receiving an invitation to a buffet dinner and candlelight service on New Year's Eve.

When they returned, *Luna* was in a small uproar. The tide was in, and eight or nine people were trying to push a large, dark *something* into the water. By the time Carolyn changed clothes and hurried down to the beach, Ward was already there. She still couldn't identify the thing, but whatever it was, it *smelled*, a stench powerful enough to give her a reeling moment of nausea.

"What *is* it?" she asked Ward.

"Dead dolphin. Dead for quite a while, given the smell. It floated in on the high tide, and they're trying to push it out so the tide will take it away again. The whole place is going to smell if it's stranded here." He was just standing there watching which seemed out of character for one always so willing to help.

The efforts of the workers were not accomplishing much. With poles and shovels and rakes, they'd push the six- or seven-foot-long creature out. The more powerful sea would push it right back in again, almost as if this were some playful game. Carolyn wondered what had killed the poor creature and felt sorry for it, but at the same time she didn't want the awful scent here, either. She picked up a wooden pole someone had dropped, held her breath against the stench and started trying to help shove the bloated body of the animal back into the sea.

Yet when she looked around a minute later, she was a little indignant to realize Ward not only wasn't helping, he'd disappeared. Was the stench too much for him?

A few minutes later, however, he was back, not with pole or shovel like everyone else, but with a coil of rope over his shoulder. Carolyn had no idea what he intended, but he conferred with several men who were by now just standing around watching helplessly, and together they got the rope tied around the dead creature's middle.

Ward waded into the water, the other men pushed and shoved, and this time, with Ward holding a rope on the floating creature, the sea couldn't toss it back ashore. Now she realized that the reason he hadn't been helping earlier was because he'd been figuring out a better way to tackle the problem. He waded out waist deep, then turned and headed south, the dead dolphin bobbing along behind like some macabre pet. Everyone followed, cheering and encouraging, until he towed it around the point of the crescent, well beyond scent distance. There a couple of men waded out and helped him tie the rope to an underwater rock, so the creature couldn't drift back to *Luna*.

Ward came out of the water grimacing and shaking his hands as if they were contaminated. By now water had plastered the front of his hair to his head, but the breeze had whipped the back into an eggbeater-tangle. His clothes clung to his body, except for a flapping shirttail, and his shoes squished noisily.

Carolyn met him with a smile. "That was brilliant. A real triumph in engineering."

"Yeah, yeah," he muttered. "Man Saves Baja Beach From Stench of the Century. I don't see you rushing up to shower me with congratulatory hugs and kisses," he added. He held out his hands to her, pretending a leer, and she backed off with a little shriek.

"But I am impressed and proud of you." Then she started laughing.

"And what is it you find so funny?" he growled.

Carolyn couldn't help it. It was a sad happening, the poor, long-dead dolphin lying there on the beach. And yet there was a bizarre, morbid humor to Ward's part in it. "Because you looked like—"

"Like what?"

"Like a mad scientist out for a stroll. Normal people take their pets for a daily walk, and so does our eccentric mad scientist. But his pet just happens to be a dead dolphin bobbing along behind him...."

"Lady, you have one weird sense of humor," Ward grumbled, although she caught a twitch of amusement at the corner of his mouth.

"I'm sorry," she said contritely.

"But I suppose it's one of the reasons I love you." And after tossing out that offhand announcement, which took away her giggle and left her breathless, he added, "I need a shower," and marched off up the hill.

Watching him go, even as those three words echoed inside her, Carolyn had another thought. Ward Setlow could manage wherever the Lord guided him. Jungle or mountain or urban slum, dead dolphin or live tiger, broken faucet or leaking dam, Ward could handle anything that came his way.

Which was no doubt one of the reasons she loved him. And why he belonged in some far-off place where all his talents and abilities could be used for the Lord.

CHAPTER

Seven

❧

They built another campfire the following evening. It was a windless night, Edgar dangling lazily on his pole. Carolyn sat with her knees wrapped around her arms, trying not to feel melancholy. She'd made up her mind to enjoy this relationship with Ward just for what it was, a temporary holiday romance, and not mourn what it couldn't be. But now that the end was so near .

Ward, sitting so close that his shoulder brushed hers as he leaned forward to toss another branch of *ocotillo* on the fire, seemed preoccupied with his own thoughts until finally he asked softly, "Are you thinking what I'm thinking?"

"I don't know." She swallowed. "What are you thinking?"

"That we can't just go our separate ways on New Year's Day. That I never really thought it would happen, especially in less than two weeks, but it has. I love you, Carolyn." The words came out with a tender amazement, as if he couldn't quite believe it himself.

Moonlight, rather than shadowing his face in mystery, revealed every open, honest plane, every line of maturity and experience and laughter. She reached up and traced the clean-cut line of his jaw, the words within her echoing his. Her swallow was sharper this time, almost painful. "Ward, I have to tell you something—"

He touched her lips with a fingertip. "Wait. There's more. I love you, and I'm asking you to marry me." Again the finger on her lips, a soft caress as much as a small gesture to silence her. "I know. You're thinking he's about to dash off to some faraway place. But we can wait until there's an opening we can accept together. I know it's a tired old phrase, but I'll say it anyway because it's true. We're not getting any younger. We don't have the time younger people who fall in love do. And I don't want to waste a minute of the years we have left being without you."

"Ward, I—"

"You're an adventurous woman. You wouldn't be here by yourself if you weren't. Marry me, Carolyn, and we'll have the greatest adventure of our lives, being together and loving each other and serving the Lord together."

His voice coaxed, his smile tempted, and she felt the wild leap of her own love. For a few brief, heartbreaking moments she saw all the wonderful possibilities of life with him, all the sweetness of loving and sharing. But it was a future that could not be. "Ward, stop! I'm trying to tell you something—"

"That you don't feel the way I do, that you don't love me?" He searched her eyes, then smiled and touched her lips lightly with his. "You can't tell me you don't love me," he said with an assurance that would have been smug if it weren't so loving.

No, she couldn't say that. Her mouth could not deny what her heart felt. But what she had to say was surely as devastating.

He smiled at her hesitation. "Ah, the mysterious lady is going to reveal her deep, dark secrets. But you're too good a woman to have some terrible secret, Carolyn."

She briefly leaned her forehead against his strong shoulder, then lifted her head to look into his eyes again. "No, I don't have a *terrible* secret…but I do have a secret. I should have told you sooner, but I didn't think it was possible that we could truly fall in love in only two weeks, and I didn't want to weigh our relationship down with…irrelevant details." She paused and rubbed a damp palm across the knee of her jeans. "May I start at the beginning?"

He sounded more puzzled than suspicious or apprehensive when he said, "Please do," and squirmed into a more comfortable position in the sand beside her.

"I had a daughter, Terry, five years older than the son you know about. She was a wonderful girl, bright, vivacious, marvelously talented musically. But she fell in love with a—" How to describe Ric? "A handsome, fast-talking charmer. A drummer in a rock band. They got married, but he liked partying and drinking and having a good time a lot more than being a faithful husband and father or steady worker. Eventually he became abusive, Terry left him, and she and the children came to live with me. But she never stopped loving Ric or thinking he'd change."

"Did he change?"

"No. Terry became a Christian, but when she heard Ric was in the hospital…on a drug overdose, as it turned out…she went to him. On their way home from the hospital, there was an accident, and Terry died in it. Ric sprained his wrist." She still had difficulty understanding that, but she could say it without the savage bitterness that had claimed her for months after the accident, the bitterness that had even come between her and the Lord for a while. "Ric claimed she was driving and squirmed out of all responsibility. The authorities had some doubts but never proved anything."

Ward wrapped his arms around her and rocked her gently, his cheek cradled against the top of her head. "Oh, Carolyn, I'm so sorry—"

She rested briefly in the warm comfort of his embrace, wishing she could never leave it. But knowing he still didn't realize all she was trying to tell him, she forced herself to withdraw. "There's more. Ric asked me to keep the children until he could 'get on his feet.' Although I'd have fought him for them if he *hadn't* asked, because with his drinking and drugs he was no fit father."

"Yes, I can see that." Ward spoke slowly, as if he were warily peering around corners and seeing something he hadn't expected.

She plunged ahead. "I still have the children, Ward. Ric abandoned them. I haven't even heard from him for several years. It's not what I expected to be doing at this time of life, but I'm mother and father and breadwinner for them. I'm not a…footloose widow free to dash off to some faraway place with you."

Ward was silent as he absorbed all she'd said. His gaze was toward the fire, but she could feel him shifting perspective, seeing a wholly different view of her.

She looked into the fire too, desperately trying to push the love she felt for him into some far corner of her mind and heart where it couldn't leap out and entangle her. "I realize now that I should have told you, how wrong it was not to tell you.…"

"Taking on the job of raising three children must have been a…difficult adjustment for you." He raked a hand through his silvery hair, his face troubled in the moonlight. He did not angrily pounce on her for failing to tell him, but neither, she noted, did he protest her self-incriminating judgment of what she'd done.

"They're great kids, Ward, wonderful kids. They fill my life with joy." Her voice was almost fierce, passionate with love and protectiveness. "But they *are* kids. They're noisy and energetic and rambunctious. They catch chicken pox and colds and everything else that comes along. They break things and spill things and roughhouse and squabble. They have to go to the bathroom at the most inconvenient times. They test the limits of authority. They can be aggravating and infuriating...and then they come and give you a hug and kiss and smile, or you hear one of them asking in a bedtime prayer that Jesus bless Grandma...and you just overflow with love."

He nodded understanding. "Yes, I remember the joys, and difficulties, of parenting."

"But you were right when you said raising a family is different these days. There are fears I never had when my own children were small. Outside influences that are powerful and relentless. Even school now is a different world than what I knew. They have to check for *weapons*. Kelsey will be a teenager in a couple of years. I worry what will happen then, with all she'll be exposed to and all the pressures that are on teenagers these days. I worry about raising a little boy without a father to guide him in male things. Sometimes I feel so lost. The term 'generation gap' isn't just a meaningless phrase, and sometimes I feel on the edge of tumbling into it. I run out of time. I run out of energy. But I never run out of responsibilities. I wouldn't even be here now if Scott hadn't come to take over and practically shove me out the door."

Ward nodded again, and she was acutely aware that she was doing all the talking here, that Ward was saying little.

"Given a choice," she added honestly, "raising three children isn't what I'd *choose* to be doing at this time in my life. I'd be doing what other grandparents are doing, enjoying their grandchildren but leaving the worries and responsibilities to the parents. But that's the way things are, and with the Lord's help, I'm going to do the very best I can. He tells me to lean on him, and I do, over and over."

"What if Ric suddenly shows up and wants the children?"

"I don't think he will. But if he came back a changed man and could give the children a decent life and the children wanted to go with him, I wouldn't stand between them. I want what's best for them. But as it is now, I have legal custody. After a long battle."

"Battle? But if he abandoned them—"

"I had to battle a legal and social welfare system that doesn't necessarily think a single grandmother is the best person to raise her grandchildren." She couldn't keep a small note of bitterness out of her voice then at the memory of one particular social worker who had stubbornly tried to put the children into a foster home. "And when I got through fighting that battle, I had to fight the Internal Revenue Service for the right to take them as dependents. And then I had to fight the insurance company to add them to my health insurance. I read a report not long ago that there are close to a million children being cared for by some half million grandparents in the United States, yet instead of finding programs and institutions eager to help us, we often find ourselves battling for our rights every step of the way. But it was worth every battle," she finished fiercely, almost challenging him to argue with her. "I'd do it all over again if I had to! And I'd *never* relinquish the children to Ric or anyone else simply to relieve myself of the responsibility."

He didn't argue. Instead, with an abrupt shift to intuition, he said, "This man you were planning to marry—this had something to do with the breakup with him?"

Carolyn nodded. "He was a good man, a wonderful help in the first terrible weeks after Terry's death. But when it became obvious I would be raising the kids permanently, he backed off. I know he felt guilty about it, but he was honest. He said he'd worked hard raising one family, and he just wasn't up to doing it again. I couldn't blame him. I wasn't sure I was up to it either." She smiled faintly. "Sometimes I'm still not sure."

174

"So…where does this all leave us?" Ward sounded more stunned than angry with her revelations, like a man turning bewilderedly in a room with no doors.

"It leaves us…nowhere. You have your plans and ambitions for serving the Lord. And I can't begin to tell you how much I admire and respect your desire to give your thanks to the Lord in service to him! But I have my responsibilities to the children, the path in life the Lord designated for *me*. And the two don't…mesh."

He twisted a heel in the soft sand, digging a hole, sliding the heel to fill it, digging it again.

"Ward, I didn't, when we first met, deliberately set out to keep this a secret or deceive you—"

"But you obviously made the decision at some point to do exactly that!"

She heard the first faint undercurrent of accusation in his voice. She wrapped her hand around his arm, desperately wanting to make him understand. "I realized almost from the start that our relationship *couldn't* go anywhere, that all we could ever have were these two weeks—"

"You might have let *me* know that!"

"Yes. I was unfair and selfish. I wanted them to be the most wonderful two weeks ever, so I didn't tell you." Almost defiantly she added, "And they have been."

"In other words, it's the old case of the end justifies the means, right? And never mind what happens to my feelings in the end when you spring this on me! You could hold back, not let your heart get involved the way mine is—"

Carolyn jumped to her feet. "What are we going to do, get into some ridiculous argument about who loves who the most?" she demanded. She deserved his anger, even his scorn at her deception…but not his accusation about a lack of love for him! Not when her heart was overflowing with it, not when

175

it felt like a dam about to burst inside her.

She whirled and ran blindly for her travel trailer.

Ward didn't follow.

Carolyn leaned over the edge of the bed and looked at the luminous dial on the clock. She felt as if she had been tossing restlessly for hours, but it was only five minutes to eleven.

She got up and knelt on the other twin bed so she could peer out the tiny window. Ward's motorhome was dark, the same as all the other houses and trailers at *Luna*. Was he lying there awake, restless and resentful, angry that he'd wasted almost two weeks on a dead-end relationship?

No, it wasn't a waste, she protested fiercely. Even if what was between them couldn't go anywhere, it was still sweet and wonderful and worthwhile.

But apparently she was the only one who felt that way.

She went back to bed, but after another five minutes she gave up trying to sleep, got up and dressed, adding a jacket against the coolness of the night. She'd simply walk until she was too exhausted to do anything *but* sleep.

Outside, she walked down to the dark rocks not yet covered by the incoming tide. The moon, no longer perfectly round now that it was on the shrinking side of full, still shone with a silver glory, gleaming on the water with a metallic brilliance. Edgar drifted languidly in a faint breeze, like a slow dancer moving to silent music. Overhead, the sky was so full of stars, yet she was conscious that each one was alone and separate. She felt an echoing loneliness, and then the stars and sea and moonlight dimmed as a veil of tears covered her eyes.

"Carolyn."

She turned slowly to give herself time to blink back the tears, hands jammed in her jacket pockets, her emotions a ragged mixture of defensiveness about her unyielding dedication to putting responsibility to the children first, love for him, and regret for what could not be. And, at this moment, a simple leaping joy at seeing him again.

"I guess you couldn't sleep," he said softly. When he reached her, he didn't take her in his arms, but he rested his forearms on her shoulders. "Neither could I." His fingers tangled lightly in her hair.

"It's…that kind of night." She turned her head to press her cheek against his arm.

"Carolyn, I'm sorry." He sounded uncharacteristically helpless, this strong man who approached problems with cheerful confidence. "Sorry about the things I said, sorry about…everything."

"I'm sorry, too, for not telling you all I should have."

"I can understand why you didn't. I remember making a careless remark much like this other man's, about not wanting to raise a young family. I'm not angry."

But understanding, dismissal of anger, and their mutual apologies didn't change what *was*.

"I was just going to take a walk," she said. "If you'd like—?"

He hesitated, and she understood why. If they walked together, they'd have to talk, talk that might only slip into argument or anger, and she knew neither of them wanted that. "How about a moonlight ride in the sandrail?" he suggested.

The open sandrail was not conducive to conversation. But they would still be together. "Yes!" Carolyn agreed gladly.

They pushed the lightweight sandrail out of the garage and down to the beach, breathless and a little giggly by the time they got it far enough that Ward could start the engine without disturbing the sleepers at *Luna*.

The beach was silvery-bright, each rock or dip plainly visible in the moonlight, and he didn't turn on the headlights. Carolyn snuggled close to him, hand wrapped around his arm, head on his shoulder, and simply gave herself up to the happiness of being with him and the glory of the night. The stars no longer looked so lonely now, and the glimmer of moonlight on sea was more rippling satin than cold metal. The breeze in the moving sandrail ruffled her hair and dried her tears.

She didn't know how far they went, past clusters of dark, silent houses, past some creature of the sea briefly breaking the surface of shimmering water and disappearing again, past the outline of a twisted piece of washed-in rope that the sea had turned into graceful art.

When eventually he turned around, he switched off the engine, and they stepped out to stand with arms around each other's waists.

"Look!" Carolyn cried.

Far overhead, like some silent traveler among the stars, a satellite crossed the sky, its path arrow straight until it was lost in the distance. And then a shooting star arced across the sky, lighting up the night with incandescent brilliance, spectacular celestial fireworks that eclipsed the man-made achievement.

Carolyn and Ward looked at each other and smiled, and he turned and took her in his arms. Carolyn closed her eyes when he kissed her, shutting out the glory of the night, opening herself to the tenderness of the kiss, the warmth and passion, the love that flowed between them with the strength of the moving tide and the magic of the shooting star.

Yet back in her bed, Carolyn was achingly aware that from this wonderful high point there was nowhere to go but down. The situation was the same, the canyon of circumstances separating them unchanged. They were supposed to attend the buffet dinner and candlelight service the following evening, New Year's

Eve. But it was an evening that must inevitably, with the following day's parting looming over them, be strained and awkward.

No, she didn't want that, didn't want their relationship to end that way, didn't want bittersweet goodbyes! She only wanted to remember these wonderful days, this magical night.

She tossed and turned again, hearing the breeze rise from gentle whisper to howling gusts, shrieking around the trailer as if it were chasing something. And she made a decision.

She didn't bother to sort and pack. She simply threw everything haphazardly into the van, battling to keep the wind from tearing the doors and her armloads of possessions away from her. She turned off the water and propane, pulled the bamboo shades on the windows and locked the doors. Then, one final task.

She huddled in the van to write the note, feeling even the metal bulk of the vehicle shudder under the assault of the wind. She didn't write much. *Thanks for the most wonderful two weeks ever. May the Lord bless you wherever you go and whatever you decide to do to serve him. I'll always remember you. With love, Carolyn.* She put the note in an envelope addressed to Ward and fastened it firmly to the door with a half dozen pieces of tape so it couldn't blow away.

The last thing she saw as she drove away was that Edgar no longer whirled from the cord on the pole. He had blown away, vanished in the night, the end of his dancing tenure here somehow a fitting symbol of the end of the brief, sweet love that had temporarily blossomed between Carolyn and Ward.

Eight

❧

At home, the kids introduced Carolyn to their new cat Henrietta and engulfed her with hugs and kisses and tales about their experiences while she was away. Before he left, Scott inspected her thoughtfully and asked, "Everything okay, Mom? You've looked a little glum since you got home." She assured him that it was just a minor after-vacation letdown. She called Helen and gave her a report on *Playa Luna de la Creciente*, mentioning Ward only in the most casual fashion.

She jumped back into the usual hectic routine of her life. Work, children's school and social activities, a scare about an almost-broken nose when daredevil Erin took a flying leap off the garage roof into a snowbank. The Christmas sunshine of Baja and Ward felt almost like some romantic flight of imagination.

She kept assuring herself, as she had on the long drive home, that her feelings for Ward would soon fade. The relationship would look different through a veil of time and distance. It was, after all, just a temporary holiday romance.

But the feelings didn't fade. Ward was in her mind all the time, hovering in the background even as she worked with a complicated real estate transaction or sympathized with Kelsey's blues about her best friend moving away or coped with a shower head that suddenly decided to spray water bullets. Ward could fix that in a minute!

Finally she had to admit what she'd known deep down all along. This was no holiday fling. She'd fallen in *love*, the kind of free-fall plunge the young thought was reserved only for them, the kind of love that permeated nights with bittersweet longings and days with an upsurge of hope when she thought she spotted him, followed by a downswoop of disappointment when she realized it wasn't him.

Then a little thought began to flutter in the back of her mind. Perhaps Ward desperately wanted to get in touch with her and just hadn't been able to find her! Maybe he couldn't remember the name of the town where she lived. Maybe a telephone operator had given him a wrong number.

The logic of all that was weak, she had to admit. Ward was so competent and resourceful that confusion about a town name or phone number would not deter him for long.

But weak logic or not, it *could* be, she decided with a rush of excitement. So she would contact him! She couldn't reach him personally, of course, but she could leave her name and number with the nephew who was living in the Atlanta house. She was on the phone, eagerly dialing the long-distance information service, when she had to pause to ask herself, Just what did she plan to say when...*if*...he called?

She wouldn't gush impossible words of love. There was no point in that because the situation was no different than before. But she could suggest that they stay in touch, exchange letters from wherever the Lord sent him. Be friends. And perhaps, sometime far in the future when their situations were different... She sat poised with pen over scratchpad as she waited expectantly for the long distance service to give her the number.

She hung up the phone a minute later, trying not to be desperately disappointed. There was no number for Ward Setlow. It had been disconnected. Which must mean the house was sold, and Ward was off on his faraway adventure for the Lord. But just to be certain, the following day she faxed a title company in Atlanta a request for information about any recent sale by a property owner named Ward Setlow. She had an answer that same day. Yes, a sale on the property had closed a week ago, a quick cash deal.

She slowly crumpled the fax sheet. This was it, then. She couldn't keep clinging to some wild hope. Where had he gone? Latin America, Korea, some primitive African country? *Appreciate that you have him, whoever you are, wherever he is,* she thought fiercely. *Because he's the best.*

Somehow she managed to get through the day at the office, go shopping, cook dinner, talk and laugh cheerfully with the kids.

But inside she silently begged, *Help me deal with this, Lord. Help me accept your will. And watch over Ward, please, wherever he goes.*

It was a prayer she repeated frequently in the next few days. A raging snowstorm knocked out the electricity, and the flickering light of her emergency lamps reminded her of Baja and Ward. Mike's kindergarten teacher called her in for a conference because of his fights with another boy, renewing her awareness of the difficulties in raising a boy without a strong male figure in his life. She read a newspaper story about two missionaries being abducted and killed in a Central American country and thought of the dangers to Ward. And on Saturday afternoon, when she backed the van out of the garage to take Henrietta to the vet for her shots, she discovered a flat tire.

The kids piled out of the van, happy to play in the drifted snow in the yard. More snow was already falling, a flutter of

182

dime-sized flakes thickening to a white veil as Carolyn got out and contemplated the disabled vehicle. She rubbed a gloved hand across her eyes as tears prickled there. She didn't know why she felt so close to crying, so indescribably weary. This was no earth-shaking disaster. She knew how to change a flat. She was accustomed to snow. She even appreciated its cold beauty. It was just that...

She looked at a figure coming up the sidewalk through the swirling snow, like some ghostly figure emerging through the mists of time. But when he got a few feet from her he wasn't ghostly. He was solid man, husky body clad in down jacket and snow boots, hands in his pockets, snowflakes blending with the silver of his hair. She stared at him warily. How often had she thought she'd seen him striding toward her and been wrong?

"Need a man who's handy with a wrench?" he inquired almost lazily as he inspected the drooping van. The outline of the motorhome, indistinct in the falling snow, loomed on the street.

"*Ward?*"

He held out his arms to her, but just then the kids came running up, curious as always, to look him over. She made quick introductions, hoping she didn't sound as breathless as she felt, wondering if she would have recklessly rushed into his arms if the children hadn't interrupted.

"Ward is a friend I met on my vacation," she added in explanation to the kids. He shook hands with each one, giving them a grown-up importance as he acknowledged each name individually.

"What'd you come here for?" Mike asked with blunt curiosity.

"I brought this to your grandma." Ward pulled Edgar out of his jacket pocket, and Carolyn laughed in spite of her tenseness. Silly, flamboyant Edgar, with his frivolous purple eyes, his tropical colors now freckled with falling snowflakes. "Among other reasons I'm here," Ward murmured in a softly meaningful aside to Carolyn.

"Hey, neat!" Erin grabbed Edgar and started racing around the snowy yard with the flying-fish windsock dancing behind her, Kelsey and Mike in noisy pursuit.

"I found Edgar on the beach the same day you left."

"Yes, I...saw that he'd blown away."

"I wondered if you'd cut him loose. As you did me." His smile softened the small accusation in the words.

"No! I mean—" Big snowflakes hit his face and turned to tiny rivulets. Her tan had faded, but the bronze glow of the Baja sun still lingered on his.

"Never mind. First things first." He efficiently dug lug wrench, jack, and spare tire out of the van and changed the flat in less time than it would have taken her to figure out how to put the jack together.

Carolyn unloaded the pet carrier and, deciding to let the shots go for now, returned a relieved Henrietta to the house. Ward followed her inside, stamping his feet on the mat to shake off the snow. His masculine presence seemed to fill the kitchen with an unfamiliar but almost heady warmth and strength. She made coffee, but there was no private conversation between them with the kids milling around curiously. Then they asked if they could call some friends over to play, and within minutes the house was full of the usual childhood shrieks, squeals, and laughter, with occasional small, live bodies hurtling through the kitchen for one reason or another.

"Are you on your way to somewhere?" Carolyn asked tentatively during a small lull as they sat at the kitchen table with refilled coffee cups and an open package of Oreos.

"No. I'm here to—" He paused and laughed as a hide-and-seek player squirmed around his feet to get under the table. "I had a, ummm, somewhat more romantic setting in mind for this, but, since you asked—"

"I'm afraid this is as romantic as it gets," Carolyn said ruefully as Henrietta jumped into Ward's lap to look him over.

"Okay, I won't waste time or beat around the bush. Carolyn, did you disappear so abruptly because you decided you didn't love me?"

"No! Ward, I'm sorry! I just couldn't see any future for us, and I wanted our time together to end on that last wonderful midnight ride on the beach, not in bitter accusations or arguments." She shook her head helplessly, feeling again the painful dilemma of that night. "I'm sorry," she repeated.

He nodded, as if her answer perhaps confirmed some thought already in his mind.

"I didn't think I'd ever hear from you again. And when I learned your house had been sold, I thought you were off to some faraway place."

"You checked on the house?" He sounded surprised, and then his grin widened with satisfaction at what that implied. He scooted his chair closer and took her hands in his. "Carolyn, when you left so abruptly I was angry and hurt. I felt as if my heart had been used for target practice. I was torn between trying to forget you...and roaring across the border to catch up with you." He paused. "I decided to forget you."

She blinked at that flat statement.

He laughed softly. "I guess, because I'm here, I don't have to tell you how successful I was at *that.*"

"I've never stopped thinking about you, either, not for a day." Her smile wobbled. "Hardly for a minute."

"Carolyn, my first proposal may have been a bit premature. The kids need time to get to know me. Maybe you need more time, too. But I know my feelings for you." He reached across the table and took her hands in his. "I'm here because I love you, and it won't be long before I'll again be asking you to marry me."

A new thought brought sudden dismay. "Ward, are you turning this into a situation of choosing between me and the Lord? You mustn't do that!" She yanked her hands from his, refusing to grab and hold on for dear life as she so desperately wanted. "I won't *let* you do that! What you want to do is too important—"

"It isn't an either/or choice between you and the Lord." His tone was decisive. The child beneath the table squirmed out, racing for the *Home Free* spot on the living room sofa, and Henrietta, fur electrified, dashed in the opposite direction. Ward didn't let the action stop what he had to say. "Carolyn, along with being hurt, I was also puzzled and frustrated. I got an offer on the house, and I rushed back to Atlanta to take care of all the final details, sure that this was the Lord finally shifting into high gear. And nothing more happened. All my applications seemed to have fallen into some cosmic trash can. I was all ready to make my grand gesture of serving the Lord by dashing off to the far ends of the earth, and instead I found myself twiddling my thumbs."

Carolyn couldn't help smiling, easily picturing his impatience with thumb twiddling. But this was no lighthearted matter. "Ward, simply because none of your applications have been accepted yet doesn't mean one won't be soon—"

"I also got stuck on the confusing problem of our meeting and falling in love. On a beach in Baja, of all places. Do *you* think that was all just chance or accident?"

Carolyn couldn't answer. She'd thought about this, too. Yet she also knew that it was all too easy to read the Lord's will into what *you* wanted. "Ward, don't let impatience lead you astray—"

"I'm sometimes an impatient man," he admitted with a rueful smile. "But then the Lord sent someone with a message to me."

"Someone with a message?"

Ward laughed lightly. "Well, it was nothing as dramatic as an angel writing words across the sky with a flaming sword, or even a fax in capital letters. I just ran into this guy I used to know, and right there on a busy street in Atlanta he told me how dealing with me as a Christian businessman had changed and influenced his life. And I got a glimmer that those plumbing-fixture years were more important than I thought in serving the Lord."

"Of course they were important!"

"And then I looked behind my hurt and anger, stopped trying to forget you, and started praying for the Lord to reveal *his* will to me, because it was finally getting through to me that dashing off to some faraway place to serve him was *my* idea, not his. That sometimes what seem to us like the most worthy of plans and decisions are not *his* will."

Carolyn nodded slowly and absentmindedly stroked Henrietta, who had claimed her lap this time.

"I remember your saying to me once, when I was expressing impatience with the Lord's slowness in sending me somewhere, that maybe I hadn't made the right application yet." He reached across the table and cupped her chin lightly in his hand as he said softly, "I think I'm making that right application now. Sometimes the Lord does want someone to dash off to a far corner of the earth for him. But sometimes what he has for you to do is right under your nose. Like helping the woman you love raise her grandchildren."

Carolyn felt a brief flare of indignation in spite of the tenderness in his voice. "You're going to make an assigned chore out of me and the kids? Something you're grimly willing to do because you think it's the Lord's will?"

He smiled at her outburst and curled a hand around her neck. "Do you love me, Carolyn?"

She lifted her head, defiantly refusing to answer that. "I remember you saying you wouldn't want to be raising a family again—"

"The Lord is pretty good at changing perspective along with circumstances. And love makes a whole new perspective." His hand tightened around her neck with fierce tenderness. "And I do love you, Carolyn, and I want to marry you, even if saying that is still premature. I'm not asking for an immediate rush to the altar. I want to get to know the kids and have them know me. We need time together, too, with no secrets between us. But I already know that I want to be part of your life and your grandchildren's lives." He looked down at Henrietta, who was now straddling laps, forefeet kneading his knees, hind feet dug into Carolyn's. "I even want to be part of this pesky cat's life. And I rather think Steele may offer a few other opportunities for a man with a powerful faith and a strong wrench. Maybe someday there will even be faraway adventures for us together."

Carolyn wasn't conscious of making a decision to stand, wasn't aware of deciding to step into his arms, but she was there, wrapped in his embrace, lost in his kiss, feeling the love that had been a bittersweet pain explode into a fountain of joy. He lifted his head, looked into her eyes, and smiled at what he saw there.

"With that," he whispered huskily, "I can wait for however long it takes."

He kissed her again, and she felt the wonderful *zing* of youth and the satisfying glow of maturity in the love that flowed between them. She wrapped her arms around his neck and returned the kiss with all the love in her heart. A kiss of romance and love, passion and tenderness—

A kiss interrupted by giggles. Carolyn and Ward broke apart and turned to look, and the half-dozen pairs of eyes that were watching them suddenly scooted in as many different directions. Something crashed in the living room, and guilty silence followed.

She looked at him a little helplessly. "I could tell you it isn't always like this. But usually it is."

He just held his arms out to her again, and she stepped into them, heart and body, and lifted her face for his kiss. Outside, snow might be falling, but here, here there was warmth and love and happiness.

Christmas sunshine had followed her home.

AN UNLIKELY ANGEL

KAREN BALL

One

❧

Seattle, A Christmas Party

A gentle snow was falling outside, blanketing the night in sparkling white, giving the city a stunning, almost storybook appearance. Men and women stopped their holiday shopping and stared in wonder at the glittering display; children squealed with delight, reaching up to capture the large, fluffy flakes as they floated down.

It was a rare occurrence: snow in Seattle. A once-in-a-life-time glimpse of near ethereal beauty, and those who saw it were filled with wonder. Yet this exquisite scene went virtually unnoticed by the party-goers milling about the spacious, elegantly decorated ballroom on the top floor of the Hirsch, Tesler, and St. John building. For all its beauty, the night scene couldn't compete with the elegance, sophistication, and glamour of the annual employee Christmas party of Seattle's most prestigious efficiency consultant firm. Snowfalls in general were commonplace; this party was not. Everyone knew that.

Or at least, almost everyone.

One young woman, dressed in a stunning sequined gown of electric blue that showcased her slim figure with style and elegance, pressed her perfectly powdered nose against the glass of a tall, beveled window and stared at the sparkling display with delight.

"Andrea, get a grip. It's just snow."

At the tart reprimand, the young woman swiveled around, her blue eyes still glowing with pleasure.

"But it's so beautiful," she said on a wistful sigh. "Even you have to admit that, Maris."

"Actually," her companion responded in bored tones, arching her dark, perfectly shaped brows with disdain. "I don't. Nor do you, unless you want everyone at the party to know just how new you are to the city."

A slight flush crept into Andrea's cheeks, and she glanced around quickly.

"Oh, don't worry," Maris assured her as she brushed a crumb from her velvet jacket. "I stopped you before you made too much of a fool of yourself." Her brown eyes rested on the younger woman's sweet features, and she frowned slightly. "But, really, Andrea, you must learn to control yourself. You're working at one of the largest, most successful firms in Seattle now. Don't you think it's time you started acting a bit more...controlled?" She swept the room with a calculating gaze. "Believe me, darling, men like these won't have the patience for sweet, innocent, naive little girls." She turned back to her chastised friend and smiled humorlessly. "They'd chew you up in a second."

Andrea nodded miserably, biting her lip. "I know." Her traitorous eyes drifted back to the window. "But it's so beautiful...."

"For heaven's sake!" Maris reached out to take Andrea's slim arm in a firm grip and propel her toward the buffet table. "Look around you, darling! This is your chance. There are men all around you...sophisticated, intelligent, ridiculously well-paid. And some of them are even single."

Andrea glanced around dutifully, then sighed. "But does any of that really matter if he doesn't...," she shrugged, "you know, make your toes curl." She could see another reprimand coming and forestalled quickly. "Like him, for instance."

Maris turned to inspect Andrea's supposed toe-curler—took in the broad shoulders and well-built frame draped in an Armani suit, the tawny hair tinged with blond highlights bearing mute witness to days spent in the out-of-doors (or a very skilled hair stylist), the aristocratic profile—then shook her head emphatically. "Oh, good grief. Anyone but him."

"Why? He's very clearly wealthy—"

"Yes, quite," Maris cut in dryly as she picked up an elegant crystal glass. "That's Mackenzie St. John. As in Hirsch, Tesler, and..." She directed a disgusted look at the man. "He's one of the partners."

Andrea's brows raised. "Really?" She studied her selection again with even more interest. "*That's* Mackenzie St. John? I thought he was an old man."

"Only at heart, dear," came the dry rejoinder. "Only at heart."

Ignoring her friend's comment, Andrea studied the man who had become a virtual icon in his field. From what she could see of his features, he wasn't drop-dead gorgeous, but he was definitely attractive. She turned to Maris. "Good-looking, tall, wealthy...single?" she thought to ask.

Maris snorted. "Count on it."

"Well, then, what on earth is wrong with him?"

"Oh, not much. Just that he's cold as ice, unfeeling, demanding...you know, basically inhuman."

Andrea looked at her, stunned. "Come on! He can't be that bad."

"Probably worse." Maris's tones were filled with disdain. "Look, Andrea, I've been with this company for almost five years, and if there's one thing I've learned, it's to stay as far away from that man as possible."

"I thought he was supposed to be the best of the best."

"Oh, he is that. There isn't a better efficiency or management consultant in the field than Mackenzie St. John. When a company calls him in, they know they'll get their money's worth, and then some. He knows exactly what to do to bring a company back to life and fiscal viability. And he doesn't let anything get in his way. Not compassion. Not consequences to others. Not anything."

Andrea shuddered slightly, casting another glance at the oblivious object of their observations. "He sounds perfectly horrid."

"Bingo." Maris carefully ladled champagne punch from a stunning crystal bowl into her glass, expertly capturing one of the floating brandied cherries as she did so. "I was assigned to work for him for a few months last year, when his regular secretary was out on maternity leave. It was an interesting job, but not one I'd care to take on for long."

"Too much work?" Andrea asked with a grin.

"Too much hostility. I received dozens of calls from angry people—'idiots and malcontents,' St. John calls them—," she pursed her lips with distaste, "among other things. But they all had one thing in common: they wanted to give the man a piece of their minds." She slanted a glance at her friend. "Several left messages. I recall one in particular, from an older man who wanted to…let's see, what did he say? Oh, yes, 'rip the devil's heart out.'"

Andrea's eyes widened. "How did Mr. St. John react when you told him?"

Maris shrugged her slim shoulders indifferently. "He didn't even blink. But I wasn't too surprised. I mean, it was hardly a believable threat."

"Why? Wasn't the caller serious?"

Maris took a sip of her sparkling punch. "Oh, he sounded

quite serious. But he made a tactical error."

Andrea's pretty forehead creased in a confused frown. "An error?"

"Of course." The older woman's full lips lifted into an amused smile. "It's hardly going to concern a man to threaten something he doesn't have." She angled a look across the room at her distinguished employer. "And believe me, if there is one thing Mackenzie St. John does NOT have, it's a heart."

"Heartless and hopeless, huh?" Andrea shrugged dismissively and directed her gaze toward the other men in the room. "I pity the woman who falls for him one day."

Maris snorted. "Trust me, dear, she'd have to be a total saint. Either that," she smiled wickedly, "or a total fool!"

It was well past midnight when Mackenzie St. John felt he could make a graceful departure from the company Christmas party. His two partners had made it clear to him that his presence at such events was important, a "morale-builder," they called it.

"A monumental waste of time is more like it," he muttered as he stepped out of the elevator onto the marbled floor of the lobby. "Just like Christmas. And the whole month of December."

The doorman nodded to him respectfully as he approached. "Evening, sir," he said. "Your car is waiting."

Mackenzie nodded curtly, grateful the man knew him well enough not to offer the usual trite "Merry Christmas" as he exited the building.

If there was one thing Christmas had not been for years, it was merry.

He handed the parking attendant a five dollar bill, then slid onto the leather seat of his Infiniti, sinking gratefully into its familiar comfort. This was more like it. Quiet. Solitude. A totally controlled environment where he was alone, isolated, not expected to make inane conversation with people he didn't know—or really care to know.

The half-hour drive to his house went by quickly. That was one benefit of driving at midnight: Seattle's usual rush-hour gridlock was over and done with. Another benefit of the late hour was that, at least for tonight, he wouldn't have to watch people bustling about, caught in the frenetic shopping fever that this time of year seemed to spawn. It was barely the beginning of December, but Mackenzie had had his fill of watching adults and children alike standing and staring at Christmas displays in storefront windows as though they'd never seen such a wondrous sight before. "Same preposterous displays every year," he mumbled.

Shaking his head, he reminded himself he was free. Free for an entire month! Until three years ago, he'd absolutely dreaded the arrival of December. The moment the first day of that month dawned, his job as one of Seattle's most-sought corporate consultants became next to impossible. There was something about the Christmas season that made people lose their nerve.

For the most part, Mackenzie loved his work. He thrived on bringing new life to a company on the edge of bankruptcy. It was a simple fact, though, that he'd made some enemies along the way. That had bothered him at first. A lot. He'd agonized over cuts and layoffs, wondering how people would react, how they would survive. Then he was fired from a job because they said he wouldn't make the hard decisions. "He's so worried about the people that my business is going down the tubes!" the angry owner had fumed to Mackenzie's bosses. At that time he'd been with Hirsch and Tesler for only a few years. The two older men had stunned him by taking him out to lunch after the fiasco. They said they'd been watching him, that he held great promise—but that he needed to toughen up.

"You're not a babysitter, Mackenzie," Abe Tesler had remarked quietly. "Corporations don't call you in to help them deal with their people. They want you to save their businesses. No matter what it takes."

It had been a tough lesson, but he'd learned it well. Within the next year he'd become the most-requested consultant at the firm. Three years later, he'd been offered a partnership. Since that time, he'd never again allowed himself to consider the emotional aspect of what he did—unless, of course, it helped him in his strategy. It was a simple fact: sometimes people had to be sacrificed to keep a company afloat. Those in management generally understood and followed his recommendations to the letter.

But let the calendar turn to December, and suddenly those same attentive, acquiescent executives were balking and offering excuses.

"I can't fire him, it's Christmas!"

"Let her go? How can I let her go now? It's Christmas!"

"What do you mean, 'downsize'? Don't you know this is Christmas? What will they think of me?"

For the life of him, Mackenzie could not understand the eternal fascination people had with this time of the year. Okay, so it was the celebration of Jesus' birth. Fine. That accounted for Christmas Day. Maybe even Christmas Eve. But Mackenzie was a firm believer in keeping things in perspective. His faith was real, but it was kept where it belonged: in church on Sunday morning.

Oh, there might have been a time, long ago, when he, too, thought this season held something special. But that was before he'd seen the way people treated each other every other day of the year, before he'd seen the hypocrisy and cold, calculating ways of the world in general. It hadn't taken long to realize that

Christmas—and so-called "good will to men"—were nice little myths shared with children around a light-decked tree. He'd seen too much.

In his line of business, one saw the worst in people every day. Let a company fall into serious financial trouble, and men and women scrambled to abandon honor and integrity in the name of the bottom line. Let a rumor of cutbacks float on the air, and employees began saying one thing to a person's face then cutting him to the quick when he left the room. Mackenzie had started out believing in the importance of treating others fairly and with honor, but "Christian demeanor" just didn't have a prayer when a company was facing financial ruin. He learned early on not to let himself get involved in the emotional side of what was happening in the companies who needed him. It was far better to concentrate on the nitty gritty, the facts—logic was the name of the game, not compassion. Do what had to be done, and let someone else worry about how people *felt* about it.

Which was why the Christmas season was so irritating. No one seemed able to stay rational and logical in the face of the holidays. This month-long indulgence in frivolity hidden under the guise of "holiday cheer" was enough to drive a man crazy. Particularly this man. Finally he'd gone to talk with his partners, and they'd all agreed. Rather than beat his head against "The Christmas Spirit," he would take the month off, using the time to review the past year, evaluating the direction of his professional and personal life, and preparing for the coming year.

So far it had worked well. Every December he ended up with a list of goals which he then tracked throughout the year. It made life much easier, much more organized, much more logical.

As he turned his car onto his street, he shook his head yet again at the holiday frippery on the houses and lawns. At least a few of his neighbors showed some restraint, sticking to white lights in the trees and elegant wreaths on the doors. Others, however, had gone all out. Baubles and lights dangled from the eaves of the houses, and Santa or crèche displays left scant inches of lawn without some kind of holiday raiment. All of which had the irritating effect of turning Mackenzie's normally quiet, refined neighborhood into some kind of mutant carnival gone wild.

"Ridiculous," he muttered. "Can't these people find a better way to utilize their time than putting plastic reindeer on their lawns?"

He pulled into his driveway, noting with a certain measure of satisfaction that his home alone had retained its bare, unadorned sophistication. At least here he could rely on things being organized. Well-ordered. In control.

If only the rest of the world would fall in line.

But as he eased out of his car, Mackenzie had to admit he was asking too much. The rest of the world would never see things his way—especially during the peace-on-earth, have-a-holly-jolly holidays. They were too busy being filled with good cheer to think straight.

Mackenzie cast one last glance at his neighbors' lawns as the garage door slid shut. "Good thing Christmas only comes once a year," he muttered darkly as he went inside the house.

CHAPTER

Two

I wish Christmas would last forever!"

Karlee McKay wrapped her arms around herself, reveling in the anticipation the holiday season always brought her. "What do you say, Zsuzsi? Isn't this the greatest time of year? Don't you wish it would just go on and on?"

The large white dog, who was sitting beside Karlee's rocking chair, responded with a happy *Woof!* Karlee grinned at the Komondor, then uttered a contented sigh, and rocked back and forth gently. Turning her head, she gazed out the bedroom window at the early morning, noting the cloud-covered sky with pleasure.

"Looks as though we're going to have snow again today, girl."

The dog tilted her head, as though carefully considering her mistress's softly-spoken words. Karlee laughed, reaching out to rub the dog's long ears, loving the feel of her soft, corded coat.

She glanced down to the Bible in her lap. Several years ago she had decided to read through Isaiah during the Christmas season. It had been so moving that she'd made it a tradition. Normally she settled for reading two or three chapters a day.

But this morning she'd found herself paging through the book, as though looking for something. And so she had. Once again she read over the section in Isaiah 40 that had seemed to jump out at her when she'd turned to it:

"A voice says, 'Call out.' Then He answered, 'What shall I call out?'...Get yourself up on a high mountain, O Zion, bearer of good news, Lift up your voice mightily, O Jerusalem, bearer of good news; Lift it up, do not fear. Say to the cities of Judah, 'Here is your God!'"

A shiver passed over Karlee. She'd been reading the Bible most of her life, but seldom had she felt such a strong impression—as though God wanted her, Karlee McKay, on this specific day in early December, to read these specific words. As though he had something special in store.

"I'm listening, Father," she whispered. A strong, sweet awareness swept over her, and she closed her eyes, filled with wonder. God was there. She could feel him touching her heart and spirit, overflowing her with his presence. And a certain conviction settled in her heart that this Scripture was more than just a morning reading. It was a message she needed to share.

But with whom?

"Show me, Lord—"

Be-weep!

The sharp sound startled Karlee from her whispered prayer, and she turned her head to glance out the window. Her neighbor was walking toward his sleek, expensive car. He must have just disabled the alarm, which explained the sound Karlee had heard. She watched as he opened the car door, absently taking in the man's tall frame, confident stance, and probably tailor-made overcoat.

Mackenzie St. John, the quintessential "man who has everything." She started to turn back to her prayer, but something stopped her.

"Call out."

She frowned, watching the man as he retrieved a file folder from within his car, then pulled the door shut and reset the alarm.

"Call out...say to the cities of Judah, 'Here is your God.'"

Karlee's breath caught in her throat and her eyes widened.

"You've got to be kidding, Lord!"

"Call out."

She shook her head. "No way. Not this man." She lifted her gaze heavenward. "I've tried before, Father. You know I have." She crossed her arms, recalling how she'd tried to be friendly after moving next door to the man. Every conversation she tried to start had been met with monosyllabic responses. The record to date was a three-minute conversation in which he'd stopped her while she was on a walk with Zsuzsi and asked her to please keep her sunflowers from leaning over the back fence into his yard.

"They drop seeds," he'd said, his expression clearly one of distaste. "And the birds are all over them."

"I know!" Karlee answered excitedly. "Aren't they fun to watch?"

His eyebrows arched a fraction. "Fun?" He turned to look at the flowers, a frown creasing his forehead. "You like having birds spreading seeds all over your lawn?"

"Well, yes. That's the point."

His dark eyes, when he turned back to her, were filled with pure bafflement. She wasn't sure if she wanted to laugh or cry. "More flowers means more birds," she tried explaining.

"And more mess," he added.

She'd opened her mouth to debate but realized it was no use. He just didn't get it. With a deep sigh she told him she'd do her best to keep the flowers on her side of the fence.

"I'd appreciate it," he said.

Nearly every other encounter she'd had with him had ended

in the same way: with him looking at her as though she were from Mars, and her sighing and shrugging her shoulders. "He thinks I'm a nut, Lord!" she protested.

The room resonated with silence, and after a moment Karlee let out a slow, deep breath. "Okay, if you say so," she murmured, reaching down to stroke Zsuzsi's broad head, finding comfort in the action. "But I sure hope you intend to send me some help with this. Because one thing's for sure, I'll never get through to Mackenzie St. John on my own!"

Three

The next afternoon Mackenzie had just finished preparing his usual lunch of salmon salad when the doorbell rang. Frowning, he went to glance out the window. He wasn't expecting any visitors.

A bright, candy-apple-green Del Sol sat in the driveway. Lindsey was here.

With an indulgent smile he went to open the front door and found himself staring at a large, full, blue spruce.

"Merry Christmas, brother mine!" a sweet voice sang out from amidst the branches. "I come bearing gifts."

"How nice," he remarked, stepping aside as she staggered inside, tree in tow. "You brought me a bush."

"A *bush?* This, my poor, unenlightened, brother, is a Christmas tree of the finest quality."

"Ah. Of course." He watched her deposit the tree in the middle of his Berber rug. "And what exactly am I supposed to do with this fine quality tree?"

She dimpled. "Decorate it, goon. Now stop being obtuse and come give your sweet sister a kiss."

Chuckling, he moved to do as he'd been told. He gave her a

quick peck on her smooth cheek, and she threw her arms around him in an exuberant hug.

She was petite, but she was strong.

"Lindsey, give the ribs a break," he gasped.

She giggled and stepped back. "If this beauty doesn't get you into the Christmas spirit, I'm inclined to think you're hopeless." The gaze she turned on the tree held an adoration that most women—at least, those he knew—generally reserved for precious gems.

"I keep telling you that's the case, Changeling," he said affectionately. "The sooner you realize it, the happier we both will be."

"Not so, Bear." She grinned at him, and he shook his head. He'd given up trying to quell the nickname years ago. An avid Winnie the Pooh fan, Lindsey had decided, at the ripe old age of eight, that her big brother reminded her of Pooh. "You're cute and cuddly," she'd said, her eyes gleaming.

"And I have very little brain, eh?" he'd demanded.

"About some things," she'd retorted with a chortle. He'd argued for a short time, but there was no putting a lid on Lindsey when she had her mind and heart set on something. She had been adamant that he needed a nickname. Fortunately, she'd been willing to compromise, so "Pooh" (a nickname that still made Mackenzie shudder) gave way to "Bear." Exactly why a nickname was so vitally important, he'd never fully understood—but then, not understanding Lindsey was par for the course.

Ten years his junior, Lindsey was a mystery to her brother. She lived life to the hilt, going from one adventure to the next, finding—and producing—delight everywhere she went. Mackenzie couldn't remember the last time he'd seen her without a smile on her face. It was hard to believe they were related.

She stood on tiptoe and tweaked his nose playfully. "I know

207

there's a heart in there somewhere, dear brother," she said, then headed for the kitchen. He followed her dutifully, closing cupboard doors and drawers in her wake as she helped herself to sandwich fixings.

"Mmmmmm," she said with glee as she applied another helping of Miracle Whip to her bread. "Peanut butter, Miracle Whip, and pickles. A lunch fit for a queen."

Mackenzie grimaced, but she ignored him, going to the breakfast nook, pulling out a chair, and plopping down. "So, what do you hear from the folks lately?"

Mackenzie smiled wryly. Only his much-adored sibling could get away with calling Eudora and Oren St. John "the folks." Professors of logic and physics, respectively, at Harvard University, his parents were well-known as somber, cerebral, and introspective individuals. Certainly not "folks" kind of people.

"The usual," he answered. "They're in high demand as speakers." He smiled. "And as dinner guests. They told you, didn't they, that they've been invited to a forum on modern philosophy?"

"Hmmmm," she said around a mouthful of her monstrous sandwich creation. "That's right. Paris, isn't it? They'll be gone all month. Ah, yes, nothing so enjoyable as stimulating discourse with the intellectual elite, is there?"

Mackenzie smiled. His parents' position in the world of academia had been established long before either he or Lindsey had come on the scene. When Mackenzie was born, they simply brought him along. Quiet and undemanding even as an infant, he fit in perfectly. When most children his age were racing around playgrounds, he was learning to sit quietly and listen. By the time he was ten, he was even taking part in some of the discussions, demonstrating a remarkable grasp of logic and reasoning. A fact that delighted his parents to no end.

Then Lindsey showed up, a complete surprise from the get-go—and as different in nature to the rest of them as it was possible to be. Impulsive, dramatic, emotional, she took their family by storm. Neither Mackenzie nor his parents could begin to understand her. By the time she was a toddler, Mackenzie had become convinced she was some sort of alien, planted in their family to keep things in an uproar. Hence her nickname: Changeling. She brought chaos—and uproarious laughter—into their home. So it was that, by the time Lindsey was four, Mackenzie and his parents shrugged their shoulders and accepted her as an enchanting anomaly. They couldn't explain or comprehend her, but they had no trouble at all adoring her.

An adoration that had never wavered, even into adulthood, Mackenzie realized as he watched his sister polish off her sandwich with evident pleasure. He might be skeptical about a lot of things, but this he knew: his sister was going places. As an up-and-coming interior decorator, she'd been gaining steady recognition for the work she was doing around the Seattle area. Her design concepts were being touted as some of the most innovative and creative to hit the city in a long time. Considering how unique Lindsey was, that came as no surprise to Mackenzie.

"So I guess that leaves just you and me for Christmas, eh, Bear?"

He opened his mouth to reply when the air was split by loud, raucous barking. Mackenzie groaned, but Lindsey's face lit up with pleasure.

"Karlee's out, huh?"

Mackenzie grimaced. "She must be. The creature only sounds that excited when they're outside together." Lindsey jumped up and went to peer out the window.

"You've got to stop spying on my neighbors, Lindsey," he said halfheartedly as he followed her. When Karlee McKay had moved next door last spring, she'd piqued his sister's considerable curiosity. Before long the two were getting together on a fairly regular basis to share tea and conversation.

Apparently Lindsey had found a kindred soul in his colorful neighbor.

"You've got to see this!"

He came up beside Lindsey and glanced out, his eyes widening with disbelief as he took in the scene next door. "She's building a snowman," he stated flatly.

Lindsey laughed. "She is indeed."

"Where did she ever find that monstrosity?" he muttered.

"What monstrosity? Her dog?"

"You call *that* a dog? It looks more like some kind of mutant dust mop!" The beast had to weigh one hundred pounds or more and was covered with a white, corded coat that danced and bounced around it as it played.

Lindsey's face lit with an affectionate smile. "For your information, I think Zsuzsi's cute."

"You think anything with four legs and fur is cute. I'm telling you, that animal is some kind of genetic experiment. A twisted mix between a lion and an unmade bed." He shook his head. "Not that the beast doesn't fit her well. Her hair is as out of control as her dog's!"

"Her hair is to die for!" Lindsey exclaimed. "It's like something out of a hair care commercial. You know, 'Use our product and your hair will look like this, all curls and waves and sun-kissed golden highlights cascading almost to your waist....'" She angled a look at her brother. "Face it, bro. She's positively gorgeous."

"She's positively peculiar." He studied the petite, slim woman who was rolling what was apparently the head toward her snow creation. "I realize she's a designer of some sort—"

"Children's clothing," Lindsey supplied, looking at him with patient tolerance. "Remember? She's very successful, though she doesn't flaunt it." She smiled, a tinge of admiration in her expression. "Karlee happens to be that rare combination of talent and humility."

"With more than a touch of quirkiness thrown in. She wears those odd dresses that drape over her and cover her from head to toe. And those crazy boots—"

"Prairie boots, Bear. They're very much in style now."

"Yeah. Right," he said dubiously. "She looks like some kind of refugee from a John Wayne movie!" He narrowed his eyes. "I can see her now, walking beside her Conestoga wagon, the quintessential prairie woman."

"Karlee is the picture of relaxed elegance and comfort—" Lindsey broke off, her eyes gleaming. "Which clearly explains why you don't get it."

He arched his eyebrows. "Oh, I *get* it. Relaxed. At ease. Spontaneous." He looked upward. "All nice little metaphors for undisciplined and wanton."

"*Wanton?*" Lindsey hooted. "Did you just say *wanton?* Nobody uses that term anymore. Besides," she went on, struggling to contain her mirth, "if there's anyone who isn't wanton, it's Karlee."

"Ah, yes," he said. "The paragon of Christian virtue."

Lindsey cast him a chastising look. "Be nice. She's the real thing."

"So you've told me."

Lindsey leaned back against the wall, crossing her arms and regarding him with a perplexed expression. "She really gets to you, doesn't she?"

"Not at all," he denied quickly. "I just find her...eccentric. Odd. And the way she talks about God is—"

"Intimate?"

"Overly familiar."

"It's the way I often talk about him," she returned, a touch of sadness in her gaze. "And the way you used to talk about him."

He shook his head. "That was a long time ago. I was much younger, more naive then."

"Seems to me you could use a bit more naiveté in your life," she offered. "You've grown...hard, Bear. Sometimes I'm not quite sure who you are anymore."

He turned away, not wanting to see the pained expression he knew would be in her eyes. They'd had this discussion several times over the last year...since Karlee had moved in.

"You know how I feel about faith issues," he said, keeping his tone light.

"It's how you feel about God that concerns me."

He turned to her. "Lindsey, I'm not like you are. I believe in God and in Jesus. A man would have to be blind, or a fool, not to. I am neither. But I'm not as convinced as you that God is so very interested or involved in our everyday lives." He glanced out the window again. "Too many people are doing too many rotten things to each other, Linds. If God's here, if he's involved, why is that happening?" He met her troubled gaze. "I've talked with people who profess faith, who talk about prayer and God as though it's all a big part of their lives, and I've watched those same people act and speak in ways that make *me* blush!"

"Bear, you can't base your feelings about God on a bunch of desperate corporate managers and owners—"

"I know that," he cut her off. "And I'm not. It's across the board, management and on down. Last year, there was an older gentleman at a small business who told me that he was praying for me, asking God to give me wisdom. But when he lost his job, he called me at the office, ranting about me being the devil and needing to have my heart ripped out." He shook his head distastefully. "I've seen too many people who just toss their faith out the window if circumstances aren't to their liking."

"Karlee's not like that, Bear. And neither am I."

He looked at her. "I know that. About you, anyway. But it's

all made me a whole lot less sure of things. And I certainly don't believe in talking about the Almighty as though he's some bosom buddy."

She came to lay a gentle hand on his arm. "But in many ways that's exactly what he is," she said. "You used to believe that, Bear."

"I used to be a child. It's like the Bible says, 'When I was a child I thought like a child, I reasoned like a child.'"

"That's *not* what that verse means."

"'When I became a man, I put childish ways behind me.'" He smiled at her tenderly. "Lindsey, you see life far differently from the way I do. But you're...well, you're you."

Lindsey laughed shakily, and a pang shot through him when he saw her eyes shining with unshed tears. "That's what I like about you," she quipped. "That keen sense of the obvious."

He tapped her nose with a finger. "You know what I mean. You have the heart of a child. And that's a good thing. But I've seen a lot of life that has made me less certain about some things."

"Like God's love."

"Like his involvement," he corrected. At the forlorn look on her face, he reached out to pull her into a comforting hug. "Don't look so worried. We'll be okay." He leaned back and smiled down at her. "Who knows? Maybe you and your crazy pal are right, and I'm all wet. If so, I'm sure God will let me know."

She gave him a watery smile. "You can count on it. After all, Karlee and I pray for you often enough. God's bound to do something."

He groaned. "You two pray for me?"

She leaned her cheek against his chest. "All the time. Does that bother you?"

He chuckled. "If it did, would you stop?"

Lindsey punched him lightly in the ribcage. "Of course not, idiot. You'd need it more than ever."

"Well, then, you do what you think is best, and I'll just have to put up with it. After all, you are family. So I'll love you no matter how emotional, excitable, and extreme you get. As for your friend out there, well, she's another matter entirely." He stepped away from Lindsey and went back to his salmon salad. "She's certifiable. You do realize that, don't you?"

"Bear—"

"Do you know what your paragon of fashion and comfort did yesterday?"

"Something awful, I'm sure," she said, barely restrained laughter in her tone.

He fixed her with what he hoped was a somber stare. "She was out there, in her long dress and crazy boots, with that mutated dust mop barking full volume and jumping around her, having a snowball fight with the neighbor kids. *All* of them." He shuddered. "There were screaming, snowsuit-clad midgets everywhere." He fixed his still grinning sister with a glare. "The woman clearly doesn't know the meaning of the word *restraint*. Or order. Not only that, she's so…happy all the time. I've always assumed her eternal good mood stems from being a bit…removed from reality, shall we say."

Lindsey chuckled wryly. "Removed from your reality, maybe. But she's quite in touch with her own. And quite content." She leaned against the wall. "All the more reason for you to ask the woman out."

He stared at her, dumbfounded.

"After all, it's the first time I've seen you really take an interest in the right kind of woman."

He shook his head, confused. "Taking an…in *what* woman? When?"

"Just now. In Karlee."

"I was not—" he began, but she cut him off.

"Argue all you want, brother, but you've been standing there for ten minutes watching her. Analyzing her dog. Her clothes. Her hair." She crossed her arms. "I'd say that qualifies as interest."

"Morbid fascination is more like it." Almost in spite of himself, his gaze wandered back to the snowman scene. The head was in place, complete with eyes, a big stone smile, and an old hat. As for his crazy neighbor, she was now kneeling in the snow, hugging her ridiculous dog, laughing so hard tears were running down her face.

She had to be a lunatic.

Mackenzie turned back to his sister. "Seriously, can you see me with a woman like that?"

"Only in my dreams."

He felt his jaw go slack. She couldn't be serious. Even Lindsey couldn't think such an incongruous match would work.

The gleam in her eyes told him he was wrong. "Like it or not, Karlee McKay is perfect for you. If you ask me, she's exactly what you need. Much more so than that human computer you've decided is the apple of your eye." She grinned cheekily. "No pun intended, of course."

He turned his back on the window and moved to the couch. "Amanda is not a human computer."

She followed him. "Of course she is. She's even more structured than you are, though I didn't think that was possible until I met her. Good grief, she thinks you're positively frivolous! I'll bet she hasn't got a spontaneous bone in that sleek, sophisticated body of hers."

He sank into the cushions of the couch. "Listen, Changeling, Amanda and I suit each other well. As for your designer friend, I can guarantee you we'd have absolutely nothing in common."

215

"Even if you didn't, I'll bet you'd have fun."

He leaned forward, sincerely wanting her to understand. "Fun isn't enough, Lindsey. Karlee is always smiling and laughing. Last summer, when my windows were open, I could hear her singing."

"Clear evidence she's a psycho," Lindsey remarked dryly.

He sat back. "Lindsey, I watched that woman sitting in her backyard once, picking daisies and making them into some kind of ridiculous necklace. From what you've said she must be making good money. Why on earth wouldn't she just buy jewelry? Why form it out of weeds that probably gave her fleas or something equally unsavory."

"Better a case of fleas than one of frostbite," she quipped. At his dark look, she inclined her head. "I'm sorry, Bear. Karlee's always telling me I need to control my tongue." She sighed. "It's just that Amanda is always so…regulated." She shrugged, adding softly, "I can't imagine her feeling passion, let alone expressing it."

"Amanda's passion is none of your concern," Mackenzie admonished her more sharply than he'd intended.

"No," she agreed slowly, "it isn't. But it should concern you. Do you really want to spend the rest of your life in this austere house living a ho-hum life with that ice queen at your side? What kind of life would that be? I think God has better plans for you. At least, I hope he does."

Caught off guard by her words, he leaned his head back and stared at the ceiling. Austere? Ho hum? Was that how she saw his life? If so, why hadn't she ever said so before? Sure, she'd told him often enough that he needed more spontaneity, but she'd never called him ho hum before!

The image of Karlee sitting in the grass floated through his mind—as it had many times since the day he'd seen her—surrounded by flowers, serene contentment on her face, her cheeks kissed with the sun, her golden hair cascading down her shoulders, her eyes glowing with pleasure.

The picture filled him with an odd sense of restlessness. Impatient, he pushed it away and regarded his sister. She was looking at a piece of paper with a slightly stunned expression on her face.

"Lindsey?"

Her gaze moved to meet his. She was clearly upset. "I don't believe you."

The hurt tone in her voice startled him, and he sat up quickly. She handed him the paper, and he looked at it. It was his To Do list for the next month. He frowned, his gaze coming back to his sister's now flushed face. "I'm sorry," he said gently. "I don't understand."

"That much is painfully evident," she whispered.

A frown creased his forehead. "Lindsey, please. What have I done that's so terrible?"

"Item number five." Her tone was flat.

He looked down. "'Propose to Amanda.' Do you have a problem with that?" When she didn't respond, he looked up to see her staring at him as though he had sprouted a second head.

"Do I—?" She broke off and sat back, her breath coming out in a frustrated hiss. "You've got to be kidding. I mean, it's one thing that you're thinking about marrying that woman. That alone would make me nervous. But you've got it on your To Do list!"

"What's wrong with putting that on my list—"

"It's number *five*, Bear! One of the most important decisions of your life and you've got it listed as number five! After—" she leaned forward abruptly and grabbed the list from his hands— "*After* going grocery shopping and balancing your checkbook!" She threw the list at him and stood. "I do not...believe you."

She strode to the door and pulled it open, then paused and looked back. Mackenzie was stunned to see tears—and disappointment—in her eyes. "I'm sorry." Her voice was husky with emotion. "It's your life. But if a man was going to propose to me, I'd sure want to be more important to him than grocery shopping."

He sat there, unsure what to say. But before he could formulate an appropriate response, she went out the door, pulling it closed behind her.

Four

L indsey stood leaning against the side of her brother's house, tears running down her face.

Her brother was hopeless. It was time she admitted and accepted it. "Hopeless," she said miserably.

"Nothing is hopeless, Linds."

She looked up to see Karlee watching her, compassion clear in her green eyes as she leaned on the white fence separating her yard from Mackenzie's. "Wanna talk?"

Lindsey wiped the tears from her cheeks and shrugged. She pulled her coat closer about her and moved to the fence. "He's so sure he's right," she said sadly.

"Your brother?"

"Who else? He's bound and determined to wreck his life, and he doesn't even see it."

"Wreck his life?"

Lindsey crossed her arms. "He's going to ask that woman to marry him," she said, torn between anger and regret.

Karlee's eyes widened. "You mean Amanda Carr?"

Lindsey nodded, feeling more miserable by the minute. She met Karlee's concerned gaze. "He can't do it, Karlee! She's not the right woman for him. I just know she isn't. But he's so blind—he can't see how wrong it would be for him to do this."

Karlee reached out to take her hand in a warm grasp. "God sees," she said. "And he's in control. Not your brother." She tugged on Lindsey's hand and smiled gently. "Not even you."

Lindsey inclined her head. "I know." Tears misted her eyes again. "It's just that he's so wonderful, and I care so much, and I want everything to go right for him."

A sweet smile played over Karlee's features. "And they will, Linds. As much as you love your brother, it's only a fraction of the love God feels for him. And he's at work on Mac's behalf." Her smile became a playful grin. "In fact, knowing your brother, God's probably mobilized two or three brigades of angels already."

"Hey, Karlee! Are we gonna play hide 'n' seek or what?"

Karlee glanced behind her, then patted Lindsey's arm. "Sorry, friend. I've got to go. The munchkins await."

Lindsey looked toward Karlee's backyard and saw a group of neighborhood kids gathered. With a wave of her hand, Karlee went to join them in their game. Zsuzsi dashed and dodged playfully, her corded tail wagging.

Lindsey smiled as she went to get in her car. The laughter from Karlee's backyard floated around her as she slid in and reached forward to put the key in the ignition—then her hand froze in mid-air. Her eyes widened, and she turned again to watch Karlee and her troops. A surge of excitement began to build deep within her. Her mouth fell open in a breathless "O."

Her eyes gleaming, she turned the key, threw the car into reverse, and gunned the engine.

The next morning, when five-thirty rolled around, Mackenzie did the unthinkable. He ignored his alarm. Instead of throwing back the covers and getting up to get started with the day, he rolled over and stared at the ceiling.

He hadn't had a night this bad in years. His eyes felt like they were full of sand; his mouth, like he'd been sucking on sweat socks. He'd tossed and turned, exhausted and in need of sleep. But every time he closed his eyes, Lindsey's face, so full of disappointment, filled his mind.

He'd hurt her. If only he could understand why.

The sound of the doorbell brought him to his feet, and he jumped out of bed, pulling on a shirt and jeans as he hurried to the door. It had to be Lindsey. She couldn't stand fighting any more than he could. He pulled the door open, then stood and stared.

"Merry Christmas!" It was Karlee, dog in tow. A brown suede crusher was pulled down over her unruly hair, but rebellious wisps snuck out to frame her wind-kissed face with a golden glow.

She grinned at him, holding out a plate wrapped with brightly colored cellophane and topped with a large Christmas bow. Mackenzie stared at her, then at the plate, then back at her. Her grin broadened.

"May I come in?"

"Oh, uh, of course," he said, stepping aside. His gaze came to rest on the dog at her side.

"Don't worry, Zsuzsi will wait outside, won't you, sweetheart?" she said, leaning over to plant a quick kiss on the dog's broad, furry head. "Stay, girl," she ordered, then sailed inside.

Mackenzie followed Karlee as she set the cookies on the counter. He cast one glance back at the dog. It sat there, perfectly content, regarding him with the oddest expression. If he hadn't known better, he'd swear the beast was watching him with a strange sort of pity in its dark eyes. He shook his head. This conflict with Lindsey—and a totally rotten night—was making him imagine things.

"Normally I'd never invade someone's home this early in the morning," Karlee was saying in that lilting voice of hers. "But Lindsey told me you get up at five-thirty most days—"

"Every day," he corrected automatically.

She nodded slowly. "Right. Every day. So I figured you wouldn't mind being the first stop of the day."

"Not at all," he said, not really understanding what she was talking about. He lifted the cellophane cautiously and peered beneath it. "What are these?"

She grinned. "Christmas cookies. It just isn't Christmas without them." She leaned her elbows on the counter, cupping her chin in her hands as she went on. "To be perfectly honest, I didn't think you'd be all that thrilled to receive them, but God disagreed, so there you have it."

He stared at her. *God disagreed...?*

She went on. "There are Santas, snowmen, stars, reindeer—," she pointed at the cookie on top—,"even a Rudolph complete with candied cherry nose. Ron, my brother, always saved his Rudolph until last. But I couldn't. He was always the first to go." She leaned toward Mackenzie. "There was something *so* satisfying in biting off his nose." She waggled her eyebrows, and he stared at her, speechless.

What kind of response could one make to that?

Fortunately, Karlee didn't seem to expect a response. She straightened up and glanced around, a pleased expression flowing over her face. "What a beautiful place you have here. A nice clean palette just ready to be worked on." She angled a compassionate look his way. "I know you haven't been around much. You really do work too much, you know."

He opened his mouth to inform her it was none of her business *how* much he worked, but she sailed on.

"Maybe you can take a few days during the holiday to start fixing everything up."

Mackenzie frowned, looking around defensively. "It's already fixed up."

Her surprised gaze roamed the spartan room, as though searching for something to confirm his words.

"This is how I like it."

She continued her careful study.

"It's simple," he insisted.

A slight frown creased her forehead, as though she were pained.

"Well-ordered," he added, his teeth clenching slightly.

Her wide-eyed gaze came back to meet his, and the slight disappointment he saw there took him aback—then annoyed him.

"It's certainly...clean," she responded, as though desperately searching for something complimentary to say.

"It's perfect for me." His words came out more forcefully than he'd intended.

She looked away somewhat uneasily, then her whole face seemed to light up. "Oh! What a beautiful tree!"

Before Mackenzie could respond, she had gone to bury her face in the fragrant branches. When she lifted her head and looked at him, her eyes were glowing with a kind of relief— which only confused him all the more. Why on earth should his neighbor care what his home looked like?

When she turned those amazing eyes his way, they were filled with delighted wonder. "You must have just brought it in. It still smells of the forest and the cold."

His eyebrows drew downward. "I wasn't aware it smelled at all."

She stepped back, inspecting the tree critically. "Yes, it's perfect. It quite suits you. Big. Bold. Filled with strength and vitality." Unexpected pleasure swept over him at this assessment of his character, but before he could respond, she clapped her hands and turned to face him, her eyes glowing with excitement. "I can hardly wait to see it decorated!"

He cleared his throat uncomfortably. Decorated?

"Well, thanks so much for inviting me in." She breezed past him, not even noting his stunned face. Inviting her in? He didn't recall getting the chance. "But Zsuzsi and I have to be going."

He followed her to the door, feeling a bit as though a small tornado had just swept through his house. Eyeing the large dog who sat so patiently on the stoop, he cast a curious glance at Karlee.

She grinned. "Pretty unique, isn't she?"

Unique was not the word he'd had in mind.

"She's a Komondor, a Hungarian breed."

His gaze went back to the dog. "You mean someone intentionally bred a dog to look like that?"

She laughed at his incredulous look—a soft, silver peal of delight that drifted around him. "Actually, they've bred a lot of dogs to look this way. Komondors aren't especially well-known, but they're getting more popular all the time." She paused to lay a gentle hand on the large dog's cord-covered head. "They're intelligent, loyal, and protective, which is pretty common for herding dogs, isn't it, sweetie?"

Zsuzsi gave a deep "Woof!" as though to agree with her mistress's assertion. Karlee laughed again.

"So the fur is supposed to look like that?" The question came out before he'd realized he was going to ask it.

Karlee nodded. "It helps them blend in with the sheep." She grinned. "Can you imagine being a predator moving in on a seemingly defenseless herd of sheep when one of these beasties suddenly jumps up to take you on?" She scratched the dog's ears with affection. "A hundred pounds of protective fury, that's what she would be. Well, see you later. We've got a full day of delivering ahead of us."

He nodded briefly, then watched her leave. Even the woman's walk was bouncy and energetic.

Closing the door, he turned to study Lindsey's tree. He strolled toward it, leaned forward, and took a deep breath. His eyes widened in surprise. It *did* smell like the forest and the cold.

He moved to pour himself a steaming cup of coffee, then sat at his desk, flipped on his computer, and prepared to get to work. December wouldn't last forever, and he had a lot to accomplish.

A few minutes later he realized he was staring at the computer screen in a daze. He stood quickly, frustrated, wondering why it was so difficult to concentrate, why the image of Karlee's face and the echo of her laughter kept nudging at him. He flopped down into a wide leather chair, staring into the dark cold fireplace. Pursing his lips, he went over her visit, recalling the way she talked about God, in those intimate tones, as though he were a cherished friend, someone with whom she spent a great deal of time.

Was that what made her seem so different from anyone he knew? So...alive?

As he wondered these things, he gradually became aware of an odd sensation deep inside...a nagging longing, a sense that he was missing out on something wondrous.

With a whoosh of air he catapulted himself out of the chair and strode to his computer. He knew he was punching the keys with more force than was necessary, but the action felt good.

Far better than sitting around and getting morose over some imaginary lack in my life, he thought half-angrily. Setting his shoulders with determination, he promised himself that the next time Karlee McKay appeared on his doorstep, he would courteously but firmly shut the door in her face.

Five

Mackenzie stepped back to admire his handiwork. His breakfast nook table had been transformed. A white linen tablecloth covered the surface. Elegant china plates and bowls were flanked by filigreed silver utensils; crystal juice glasses sparkled and reflected the candlelight of tall tapers that sat in the middle of a fresh flower centerpiece.

"Let's see you call *this* ho hum, Lindsey," he said, a satisfied smile lifting the corners of his mouth. Everything looked perfect. A beautiful setting. Romantic music playing in the background. A delicious meal. It was all just right for taking care of item number five.

At the sound of the doorbell he strolled to pull the door open. "Good morning, Madame. Your breakfast awaits."

Amanda Carr, the only daughter of business tycoon Alexander Carr, stood on the threshold, the picture of refined beauty. Her facial features were delicately carved, her mouth full though unsmiling, her bearing poised and controlled. Mackenzie had first met her at an art gallery opening. They'd collided while studying a sculpture. Startled from his contemplation, he'd turned and found himself staring into a pair of beautiful, blue eyes. The rest of the woman was equally attractive—as was her intelligence, which he discovered while they shared their interpretations of what the sculpture was trying to express. Before he'd realized he was going to do so, Mackenzie asked Amanda out to dinner. Much to his surprise, she accepted.

Their relationship had built slowly, but Mackenzie felt they were a good match. Capable, reasonable, well-read, intelligent, prone to logic over emotion...every facet seemed to mesh well. And if Amanda was a bit more driven, a bit more determined than he, then it was only because she'd had to become so as a woman CEO in a fairly large Seattle advertising corporation. Mackenzie knew those same beautiful blue eyes that had so captured his attention could turn positively glacial, which helped her many a time to face down more than one stunned male in a board room. Amanda was a woman who knew what she wanted and went after it with steely determination; she never allowed herself to be distracted by sentimentality or misplaced altruism.

It's like we came from the same mold. Oddly, he felt little pleasure at the thought.

"Mackenzie, dear," she remarked as she stepped inside and tilted her head back, inviting him to kiss one smooth cheek. He did so, then reached for her coat. As she slipped from her wet London Fog raincoat, he noted that not a strand of her silky black hair seemed out of place.

Quite a contrast to Karlee. She'd probably be dripping wet and loving every minute of it. The thought—and the sudden picture in his mind of his neighbor's golden, unruly hair—startled him.

Amanda caught sight of the carefully laid table, tilted her head to listen to the music, then turned to him with an indulgent smile. "Darling, really. Such extravagance so early in the morning." There was a hint of censure in her voice, and a flash of irritation shot through him.

"I'll bet she hasn't got a spontaneous bone in that sleek, sophisti-cated body of hers."

He pushed the echo of Lindsey's words away as he pulled out Amanda's chair for her. "It's a special morning," he explained, wondering as he seated her why he felt the need for explanations.

"So you told me when you invited me." She carefully smoothed out her crepe pantsuit, then laid a cloth napkin on her lap and smoothed that as well.

"I can't even imagine her feeling passion...."

The words stuck in his mind. He shook his head sharply to dislodge them, with little effect. Drawing a steadying breath, he settled into his own chair. Amanda watched him coolly, her expression one of tolerant patience.

"Really, dear, isn't it about time you told me what's going on? You know how much I dislike being kept in the dark."

"Austere...ho hum...."

"I...wanted to ask...." His throat suddenly felt dry and con-stricted.

"Yes?" she prompted.

"Ice Queen...rest of your life...God has better plans...."

"Shut up!" he muttered fiercely.

"I *beg* your pardon?"

Oh, good grief. Did he say that out loud? "No, I'm sorry, Amanda—"

She sat there, her features frozen with disapproval, and he had the sudden urge to pound his forehead on the table. This wasn't going at all as he'd planned.

The doorbell sounded, and Mackenzie jumped to his feet. "I'll get it!" he announced unnecessarily, grateful for the unex-pected reprieve. He paused to draw a steadying breath, then jerked the door open—and stared at the rainy morning. No one was there. Then he glanced down, and his eyes grew wide.

There was a wolf on his stoop! A soggy, muddy, whining wolf. He stared at the beast. No, not a wolf. A dog. With heavy, reddish-brown and white fur, large pointed ears atop a squarish head, and striking eyes—one brown, one a pale, ice-blue.

Mackenzie looked at the animal, dumbfounded. He thought it was some kind of sled dog, though he was far from an expert. He glanced around. No one in sight. He stepped out to look farther down the street. He looked back down at the dog, who was now whining only slightly.

"Beat it," he said firmly. "Go away. Lassie, go home."

Those intense eyes stared up at him. Then, as though in supplication, the animal lifted one soggy paw and gently laid it atop Mackenzie's leg.

He brushed the paw away and stepped back quickly, shutting the door.

"Who was it, darling?"

"No one," he muttered, slipping into his chair. "What do you say we eat before the food gets cold," he suggested, pasting on a smile that even he could tell was stiff. "Then we can talk."

"If you say so," Amanda replied, her tone filled with restraint.

Mackenzie nodded and picked up his silverware. All he needed was some food in his system to clear out his fogged brain. And a little time to figure out exactly what he wanted to say.

Two bites of his perfectly made omelet later, a horrific, sorrowful sound resonated throughout the house. The dog was howling.

"What in the world?" Amanda's delicate brows arched. Mackenzie gritted his teeth and held up a hand.

"Just…just a minute." He went to the door again, pulled it open with tightly controlled movements, and stepped outside, carefully closing the door behind him.

"GO AWAY!" That bellowed, he composed his features, opened the door, and stepped back inside—and ran right into Amanda, who had followed him to the door.

She stepped around him and glanced outside. The dog was sitting there, a morose look on its furry face. "Whose creature is that?" Her voice dripped with abhorrence.

"Your guess is as good as mine."

Amanda turned to study him. "You don't need to get emotional about this, dear," she chided.

"I am *not* getting emotional," he exploded.

Clearly startled by his tone, Amanda stepped back.

He looked down, closing his eyes. "I'm sorry."

"Perhaps you should call the police, Mackenzie. That seems the most logical solution."

He nodded. She was right, of course. He moved to the phone, then returned a few moments later. "The police transferred my call to Animal Control."

"Good. When will they pick him up?"

Mackenzie shrugged. "They're booked up and can't make it right away. They told me to watch the dog and they'll get there as soon as they can."

"Well," she said, a pained smile stretching across her features, "then why don't we finish our breakfast?"

Half an hour later, the dog was still howling soulfully, and Mackenzie was wishing mightily that Karlee was home. He'd been sure she would show up when the dog started its cater-wauling and had fully intended to hand the creature over to her. Why couldn't she be around when he needed her?

"Mackenzie, isn't there something you can do?" Amanda finally asked, her fingers gently probing her temples. "That creature's unholy noise has given me the most horrendous headache."

He stood slowly, went to the door again, and jerked it open.

The dog stopped howling, and looked up from where he was lying on the porch. His chin rested on his paws, his heavy fur was soaking wet, his face was filled with misery. At the look in the animal's eyes, something inside of Mackenzie gave.

Even a dog shouldn't be treated like this.

He knelt down and cautiously reached out one hand. The dog lifted his head and licked Mackenzie's hand gently—almost as though in forgiveness.

An unfamiliar tightness formed in Mackenzie's chest, and he felt beneath the fur on the dog's neck. There was a collar! Quickly he examined it, but found no tags. Instead, what he discovered was a piece of clothesline tied from the collar to the railing of his porch. The dog was tied to the railing!

"Who did this to you, fella?" he asked. The dog stared at him in sorrowful silence. Making a sudden decision, Mackenzie untied the clothesline and stepped inside. The dog followed him willingly.

"Mackenzie! What in the world are you doing? You can't bring that creature in here!"

"He's wet, Amanda, and cold. I can at least get him dried off."

"With what? I hope you don't plan to use any of your good towels on that...that thing!"

"Of course not," he said, tying the clothesline to the leg of the couch. "I've got some old torn towels that I use to wash the car." He hurried to the garage, then returned with a pile of ragged towels. The dog was still sitting there, looking very much like a perfect gentleman. Mackenzie directed a smug smile at Amanda.

"See? This won't be so bad." He stepped forward, the towel spread open, and the dog stood and proceeded to shake himself vigorously. Mud and water flew everywhere.

With a frustrated roar, Mackenzie dove for the dog, trying to throw the towels over him and protect his mostly white furniture and walls. The dog scrambled back frantically, tugging on the cord with such force that it came untied. Realizing he was free, the animal tore away, his claws scrabbling over the polished wood floor.

"Come back here!" Mackenzie bellowed, further frightening the dog. With a startled yelp, he vaulted the coffee table, his muddy paws touching down only long enough to smear everything in his path. Thus began a wild chase. Mackenzie followed the rampaging dog as the animal jumped the couch, scrambled across the tiled kitchen floor, circled and knocked down a screeching Amanda, raced down the hallway, and leaped into the middle of Mackenzie's king-sized waterbed.

Momentarily startled by the uncertain footing, the dog paused, which gave Mackenzie the opening he'd been watching for. Quickly he grabbed the edges of the silk comforter and enveloped the dog as neatly as if it had been a net. Muttering threats the entire way, he dragged the struggling, yelping dog to the bathroom, pushed him in—comforter and all—and slammed the door.

Leaning against the door, he wiped a hand across his face—then his jaw dropped as he took in the damage to his once immaculate home. Streaks of mud covered everything, from smudges on the rugs and floor to hair-encrusted splatters all over the walls and furniture. Slowly he walked into the living room. There were muddy paw prints everywhere.

"Well, I certainly hope you're satisfied."

At Amanda's cold, critical remark, he turned to give her a scathing reply, and stopped cold. She stood there, covered with mud splatters; her hair was a snarled, mud-speckled mess. At the sight of the usually picture-perfect Amanda in such disarray, a sudden smile quirked Mackenzie's mouth.

"What are you smiling about?" she fumed furiously. "Your

house is destroyed, but it looks far better than you do!"

He glanced down and saw what she meant. He was as wet and muddy as the dog. His hands were covered with black, which probably meant his face was as well. He shook his head slightly, struggling against the surprising urge to laugh himself silly.

"Mackenzie St. John, you wipe that absurd look from your face this minute!"

His head came up and his suddenly angry gaze met her glacial one. Before he could respond, the doorbell rang.

"Saved by the bell," he muttered, then went to jerk open the door. "What?"

Karlee stood there, eyes wide, clearly startled at his unkempt appearance. She scanned the living room, taking in the cushions strewn about the room, the turned-over furniture, and, finally, Amanda's glowering visage. "Oh my." Her gaze came back to him. "Did I...interrupt something?"

Suddenly bloodcurdling screams split the air, and the two of them spun to see Amanda on the floor, with the dog in her lap, licking her face with gusto. She was swatting at him frantically—albeit ineffectively—and screeching like a banshee.

"Oh!" Karlee exclaimed. "You got a dog! How delightful!"

Mackenzie, who was trying to figure out how the beast had escaped the bathroom, turned to Karlee in stunned disbelief. With an enraptured smile on her face, Karlee glided across the room and took hold of the dog's collar, pulling him from Amanda and leading him away, talking to him in a low, sweet voice.

Not surprisingly, the dog went along without the least sign of resistance.

Amanda struggled to her feet, sputtering. Without a look at Mackenzie, she marched over to jerk her coat from the rack. With one furious motion, she pulled it on. She attempted to smooth back her hair—but only succeeded in rearranging the mud—then headed for the door. With her hand on the doorknob, she turned to pin Mackenzie with a burning look. "Thank you, my *dear* Mackenzie, for the most horrid experience I've had in my entire life!"

Mackenzie and Karlee watched in silence as Amanda left, slamming the door behind her. He pursed his lips, turning to stare at the door for a moment, then directed a glance at Karlee where she sat beside the now docile dog.

"Don't worry," Karlee said gently, "your friend will get used to him."

Galvanized into action, he moved toward them. "She most certainly will not! That animal isn't staying long enough for *anyone* to get used to it!"

Shocked dismay filled her features. "Surely you wouldn't get rid of him before he's even had a chance to fit in? That wouldn't be fair at all."

"Wouldn't be—" he broke off, exasperated. "Listen, Karlee, there's nothing to be fair about. This animal showed up on my doorstep this morning. Someone tied him out there, though who or why, I haven't got a clue."

"Maybe someone thought you would take good care of him," she offered, and he looked at her, slightly stunned.

"You make it sound like someone left a baby on my doorstep!"

She grinned. "Well, maybe in a way, they did. Maybe they couldn't care for him any longer, and they'd seen you and thought you looked like someone who would care—"

"Well, they were wrong!" he sputtered. "This animal is not mine. Apparently he's not anyone's! And as soon as the Animal Control people show up, he's gone!"

Karlee didn't respond, but he sensed her disapproval. "I suppose you'd keep it," he commented dryly.

234

She nodded. "At least long enough to give the owners a chance to maybe change their minds and come back for him."

"And if he's lost and someone just tied him on my steps because they were handy?"

"Then I'd want to give his owners every opportunity to find him."

"How exactly would you do that?"

"I'd put an ad in the paper. And notify area vets and animal shelters. Then I'd wait."

"Wait!"

"Three weeks. If the owners don't show in three weeks, he's yours."

"No, thanks!" He noticed the slight crease in her forehead. "What?"

Her gaze came to meet his, and the look in her eyes stirred him deep inside. "If it were Zsuzsi, I'd pray that the people who found her would give me every opportunity to claim her."

"Three weeks," he muttered as he came to sit beside Karlee on the couch. The dog shifted to lean against Mackenzie's leg, uttering a small sigh. Karlee smiled at him.

"He seems to have taken to you."

"So he does," Mackenzie agreed quietly, rubbing the dog's ears gently. At least there was one creature on the face of the earth who didn't consider him an unapproachable, heartless brute. The soft texture of the dog's fur was like velvet, and the way he tilted his square head and half-closed his eyes with pleasure made Mackenzie smile. A gentle touch on his arm brought him out of his fascinated study of the dog.

"Hmmm?" He looked at Karlee, slightly startled to find her face so close to his. "I'm sorry, what did you say?"

"Your phone? I'll call the shelter about bringing the dog in."

"Oh. On the counter, over there."

She started to rise, but he reached out. "Wait." She stilled.

He looked at the dog again. "I don't know anything about dogs," he muttered.

Karlee cast a glance around the devastated house. "Tell you what. I'll help you clean up here, and I'll help you take care of the dog. I've got an extra crate that you can use and a leash and bowls. All you'll need to do is buy him some food. And take him for a walk from time to time." She grinned suddenly. "And, of course, pray."

Mackenzie looked at her. "Pray?"

She nodded. "Sure. You'll need some wisdom to get you through this, and there's no better source of wisdom than God."

"You really think the God of the universe cares about a stray dog and what I do with it?"

"Of course," she said, clearly surprised at the question. She tilted her head, regarding him curiously. "Let me ask you this. If you had a child, would you care how he treated a stray dog?"

Mackenzie thought for a moment, then nodded. "I suppose so. I'd want him to treat it right, maybe learn something about treating other creatures with respect."

Karlee's face glowed. "Exactly! As a father, you care that your children live their lives in the best way possible, right?"

"Right…" Where was she going with this?

"Well, God is interested in everything we do, too. He's our Father, we're his children, and he wants us to live our lives in the best way."

"Seems to me the Almighty would have better things to do with his time," Mackenzie remarked, trying not to sound sarcastic but unable to help himself.

She studied him for a moment. "Maybe so, but I believe he considers keeping his promises high on the list."

"Now wait a minute," Mackenzie held up his hand. "What does this dog have to do with God keeping his promises?"

"Simple," she said, leaning against the kitchen counter. "In his Word he tells us, 'If any of you lacks wisdom, he should ask God, who gives generously to all without finding fault, and it will be given to him.' So if you pray about this situation, I believe God will answer."

Mackenzie looked at the dog uncertainly. Would God really care what he did in this situation? He didn't buy it. Not entirely. Still, what did he have to lose?

Feeling somewhat foolish, Mackenzie prayed. *Almighty Father, Creator of the Universe, if you're really listening*—he looked at the dog again—*should I keep this animal or not?*

The furry invader met his considering gaze silently, then leaned forward to deliver a gentle lick to Mackenzie's face.

He stared at the animal. Was that supposed to be a sign?

The dog licked him again.

Mackenzie closed his eyes, shaking his head. "I must be nuts," he muttered, then, "Okay. I'll keep him. But just for three weeks."

Surprisingly, he didn't really mind doing so. Somehow with Karlee's exclamation of delight floating around him and her warm, approving gaze resting on his face, keeping the dog seemed like the best decision he'd made in a very long time.

Later that evening, Karlee stepped back to study the room with satisfaction. One corner of Mackenzie's spacious living room was now a warm and welcome, custom-designed doggie domicile.

The two of them had managed to get the house cleaned up and back in order in just a few hours. Next had come the task of getting the dog cleaned up. Neither she nor Mac—she much preferred that to his full, oh-so-formal name—had had the energy to bathe the dog. They settled for brushing out the now-dried mud and rubbing the dog down, first with damp towels, then with dry ones. When they were finished, he looked remarkably presentable.

Once the house and dog were clean, Karlee retrieved one of Zsuzsi's older crates. The large container was constructed of heavy molded plastic, had side windows, a swinging grated door, and plenty of room for a dog of the husky's size to stand and turn around. A sleeping mat and bowl completed the accommodations.

Karlee pulled the crate nearer the fireplace, reaching out to move the still-undecorated Christmas tree as she did so. She glanced over her shoulder at Mac; he was seated on his couch, watching her every move, a bemused look in his eyes.

"You'd better get this beauty in a stand with some water," she said, "or it will start to lose its needles. And there's nothing sadder than a dried out, undecorated Christmas tree."

"There's not?" His gaze drifted to the tree, then back to her.

She shook her head, leaning the tree against the wall. *See, Father? I told you he thinks I'm nuts.* She'd seen that slightly confused look on his face before—every time he saw her, to be exact. It was a look full of perplexity, as though she were an oddity that he couldn't quite analyze or categorize.

There was something sad—and strangely endearing—in that look. It reminded her of a little boy watching a parade from a tall tower, wanting desperately to join in the fun but not quite sure how to escape his confines. It made Karlee want to make her somber, dark-eyed neighbor smile or laugh. Or put her arms around him and comfort him.

"Is something wrong?"

The question brought her out of her thoughts with a jolt, and the chagrined realization that she'd been staring at the man washed over her. He was practically engaged, for heaven's sake! What was wrong with her?

"Oh…ah…no. Not at all." She turned back to the crate.

He was silent for a beat, then said, "That thing looks like it should keep him contained."

"You'll need to let him get used to it gradually," she cautioned. "And use a happy voice whenever you put him in there, so he doesn't feel as though he's being punished."

"A happy voice?"

"Right. The same kind of voice you'd use to praise him for doing something good."

He cast a dubious glance at the dog, who sat nearby, watching them with bright, alert eyes. "Hmmm, there's a concept."

She restrained a smile. While she'd been out, Mac had lost three shoes, a towel, and a Mont Blanc pen to the husky's ever-busy jaws. Using a 'happy voice' was likely the furthest thing from the man's mind. "You'll need to keep him in the crate when you're not at home, too."

"Why is that?"

A flash of amusement flickered over her face. "Well, for one thing, huskies are famous for being escape artists. Especially males. And for another, they're incredibly destructive when they're bored, which they are when they're alone."

From his expression as he looked at the dog, it was clear he was wondering what he'd gotten himself into. "You're sure you can't take him?"

She shook her head, trying not to let her mirth show. "I'm afraid so." She moved to the table and started pulling items from a large bag.

"What did you do? Buy everything in the pet store?"

She grinned. "Hardly. That place is enormous. Next time you'll have to come along. We can even take your dog with us."

"They let dogs in the—" He broke off and fixed her with a glare. "He's not my dog."

She didn't reply. He could argue all he wanted; she'd seen the way he looked at the dog when it leaned against him or rested its head on his leg. When she'd prayed for help with Mac, the last thing she'd had in mind was a dog. But there could be no denying the fact that the man was smitten. Pure and simple. Of course, if she even suggested such a thing, he'd get all huffy again. Much better to just hold her peace and give the dog time to reach Mac's heart.

No matter what anyone else said, she was sure he had one.

CHAPTER

Seven

Mackenzie watched with increasing discomfort as Karlee rummaged in a paper sack on the table.

"I know it's in here somewhere," she muttered. Her long hair fell in a golden mass around her face, and Mackenzie felt an odd constriction in his throat. Watching her from a distance had been disturbing enough. Her eccentric actions had amused and confounded him, but he'd never felt any need to try and understand her.

Now, watching as she exclaimed with triumph and pulled a large plastic bone from the bag, he found himself struggling with the inexplicable desire to discover why she did the things she did.

Why, for example, she had stood in the middle of his living room a few moments ago staring at him, a strangely tender look on her face. It had taken every ounce of self-control not to jump up off the couch and go to her and…

Forget it, St. John! he chided himself harshly. *She's not your type. Remember? Do yourself a favor and stick with a woman you can relate to.*

Amanda. She was his type. Sleek. Sophisticated. A woman

who thought the way he did, whose every action was logical and easily understood. You'd never find her standing there, tearing the packaging of a plastic bone apart as though it were some wonderful treasure.

Karlee directed a smile his way. "It's a chew toy," she informed him. "Chicken flavored. Zsuzsi's favorite. I figured our friend here would like one, too." She held it out to the dog.

"You got him a toy?"

She angled a surprised look at him. "Of course."

"Let me get this straight. You spent good money on a toy for a dog?" Her expression told him she didn't see the problem. "I suppose your dog has a closet full of toys."

Her mouth curved. "Not exactly. She has a Nylabone that she likes to chew in her crate, and a tennis ball she loves to chomp on while we're sitting on the couch watching TV—"

"You let that beast up on your furniture?"

Karlee's bell-like laughter rang out. "Sure. A couch is just a couch. It doesn't bring me joy or comfort or laughter. Zsuzsi does all of those things and more." She shrugged. "Possessions are to be used, Mac. What does it matter if it's me using them or Zsuzsi?"

"Mackenzie."

She didn't seem to notice the correction. She was too busy kneeling beside the dog, petting him gently.

"Don't call me 'Mac.'"

She stood to brush the fur from her dress—the dog seemed to leave a cloud of it wherever he went!—and moved to lay out a small rug near the crate.

"I don't like nicknames."

The sternness he'd injected into the sentence seemed to have no effect. She filled one bowl with water and watched as the dog trotted over to circle the rug three times, then plop down with a contented sigh. Karlee turned and beamed that

242

beautiful smile at him, but he refused to be moved.

"I don't believe in them." He was talking through gritted teeth now.

She blinked. "In what?"

"In nickna—" He frowned. "Have you heard a word I've said?"

Her expression was one of utter innocence. "Oh dear, were you talking to me? I'm sorry! I thought you were scolding the dog again." She directed her entire attention to him, and for the first time since he'd met her, he felt the full impact of her gaze. Her eyes were an extraordinary shade of green, and they were fixed on his face as though he were the only person in the world.

She smiled warmly. "Now, I promise to listen. What were you saying?"

He stared at her. He'd never seen eyes quite that color before.

"Mac?"

They were hunter green in the center, with a darker ring of aquamarine around the outer edges. But what struck him even more than the startling color of her eyes was the artless serenity they held.

"Beautiful," he murmured, and she started slightly, her eyes widening a fraction. Then a slight grin quirked her mouth. She reached forward to gently rap her knuckles against his forehead.

"Hello? Anybody home?"

The warmth of her touch jarred him, and he stepped back quickly. He'd never wanted to reach out for someone so badly in all his life!

She regarded him quizzically. "Are you okay?"

"Fine. Absolutely. No problem."

"Okay, then what did you want to tell me?"

"About what?"

"About whatever you were saying to me."

"When?"

She laughed. "When I wasn't listening."

Oh yes. The nickname.

"Are you sure you're okay?" she asked again.

"Yes, I'm fine," he said, feeling far from it. "As for whatever I was saying before, well, never mind. It doesn't matter." If he and his peace of mind were lucky, she wouldn't be around often enough to call him much of anything.

She nodded slightly, then studied the dog thoughtfully. "So, what are you going to name him?"

Mackenzie raised one eyebrow. "Why would he need a name? I'm not going to keep him."

"You have to call him something."

He looked at the now sleeping animal. "'Dog' should suffice."

"It most certainly will *not* suffice!"

Mackenzie looked at her, surprised at the vehemence of her response. He noted with growing amusement the spark in her eyes, the mutinous tilt of her chin, and the way her arms were crossed over her chest.

"I don't know why not," he replied and was rewarded with a glare.

"Well then, contrary to popular opinion, you obviously don't know everything," she retorted.

He chuckled as she studied the dog briefly. "I know," she said, her eyes twinkling suddenly. "How about 'Bubba'?"

"Bubba?" She couldn't be serious.

Her eyes gleamed playfully. "No? Well…there's always 'Buddy.' Or how about 'Spot' or 'Rover'?"

"I refuse to call something 'Spot'!" he said with a disdainful snort.

"Fine," she said, and this time he caught the impish tone of her words. "Then *you* come up with a name. Unless, of course, that's too much of a challenge for you. You know, too creative?"

He crossed his arms and fixed her with a warning look, which only resulted in a burst of muffled laughter coming from her. He turned his back on her, then studied the dog thoughtfully. So the beast needed a name, did he? "I've got it." He turned back to her—but his words caught in his throat when his gaze collided with hers. She had the most amazing eyes....

"Yes?"

He cleared his throat. "Ivan."

She looked at the dog. "Ivan," she echoed, testing the name. The dog stretched, yawned, and looked up at them sleepily. "Ivan," she said again, and he saw excitement in her expression. "It's perfect. I had a friend in college whose name was Ivan. If I'm remembering correctly, it's the Russian form of John, which means 'gracious gift from God.'" She turned back to him, a smile lighting her face with warmth. "It fits."

He looked at the dog, then back at her. "Actually," he said, doing his best to restrain the grin tugging at his mouth. "I was thinking more of Ivan the Terrible when I suggested the name, not Ivan the gift from God."

She looked at him indignantly.

"Hey, he nearly destroyed my house."

She bit her lip.

"And my white towels—which, I might add, are *very* expensive—will never look the same."

A smile eased across her face, and she glanced at the dog and laughed. "Well, okay, so we know your meaning is appropriate. But who knows—," she waggled her eyebrows playfully—, "we could both be right."

He laughed. "Never say die, eh?" He glanced down at the dog, who watched them with an adoring look in his mismatched eyes.

Karlee started for the door, her grin even wider. "And isn't it nice that you have three weeks to discover whether or not I'm right?"

Before he could form an appropriate retort, she slipped out the door. But he could hear her laughter all the way down the walkway.

Mackenzie stretched and yawned. It had been a long day—his gaze drifted to Ivan, who sat beside him on the floor, leaning against his leg—and a busy one. After Karlee had left, he'd spent the rest of the evening cleaning up dog hair and getting the dog situated.

As though sensing Mackenzie's attention, Ivan looked up at him, his eyes wide with entreaty.

Mackenzie frowned. "What is it, boy? What do you want?"

Ivan stared at him, then at the couch, where Mac was sitting.

"Forget it."

The dog kept staring soulfully.

"No way." Mackenzie crossed his arms. "You're not getting up here."

If anything, Ivan only looked more forlorn. *Manipulator!* Mackenzie thought, fighting a sudden smile. The husky reminded him of Lindsey. She knew exactly how to get around his most determined refusals. Well, he was not going to be cajoled by a four-footed furball. No matter how appealing he was.

Mackenzie leaned down to look Ivan in the eye and inform him firmly, "Couches are for humans. Floors are for dogs."

Ivan leaned forward and licked Mackenzie's nose.

He straightened, aware of an odd warmth somewhere in the region of his heart. He glanced at the couch cushion beside him. *I can't believe I'm even considering this!* he thought. *This couch cost me a bundle! No way I'm going to let this fur machine up on it!*

At a gentle touch, Mackenzie glanced down to find the dog resting one paw on his knee. *"A couch is just a couch,"* Karlee's voice echoed in his mind.

"Just a minute." He got up and went to rummage in his cedar-lined linen closet. A few moments later he emerged, a large beach towel in hand. He came to the couch, spread the towel over the cushion, then sat down and patted the couch.

Ivan jumped up, circled three times, then plopped down with a contented sigh. By the time the movie Mackenzie was watching was rolling the credits, Ivan was sprawled out beside him, his head in Mackenzie's lap. Mackenzie stroked the soft ears gently and became aware he was smiling.

Shaking his head, he patted Ivan's side. "Up and at 'em, boy. Time for bed. Which means you go in your crate."

Ivan stretched, yawned, and slid from the couch. He followed Mackenzie to the crate and went inside without argument.

"Good boy, Ivan," he said, pleased. "Now go to sleep."

A half hour later Mackenzie was startled from sleep by a horrific wailing sound. He scrambled from bed, grabbing his robe and racing for the living room. Ivan sat in his crate, staring at him, howling his heart out.

"That's enough!" Mackenzie yelled, and Ivan stilled, but his expression clearly told Mackenzie that his heart was breaking.

"Save it for the women, buster," Mackenzie snapped.

No sooner had he slid beneath the covers than the howls began again. The mournful sound bounced off the walls and reverberated all around Mackenzie. With a groan, he pulled his pillow over his head. It didn't help. He jumped up and went into the bathroom. When he returned there were cotton balls stuffed in his ears.

It turned out to be a waste of cotton. Nothing blocked out the pitiful sound of Ivan's anguish. Finally, around 3:00 A.M., Mackenzie threw back the covers.

"All right," he said as he went into the living room. "You win."

He reached down and opened the door of the crate. Ivan bounded out, jumping in ecstasy, dancing around Mackenzie like a Mexican Jumping Bean. "I should have named you Tigger," he mumbled, fighting a smile.

Ivan raced down the hallway, and Mackenzie followed at a more sedate pace, certain Ivan would be in the middle of the bed when he got there. But, much to his surprise, the dog was sitting beside the bed, waiting for him. Too tired to question, Mackenzie slipped under the covers. Ivan rose, turned three circles, then lay down with a plop beside the bed.

Mackenzie reached down and rested a hand on the dog's soft head. Just before he drifted off to blissful sleep, Mackenzie felt a grateful lick on his hand, and he smiled.

Eight

❦

E arly the next morning, just as he was stepping out of the shower, Mackenzie's phone rang. Grabbing a towel, he went to answer it. It had to be Amanda.

"Darling," she said, her tone low and warm, "I'm so sorry for our disagreement."

"So am I." He eased his tall frame into a chair.

"That creature was terribly filthy—"

"He was, indeed." Mackenzie's eyes wandered to where Ivan snoozed contentedly on his rug, one paw curled around his muzzle.

"I've never been terribly good with animals, you know—"

"I know." At the sound of Mackenzie's voice, Ivan stirred, stretched, and yawned widely.

"Please, dear, do say you forgive me?"

"Hmmm?" Mackenzie said. Ivan had come to sit beside him, leaning his body against Mackenzie's still-damp leg. "I'm sorry, Amanda. What did you say?"

"I said—"

Mackenzie grinned. Apparently he didn't get his feet clean enough, for Ivan was now intent on licking every inch of them.

"—Give me?"

Mackenzie bit back a laugh. Ivan's tongue tickled! But from the impatience in Amanda's words, he doubted she would find the situation amusing.

"Of course I forgive you," he said, hoping that was the right response. Ivan chose that moment to climb into Mackenzie's lap and yodel into the receiver.

"Hush, you!" Mackenzie scolded, then brought the phone back to his ear.

"Mackenzie! What was that?"

He chuckled. "Ivan. I think he's jealous."

"Ivan? Who in the world is Ivan?"

"The dog—" he began, but she broke in.

"The *dog!* You still have the beast?"

He sighed, rubbing Ivan's ears soothingly. Apparently he could hear Amanda as well, and from the way he was hiding his face in Mackenzie's chest, Ivan was finding it to be a less than melodious sound.

Quickly he explained his decision. "Just for three weeks," he hastened to add at her quick intake breath.

"Three weeks? Are you mad?"

"It's not that bad. Karlee has been a big help."

"Oh, I'm certain your preposterous neighbor has done her best to make herself indispensable—"

"Now, hold on, Amanda," he broke in on her frigid tirade. "Karlee has—"

"I don't want to hear about it!" she snapped. "Any more than I want to hear about that…creature!"

He felt unutterably weary. "What would you suggest I do?"

"Get rid of it."

He struggled to hold onto his patience. "I can't very well do that, now can I? He belongs to someone, and it doesn't seem right to ignore that fact. Besides, it's only for three weeks."

"I refuse to step one foot into your house with that beast in residence!"

"He's not that bad—"

"He's disgusting! And I can't believe you'd rather spend time with some mangy dog than with me."

"Amanda, don't be ridiculous—"

"If anyone is being ridiculous in this situation, it's you!"

"I'm doing what I have to do," he said, aware his voice had hardened but unable to temper the words.

"As am I. Goodbye, Mackenzie."

"Amanda...wait." He reached up to rub his forehead. He really didn't want to end the call this way. "Look, why don't I take you out to dinner tonight?"

There was a pause, then, "Well..."

She was weakening. He lowered his voice persuasively. "Chateau Michel's shouldn't be too busy. We'll ask them for the corner table near the fireplace, away from everyone else. You can order the veal, just the way you like it...."

Nine

Mackenzie finished making his lunch—a perfectly created western omelet—and went to sit down at the table to eat. Ivan watched him avidly, dancing around him as he walked to the table, pressing up against him as he cut off a bite of the still steaming omelet.

Mackenzie tolerated the dog's actions for as long as he could, then barked, "Ivan! Lie down!"

The dog gave him one mournful look, then padded to his crate to lie down on his rug. Mackenzie stared in amazement. The animal had actually obeyed him! And without much hesitation. So little, in fact, that it didn't really qualify as hesitation. It was more of an "Are you sure?" pause before doing as his master had ordered.

Mackenzie rose and went to stand in front of the dog, who now rested with his head on his paws. "Ivan, come."

Within seconds Ivan was sitting in front of him, gazing up at him expectantly.

"Ivan, lie down."

He did so, not even pausing this time.

A smile moved across Mackenzie's face and erupted into a

full-fledged grin. He knelt beside Ivan feeling absurdly pleased. "Good boy, Ivan," he said, rubbing the dog's soft ears. The husky panted happily and leaned his head into Mackenzie's hand.

Two realizations came to him then: (1) He liked having Ivan around, and (2) he was going to miss the dog when his real owners claimed him.

Pushing these troubling thoughts away, Mackenzie gave Ivan one final pat, then rose and went to dump his omelet down the garbage disposal. He wasn't hungry any more. He'd briefly considered feeding the omelet to Ivan, but Karlee had given him a lecture on how bad it was for dogs to feed them "people food." Restlessly, he grabbed his coat from the rack. Pulling a doggie treat from the tin, he tossed it into Ivan's crate. Again, the dog obeyed, entering the crate and polishing off the tidbit before lying down.

When Mackenzie went outside, he stood on the porch, wondering where to go. He stepped off the porch and started out, but his step slowed when he came to Karlee's gate. He paused, studying the tidy, white house. True, she had Christmas decorations up, but at least they didn't cover every inch of her house and lawn. The display was actually quite attractive.

Luminaries lined the walkway, though they weren't lit at the moment. An elegant wreath adorned the door, above which was a red banner sporting the simple words "Immanuel: God with Us!" Simple white lights were strung on the two trees in her front yard and along the eaves of the house. From inside he could see a crèche set up in front of the large plate-glass window. If he remembered correctly, it was lit in such a way that those passing by at night could see it.

"Oh, good! I need an extra hand."

The warm voice jolted him from his study of the decorations, and he looked to see Karlee standing in her doorway, smiling at him in gentle amusement. Her golden hair flowed about her face, looking almost like a halo. He glanced around quickly and was surprised to discover that he'd come through the gate and was standing on her front porch. He felt a flush wash his cheeks.

"I...I was just leaving," he said uncertainly, but she wasn't listening. She stepped forward and laid a gentle hand on his arm.

"You can't leave," she said. "You haven't come in yet."

Not sure why he was doing so, he let her lead him inside. "Besides," she went on, "I need your help." He followed her into a bright, warm kitchen that was decorated with sunflowers and daisies. It was the perfect setting for her, he decided, looking around.

"Here you go," she said, pulling his hands out and sticking hot pad gloves on them. He stared down at his hands.

"What—?" he began, but broke off with a start when she reached around him from behind.

"Hold still," she ordered. "I have to get this tied on."

He looked down to see she'd slipped an apron around his waist and was tying it firmly in place.

She came around him and regarded him critically, then smiled. "Wonderful. You're all set."

"For what?"

An electronic beeping sounded, and she shooed him toward the oven. "For that! Pull the pan of cookies out and set them on the table. There's a flipper there to take the cookies off the pan and set them on the cooling racks."

He stared at her, wondering if he were hearing her correctly. "Cookies?" He cast a look at the oven. "I don't do cookies," he muttered.

There was something warm and enchanting in the look she gave him. "You'll be wonderful. But you'd better hurry or they'll burn!"

He went to fumble with the oven door, wondering in disgust how one did anything with the ridiculous mitten-like hot pads on their hands. At last he wrestled the door open, pulled the pan of golden brown cookies from the oven, spun around, and bumped right into Karlee. The sifter of flour she'd been carrying went flying, dousing him with a cloud of white.

He coughed and sputtered, then stopped in amazement when he heard her laughter. Blinking the flour out of his eyes, he stared at her, fully intending to tell her how little he appreciated being laughed at, but the words stopped in his throat.

She stood there, flour smeared on her cheek, her eyes sparkling, and he thought he'd never seen anyone more beautiful in his life. She bit her lips to stop her laughter and reached out, grabbing a damp cloth from the sink.

"Here, let me help," she said, and he could hear the barely restrained laughter in her words.

A responsive smile tugged at his lips. Lindsey was right; the woman was contagious.

She wiped at his shirt front, then rinsed out the cloth and reached up to wipe his face. At her gentle touch on his cheek, their eyes met—and all at once the very air around them seemed electrified, all but snapping with awareness.

Karlee dropped her hand slowly and stepped back. He watched her lick her lips and understood. His own throat and lips were suddenly bone dry.

"I...," she began, "I mean, maybe you should do this yourself."

She held out the cloth, and he took it from her, grateful for something to do. He moved to the sink and washed his face quickly, pondering the uproar his emotions seemed to be in. If he were smart, he'd get out of there. Quickly.

He turned to face her, and when their gazes met he was struck by yet another startling realization: he had absolutely no desire to do the smart thing. He shrugged, smiling. "Well, since I've been baptized by flour, I may as well help you finish this little venture."

The smile Karlee gave him confirmed his belief that being smart wasn't all it was cracked up to be.

R udolph, the red-nosed reindeer, had a very shiny nooooose...."

Mackenzie belted out the song, letting the water from the shower head fill his mouth and make the words sound gargled. He swallowed, laughing.

He felt good. No, great! He hadn't felt this way... He frowned. Ever. He'd never felt this good, not that he could remember. He and Karlee had spent the afternoon baking cookies. Then, when the treats were cooled and lined up on strips of wax paper, they'd decorated them. During it all, they'd talked and laughed and found that they actually did have quite a lot in common. They both held integrity and kindness in high esteem. And they both had a passion for the color green. They shared interests in books, foods, walking, camping, horseback riding, even the kinds of movies they enjoyed.

And, of course, dogs.

He smiled again as he shut off the water and stepped from the shower. He'd have to let Lindsey know she was right for once. A quick glance at his watch told him he had just enough time to get dressed and head out to pick up Amanda. He pulled on his clothes in record time, calling for Ivan as he did so.

When the dog didn't come, Mackenzie went into the living room. "Ivan," he called again, looking around. No exuberant, bounding dog responded. A small frown creased Mackenzie's forehead as he called again, fighting the sense of dread that was beginning to build inside. He went to the crate and pulled Ivan's favorite squeaky toy from inside. Feeling totally absurd, he squeaked it, hoping Ivan was just snoozing soundly some-where. He glanced around the room, and his gaze came to rest on the sliding doors.

The air in his lungs came out in a rush—the doors were open. He looked outside. "Ivan!" he called. Again, no response.

"Huskies are famous for being escape artists...."

Karlee's warning rang in his mind, and he groaned. "You dumb dog!" he muttered, going back inside. "Well, so be it. He's not my dog. If he wants to take off, I can't exactly stop him." But the words didn't ring true, even to his own ears. There was a decided ache in his chest, and he imagined the look in Karlee's eyes when he told her Ivan was gone. He shook his head and grabbed his coat.

"Five minutes," he said. "I'll look for five minutes."

An hour later, Mackenzie came trudging back to his house. Ivan had been nowhere in sight—and he felt terrible. His throat was tight; his heart felt constricted. He'd done everything he could, looked everywhere he knew to look. As much as it hurt to admit it, there was nothing else he could do.

"You could pray."

This time, he didn't even argue. "God, I'm sure you have better things to do than find a lost dog," he whispered forlornly. "But I'd sincerely appreciate any help you could give me."

He unlocked the front door and went inside—then paused, listening. Someone was in the back yard! He hurried to the sliding doors and pushed them open. A group of neighborhood kids were in his backyard, gathered in a circle around something. Mackenzie walked over to find Karlee in the center, kneeling beside a mud-encrusted, clearly happy Ivan.

"Oh, you're home!" Karlee bestowed that incredible smile on him, and her eyes lit up. "Look who the gang found at the park."

He came to kneel beside her, stunned at the relief he felt. "Thank God," he whispered. Karlee's quick, wide-eyed look brought a small smile to his lips. "When I couldn't find him, I took your advice," he admitted, "and prayed." He cupped Ivan's face in his hands and rested his forehead against the dog's furry muzzle. "I don't know how he did it, but he got the sliding doors open somehow."

"I told you huskies could be escape artists."

"Well, he definitely proved you right. And you're living up to your name, aren't you, Ivan the Terrible?"

She arched an eyebrow at him. "I could swear someone around here told me he didn't believe in nicknames."

He turned to her, arching his eyebrows. "I thought you weren't listening when I said that," he accused.

Her dimples peeked out. "Some things are better ignored."

A boy of about eight stepped forward. "Hey, mister, can we come play with your dog tomorrow?"

Mackenzie looked at the boy in surprise. "He's not my—," he began, but was cut off when the other children crowded closer in excitement.

"Yeah! He was a lot of fun!"

"Your dog is vewy pwetty," a small girl said softly.

"He's not my—"

"Is he your only dog?" the older boy asked, looking around eagerly.

"HE'S NOT MY DOG!"

Five heads turned toward him, and five pairs of eyes regarded him solemnly. He looked at Karlee, who was struggling with laughter.

"Did you steal him?" the small girl finally asked in that sweet, angelic voice.

"Of course not!" Mackenzie sputtered, and Karlee finally stepped in.

"Ivan is a stray. Mr. St. John is taking care of him until we can find his owners."

"Wow," one of the other boys exclaimed. "God must like you a lot to bring you such a great dog, huh?"

Mackenzie directed his gaze at Ivan, who seemed pleased as punch at being the center of all this attention. "Yes," he said at last, "I think he must."

CHAPTER

Eleven

❧

I t took some time, but the children finally went home.

"How about some coffee," he offered, pleased when Karlee smiled.

"I wouldn't refuse a cup of cocoa."

"You've got it," he said. "I'll get right on it." He paused with a grimace. "Right after I make a phone call."

She nodded and went to the living room, Ivan padding along beside her. Drawing a deep breath, Mackenzie lifted the phone and dialed Amanda's number.

She answered before the first ring was finished. "Mackenzie?" she snapped.

"Amanda, I can explain—"

"Do you realize I've been sitting here waiting for you for two hours?"

He rubbed his eyes wearily. "Amanda, please, Ivan got away."

"Ivan? Who in the world is Ivan?"

"The dog—"

"The *dog?*"

Her screech pierced his eardrum, and with a grimace of

pain he held the phone away. Even with the receiver at arm's length, he had no trouble hearing her. "Do you mean to tell me you stood me up for a dog? How *dare* you treat me in such a cavalier manner! Well, I have had enough. *More* than enough. I do not, I repeat, *do not* want to hear from you again until that...that *thing* is gone!"

The sound of the receiver slamming down rang in his ear, and Mackenzie sat in silence for a moment. Then, very carefully, he hung up the phone.

Karlee glanced at the clock as she slipped into bed. One-thirty in the morning. She couldn't believe she'd stayed so long at Mac's.

They had talked into the wee hours, discussing everything from family to favorite foods.

"Hmmmm, peanut butter," she said. "Now God did himself proud when he moved mankind to invent peanut butter."

Mac fixed her with an incredulous stare. "God? You really think God had anything to do with peanut butter?"

"Yes and no. I believe God cares about the things that move and delight us. Just as a father would care about the things that delight his children." She crossed her arms, hugging herself. "I remember watching once when my younger brother was sick. My dad sat by his bedside, washing his fevered face with a cool cloth, talking to him. And crying."

Surprise lit Mac's eyes. "Crying? Why?"

"Because his son was in pain and he couldn't stop it. But what my dad felt was only a small reflection of what God feels as he watches us. He's far more affected by our joys and our pains than any earthly father is with his children." She shrugged. "That's just the kind of God he is. When we hurt, he hurts. When we are in pain, he longs to help us and ease our suffering. Because he loves us."

"So why doesn't he stop the hurt?"

"Sometimes he does. But he never said we wouldn't suffer. He just promised to be with us in the hurting. And he provides us with the help we need to get through it."

"Let me guess," he said dryly. "You're talking about angels."

She smiled. "Sure, sometimes. Or people." Her gaze drifted to Ivan, who was snuggled next to Mac. "Or others who bring us joy or comfort." A rebel yawn forced her to glance at her watch. When her eyes widened in surprise, Mac leaned over to take her wrist in his hand and tilt her watch so that he could see the time. He looked at her then, and their eyes met and held.

She could still feel the way her heart had tripped, the way her breath had grown ragged at his nearness. And at the intensity of his gaze. She'd watched, mesmerized, as he slowly lifted her wrist to his lips and pressed a soft kiss there. "Thanks for all your help." His low voice had seemed to resonate through her, touching and warming her from the inside out. "If anyone's been an angel lately, it's you."

Karlee's cheeks burned as she remembered wanting to lean forward and press her lips to his. Instead she'd managed a simple, "Any time," before she disengaged her hand from his and rose to leave.

She rolled over, punching her pillow into submission, then flopped down with a confused sigh. *What is it about this man, Lord? And why is he looking at me like he did tonight? He's nearly engaged to that socialite. Shouldn't he be saving his looks for her?* She punched the pillow again. *And while we're at it, why does one look from those blue eyes almost stop my heart?*

Her own eyes widened with a sudden realization. She'd been praying for someone to share her life with since she was a child, praying for the man she would love, the man with whom she would share her life.

You've got to be kidding, Lord, she thought, stunned, her head spinning. *Mackenzie St. John?* She rolled onto her back and stared at the ceiling. Until the last week, she'd looked at Mac as someone distant and cold, someone focused on controlling his life and environment. Oh, Lindsey had told her time and again that there was more to Mac than that. But she hadn't believed her.

Until now. Now...now she'd seen another side of Mackenzie. A softer, tender side. She'd seen him smile and laugh and take a stray dog into his home. *And into his heart,* she thought, remembering how he'd rested one large hand on Ivan's head as he slept beside Mac on the couch. This Mackenzie St. John was a man she liked, a man she enjoyed being around.

A man she could grow to love.

She threw her arm over her eyes. *Father, this is impossible. He's going to ask Amanda Carr to marry him, and that's all there is to it. Right? Right.* She pictured the woman in all her elegant perfection, and her heart sank. Why wouldn't Mac want to marry someone who looked like that? Amanda Carr matched him perfectly. Far better than she ever could.

Wait, child. Wait and see that the Lord is good.

She wanted to trust the promise that whispered through her, but Amanda's image wouldn't leave her alone. Perfect hair. Perfect teeth. Perfect clothes. Perfect, perfect, perfect.

Karlee was beginning to hate that word.

With a final punch to her now-battered pillow, she reached a decision: Mackenzie St. John, in all of his charm and endearing boyishness, was off limits.

CHAPTER

Twelve

When Mackenzie pulled open his front door in answer to the doorbell, he was delighted to find Lindsey on his doorstep.

"I can't stay for more than a few minutes," she told him quickly. "But I wanted to stop by...," her voice trailed off, and he saw tears in her eyes. "I missed you, Bear."

"I missed you, too, Changeling." He reached out to draw her into a hug. He knew she was surprised by the action, but he didn't care. He was just glad to see her again.

"Well," she said, following him into the living room. "I should stay away more often if I get a greeting like that."

"Tell you what," he countered. "You forgive me for being a total goon and I'll greet you that way every time you come around."

With a tip of her head, she studied him thoughtfully. "A total goon?"

He nodded. "I've been thinking. A lot, actually. And Amanda and I...well, I'm not so convinced that we're right together."

Lindsey jumped up from her chair with a whoop and came to wrap him in a crushing hug. She rained kisses on his face, and Ivan danced around them, barking furiously.

When Lindsey finally calmed down and sank back into her chair, Mackenzie reached out and patted the couch beside him. "Ivan, lie down."

The dog jumped up on the couch, circled three times, and plopped down happily. Mackenzie reached down for one of Ivan's squeaky toys—once he discovered that Ivan would chew on them rather than shoes, he'd hadn't hesitated to buy a dozen of them—and handed it to the husky.

When he looked up, Lindsey was staring at him, a strange expression in her eyes. "So this is the stray you're keeping?"

"Watching," he corrected her. "Remember? I'm just watching him until someone claims him or Karlee finds him a home."

She nodded slightly. "I was pretty amazed by the message you left on my machine telling me about him. At first I thought it was a brotherly ploy to get me to come back so you could apologize."

He grinned and scratched Ivan's ears playfully. "Now there's an idea. I wish it had occurred to me."

Lindsey watched him thoughtfully for a moment.

"What?" he asked, and she met his curious gaze.

"Are you sure you want to get rid of Ivan?"

He looked at her, taken aback by the question. He'd forgotten about that. Ivan wasn't his. "I'm not getting rid of him," he said. "He doesn't belong to me."

She tipped her head, eyeing him thoughtfully. "Suppose he's for sale?"

The words had an odd affect on Mackenzie: his heart constricted with hope, and he felt his throat tighten with emotion. He looked at Ivan, who was watching him carefully, an adoring expression in his doggie eyes.

"You're sure not going to find anyone else in this world who looks at you like that," Lindsey said with a laugh. When he didn't respond, she rose and came to wrap her arms around his neck. "That dog has been a gift to you, Bear," she whispered. "He's made you laugh again. If for no other reason than that, you should think about keeping him." She stepped back, then went to pull a small bundle from her purse. She set it on the coffee table.

"What's that?" he asked.

"A gift. From Karlee. And the card is from me, to be opened on Christmas Eve and not before, okay?"

"Okay," he said, leaning forward. Then his eyebrows arched. "She's giving me a Bible?"

Lindsey nodded as she moved toward the door. "Karlee said she marked places that pertained to your discussion the other night." She angled a look over her shoulder. "Sounds as though you two are getting along pretty well."

He started to respond, but she halted as she noticed her tree.

It was in a stand now. Mackenzie had bought one the day after Ivan showed up. And he'd been watering it faithfully, though he wasn't quite certain why. It was still as bare as the day Lindsey had hauled it through the door.

"Bear—," she began reproachfully, but he held up a hand.

"I've had a few things on my mind," he said. "And they were a bit more important than putting tinsel on a tree."

"Hmmm," she responded. "You might be surprised how really important that is." She opened the door and cast a glance back at him. "Think hard about keeping Ivan, okay?"

"I will," he said, coming to stand by the door. "When I have time." But he knew, as he watched her walk away, that he'd probably think of little else for the next several days.

Mackenzie lifted his hand to knock on the door just as Karlee pulled it open. She stared at him, wide-eyed—and he felt his heart surge with awareness.

He opened his mouth to speak and found his throat was dry as dust. Clearing it, he tried again. "Hi."

She leaned against the door jamb. "Hi."

He frowned slightly. Something was wrong. She seemed distant. Removed. He slid his hands into his jeans pockets, suddenly uneasy. "I wondered if you had a few minutes to talk."

Something flickered in her eyes—a gladness, a warm eagerness—and then it was gone, locked behind a veil of remoteness that he'd never seen in her expression before.

"I don't know," she said, glancing around as though seeking some excuse.

"If it's a bad time…," he began, confused both by her behavior and the sharp hurt that was washing over him. He had the oddest feeling that he was losing something precious—and he didn't even know what or why. His head was spinning, and his chest ached as though an anvil were sitting on it. *Get hold of yourself, St. John!* he commanded angrily. *So she doesn't want to see you. Big deal.*

Exactly, his heart echoed. *Very big deal.*

He had to get away from there. He needed to think. "Well, never mind. I'm sorry to bother you."

He spun around and walked away with long, rapid strides.

"Mac!" Karlee called, but she was too late. He was gone. And she couldn't blame him after the way she'd just acted. She went back inside, feeling more miserable than she'd felt in a very long time. Sinking into her rocking chair, she leaned her head back as tears began to slide down her cheeks.

Father, help me. I don't know what to do.

Thirteen

❧

The jangling, jarring noise wouldn't stop. It kept nagging at her, poking her, pulling her from the warm cocoon of sleep.

The phone was ringing. Karlee forced her eyes open and tried to focus on the clock. The iridescent red numbers blinked at her gleefully.

3:30 A.M.

She grabbed for the phone, pulling the receiver from the cradle and laying it next to her ear on the pillow. "Hullo?" she managed groggily.

"I need you."

She blinked. "W...what?"

"I need you. Now!"

A frown creased her forehead. It sounded like Mac's voice. But it couldn't be. "Mac, is that you?"

"Mackenzie." The correction came automatically, but it didn't hold the arrogant tone she was used to when he chastised her. "Now stop asking ridiculous questions and get over here, now!"

"Mac...Mackenzie, what in the world—?"

"He's sick."

Karlee sat up, suddenly alert. Mac wasn't angry; he was frightened. She could hear it clearly in his voice. "Ivan?" Even as she asked, she knew it was the husky. "What's wrong with him?"

"I don't know." He sounded miserable. And desperate.

"Then how do you know he's sick?"

"Let's just say my two thousand dollar Persian rug will never be the same."

"Ah." She threw back the covers. "I'll be right there."

The sight of Ivan lying in the middle of the bathroom floor, panting rapidly, his tongue hanging out, sent a chill of apprehension through Karlee. But that was nothing compared to what the sight of Mac's haggard face did to her.

Without thinking she came to him and folded him in her arms. He stiffened, then sagged against her briefly. "Has Ivan eaten anything different?" she asked as Mac straightened and moved away from her.

He gave her a wry look, then pulled a large gold box from the trash container. "Not unless you count five pounds of the finest Belgian chocolates," he said dryly.

"Oh, wow." At her low exclamation, Mac turned to look at her, his stance and expression alert.

"What?"

She bit her lip. "Chocolate, well, it can be harmful to dogs in large amounts."

His eyes narrowed. "How harmful?"

She didn't respond, and he took her hand, holding it tightly. "Karlee."

Licking her lips, she met his gaze squarely. "It could kill him." His face paled, and she squeezed his hand. "Listen, we probably caught it in time. The best thing we can do now is take him to the emergency animal clinic." She looked back down at Ivan's limp form. "And pray."

Several hours later, Mackenzie and Ivan were back home. The husky was sick, very sick, but he would recover. Karlee had helped set Ivan up in the bathroom, then turned to leave. Mackenzie, who was sitting on the floor stroking Ivan's ears, had reached out to capture her hand.

"Karlee, I—" He broke off. He'd appreciated her presence more than he could say. She'd been a source of comfort and calm. Their eyes met, and she nodded.

"I'll check on you tomorrow," she told him, squeezing his hand gently, then she was gone.

Now he leaned back against the wall and looked down at Ivan's sleeping, exhausted form. "I didn't know," he whispered brokenly. "I didn't know chocolate could be dangerous. Or that it would hurt so much to see you in pain and not be able to help you...." His voice trailed off and he rested his head against the cool wall. "I didn't know caring so much could hurt so bad."

"God is affected by our joys and pains.... When we hurt he hurts.... That's just the kind of God he is...."

When Karlee had first said those things, Mackenzie hadn't understood. Now... He closed his eyes. "I don't know, Lord. I'm not sure it's worth it."

The feel of a wet tongue on his cheek startled Mackenzie, and he opened his eyes to find Ivan standing beside him, shaky but upright. The husky's mismatched eyes, filled with trust and devotion, gazed at him. Mackenzie slid his arms around Ivan's neck, burying his hands in the deep, soft fur. Ivan licked him again, then bent his head to tuck it beneath Mackenzie's chin.

"Good boy," Mackenzie murmured. "You're going to be okay." And as he sat there, feeling Ivan lean against him, Mackenzie knew there was nothing more worth the risk, more worth the pain, than loving.

CHAPTER

Fourteen

❧

When the morning sun streamed in the windows, Mackenzie was already slipping into his coat and heading for the door. He needed to talk to Amanda. He reached for the door just as the bell rang. Surprised, he opened it and found Karlee standing there.

She met his gaze steadily. "We need to talk."

He nodded. There was no point in pretending he didn't understand. "Yes, we do." He held out his hand, and she placed hers inside it. As his fingers closed around hers, he noticed how their hands seemed to fit together. Just like their hearts.

He led her to the kitchen. "Cocoa, right?"

She nodded. He had it ready in minutes, then handed it to her. As she took the steaming mug, he reached out to touch her face gently. "I want you to wait here for me," he said, not sure why he made the request. All he knew was that he wanted to be sure she would be there when he got back.

"You're going somewhere?"

"I have to talk with Amanda." She stiffened slightly, and he cupped her face. "I need to tell her that things have changed," he said, his voice tender. "And I don't feel right about doing that over the phone."

She held his gaze, her eyes searching his face, and then she nodded. "I'll be here."

Relief swept over him. "Good." He smiled, feeling suddenly light. "Good. I'll be back soon."

Everything was going to work out. He was sure of it. Whatever was happening between him and Karlee, it was right. For the first time in a long time, he felt as though his life was on the right track. And he could hardly wait to see where it was heading.

He pulled the door open—and ran right into a policeman who stood there, hand poised to ring the bell.

"Mr. St. John?" the officer inquired, and Karlee came to stand beside Mackenzie as he nodded. The policeman inclined his head. "I'm afraid I have some bad news, sir."

Mackenzie froze.

"It's your sister. She's been in an automobile accident." His eyes gleamed with compassion. "I'm sorry, Mr. St. John, but it's serious."

Mackenzie tried to contact his and Lindsey's parents, but two days after the accident, he still hadn't been able to locate them. "I believe they intended to take a rather rambling tour of the countryside," a woman from the Paris conference informed him. He'd called the airlines and left a message with them. That was as much as he could do.

He sat in the ICU, holding Lindsey's hand, staring at her uncomprehendingly. He understood the doctors well enough— his sister had been thrown from her car when it was rear-ended by a truck. She'd suffered head trauma and was in a coma. The prognosis was not good.

What he couldn't understand, however, was why. Why Lindsey? Why now?

"Mackenzie?"

He started at the cold tone and looked up. Amanda stood in the doorway, a nurse at her side. "Would you please tell this…woman that I'm part of the family."

At Amanda's haughty tones, Mackenzie rose and went to take her arm, ushering her back to the waiting room. She gave him a disapproving glare, but followed without comment. Until, that is, they reached the room.

"You haven't called me," she said coldly. Mackenzie stared at her.

"I believe you told me not to."

She made a dismissive gesture. "Don't be ridiculous. I only meant that while the dog was there."

"Well, he's still there, Amanda, and he's staying."

She stared at him as though he'd lost his senses. "Staying? What do you mean 'staying'? I won't allow it, Mackenzie."

His head was starting to pound. "Listen, Amanda, I can't talk about this now—"

"Not with me, anyway. I understand you've been talking plenty with your little fuzzy-headed neighbor."

Anger swept over him at the disdain in her tone. "Karlee has been an enormous help."

"Oh, I'm sure," she said nastily. "She filled me in on quite a lot when I encountered her this morning as she was leaving your house." Her eyes were even colder than her tone. "She rambled on about all you've suffered, how her God saved your dog. She actually asked me to pray for you." Her expression was one of pure distaste. "The way she talks about God is juvenile. But then, that doesn't seem to bother you. Not any m—" She broke off suddenly, her eyes wide and incredulous.

"Amanda—," he began, but she cut him off.

"You're in love with her!"

He frowned, staring at her uncomprehendingly. "What?"

"You are!" she said, her tone full in imperious disbelief. "Don't waste your breath trying to deny it. You're in love with that absurd woman." She gave a harsh laugh and turned from him sharply.

Mackenzie stood there, staring at the back of Amanda's well-tailored suit. In love? With Karlee? The very idea was ridiculous. Preposterous. He frowned. Wasn't it?

He shook his head impatiently. He wasn't sure what he felt about Karlee, but he didn't have time to figure that out now. Soon, soon he would do so. But not now.

"Amanda, listen—"

She spun around, raising an imperious hand to halt his words. "No. Don't bother. You've changed, Mackenzie. And not for the better. I hope you and that ludicrous woman are happy." She turned and stalked away, then paused in the doorway and turned to fix him with an icy glare. "But you might want to ask her one thing. Where was her almighty God in this?" She swept her hand toward the ICU. "He cared enough to save your silly dog. Why didn't he save your sister?"

With that she spun around and walked away.

Karlee set Ivan's bowl of food down, then stepped back.

"There you go, boy. Have at it."

Ivan just looked up at her, then laid his muzzle on his paws. She sighed and knelt beside the morose animal. "I know, pup. I miss him, too. But he'll be home soon." She sat back on her heels. "I just wish there was something I could do...." Her voice trailed off as her gaze came to rest on the unadorned tree.

The urging that filled her was clear, and she nodded slowly. Then she rose and went to work.

It was amazing how quiet the hospital hallways were around midnight. Mackenzie had grown somewhat used to the constant bustling of nurses, doctors, orderlies, and visitors during the daytime. Now, with the lights dimmed and the activity almost nonexistent, the hallway had a strange, melancholy emptiness to it.

Like a tomb.

The thought sent a chill up Mackenzie's spine, and he quickened his step back to Lindsey's room. He'd stepped out to get a drink of water. He knew he probably shouldn't be there, but he didn't want to leave Lindsey. He needed to see her. To talk to her.

As he entered the ICU, the only sound was the ping of her cardiac monitor and the gentle *swooshing* sound of her respirator. Mackenzie sank into the chair he'd pulled next to the bed. "Hey, Changeling," he said, surprised at the roughness of his voice. He cleared his throat, then shook his head in exasperation. There was no one here to see or hear him. What did it matter if he sounded like he was about to cry?

He stared at Lindsey's pale face. It didn't even look like her. All the animation, the luminous personality that drew people from the moment she entered a room, was gone. She lay there, passive, as though she were already gone from him.

"O God, please," he whispered brokenly. "Don't let this happen." He felt a dampness on his face, was dimly aware that he was crying. He reached out to take her limp hand and hold it between his own. Bowing his head, he placed a soft kiss on her fingers.

God, God…help us.

"It's Christmas Eve, Linds," he said softly. "Bloomingdales called me this morning all upset that you haven't been around."

He smiled, knowing she would have appreciated the joke. His gaze rested again on her face, and his features contorted with grief. "Ah, Linds, you can't do this, hon. You can't leave me. How can I face Christmas without you? How can I face life without you? Don't you know you're the only spark I've got?"

He leaned his forehead on the white sheet. "You said my life was ho hum, boring. Remember? You were right. But I don't know how to be different, Linds. I need you to show me...." Choking back a sob, he lifted his head and pressed her knuckles to his lips. Memories of their life together flitted through his mind, pictures of them as children, as teens, as adults.

"Remember that Christmas we stayed with Grandma and Gramps?" He turned his head to gaze out the window. It was snowing again. "Mom and Dad were off on some archaeological dig of some sort halfway across the world. I was so steamed they didn't take me with them, but they said you needed me. I think they knew the truth, though. It was I who needed you. I needed your laughter, your delight in every little thing. You loved being at Gran and Gramp's house. I thought they were kooks."

A sad grin crossed his face, and he could see as though it were happening again how they'd gone into the mountains, trudging through the deep snow, examining every tree in the forest—or so it had seemed to his eighteen-year-old mind— until they found The Tree. That was how his grandmother had said it. The Tree. As though it were some precious treasure.

He had to admit it, though, once they brought it home and decorated it—an event that took an entire evening—even he had thought it was worthy of such respect. It had been magnificent.

"It was like spending Christmas with Beaver Cleaver and the gang," he muttered, looking at his sister's pale face. "Christmas carols playing on the radio, the smell of fresh-baked cookies and pies in the air." He laughed lightly. "I swear we watched every TV Christmas special ever produced!" His gaze rested on her face. "You made me watch the Grinch with you five times. Five times, Linds! I should have gotten a medal of some kind." He closed his eyes, savoring the memories of laughter, singing, praying together.... "It was pretty amazing, wasn't it? You said that year was really Christmas. I pretended I didn't care, but I did. I still do."

He broke off, too choked with emotion to continue. He stood and went to pour himself some water from the pitcher on her bedside table. He swallowed the tepid liquid, willing it to soothe the tightness in his throat, in his chest. "You hounded me into going caroling with you," he went on, staring out the window again. "Told me it would be my fault if you and your little friends got mugged. I groaned about it, complained every step of the way, but do you know, I can still remember the songs?" He smiled. "I can still hear you singing, your sweet voice floating on the air...."

In a hushed, choked voice, he started to sing.

"Joy to the world, the Lord is come,
Let earth receive her king.
Let every heart prepare him room,
and heaven and nature sing,
and heaven and nature sing,
and heaven and heaven
and nature sing."

The last note came out ragged, full of agony, and he turned and left the room with quick, almost desperate strides.

Karlee leaned over to pull a sheet of cookies from the oven when she felt it...a strong sensation, an urging.

She needed to pray for Mac.

279

She set the cookies on the cooling rack and moved into the living room. Ivan padded beside her, watching her intently. She sat down, and he situated himself beside her, leaning against her leg as though offering his support.

Laying a hand on the husky's velvety head, Karlee closed her eyes and was ushered into the throne room of the Almighty.

Fifteen

Let earth receive her king…Let every heart prepare him room….
The words echoed over and over in Mackenzie's mind, accompanied by a multitude of searing questions.

How do I do that, God, when I'm so full of anger, so full of fear? How do I receive you? How do I prepare my heart? What if I don't want to do either one?

The last questions struck him hard, like a sledgehammer slamming into the middle of his chest. He believed in God, didn't he?

"Yes," he whispered, knowing it was true.

He trusted God, didn't he?

He opened his mouth, but no response came. And as he considered the questions, he saw a huge, gaping darkness within himself. Fear, sharp and piercing, sliced through him. *How can I trust you?* he asked, flooded with desperation. *If you take Lindsey away from me, how can I ever trust you?*

He waited, hoping, praying for a response. But there was only silence. And the fear grew.

The streets were dark and silent when he pulled in his driveway and into his garage. He stepped from his car feeling more weary, more bruised and abandoned than he'd ever felt in his life.

Are you there, God?

He moved inside, slipping out of his coat and letting it fall to the floor. He started down the hallway to his room...then stopped, startled by the tantalizing aromas drifting on the air. What? He turned toward the kitchen in confusion and saw a strange light in the living room, a glow of some kind. Moving as though in a dream, he forced himself forward, and what he saw took his breath away.

The tree, Lindsey's tree, stood there, resplendent in ornaments, tinsel, and delicate white lights. Gifts of all shapes and sizes were wrapped in colorful Christmas paper and piled beneath the full branches. He was dimly aware of the soft strains of Christmas carols floating around him as he moved toward the tree. He fingered the stiff needles, breathed in the scent of the evergreen, drank in the delicate beauty of the ornaments.

It was real. He wasn't going crazy. Somehow, suddenly he was a young man again, standing in his grandparents' living room, surrounded by Lindsey's "real" Christmas.

His knees felt suddenly weak, and he went to sit on the couch, intensely aware of...something. A presence. "Jesus...Jesus, please be here." His gaze fell on the Bible Lindsey had set on the coffee table. He reached out and lifted it, opening to one of the sections Karlee had marked. He reached up to turn on a lamp, then began to read.

"I will strengthen you and help you.... My help comes from the Lord, the Maker of heaven and earth. He will not let your foot slip—he who watches over you will not slumber.... The Lord watches over you.... The Lord will keep you from all harm—he will watch over your life; the Lord will watch over your coming and going both now and forever more.... God is our refuge and strength, an ever-present help in trouble.... If you make the Most High your dwelling—even the Lord, who is my refuge—then no harm will befall you, no disaster will come near your tent. For he will command his angels concerning you to guard you in all your ways; they will lift you up in their hands, so that you will not strike your foot against a stone...."

Understanding swept through Mackenzie, washing his heart with wonder, filling him with the sense that he was not alone, that God was, indeed, in that very room, touching him, loving him.

Let every heart prepare him room....

The carol rang through him again, and this time Mackenzie understood. God was present. He always had been. Day in and day out, the Almighty was there, watching over his children, intimately involved in their lives. Intimately involved in *his* life. As he sat there, scenes from his life played over in his mind—his grandparents and their solid, every-day faith; Lindsey and her unflagging determination to draw him back to faith; Karlee and all she had shared with him in the past weeks; even Ivan and the laughter he'd brought back into Mackenzie's life....

Tears coursed down his cheeks as he faced the truth: God had never left him. He had been the one to walk away.

"I'm sorry," he whispered brokenly. "I couldn't see you, couldn't make room for you because I was so sure I was right. So sure I knew the truth. Forgive me. Father, please, forgive me."

"Do not be dismayed, for I am your God."

The assurance resonated in his heart, and Mackenzie felt an overwhelming joy spread through him. He was not alone. Nor was Lindsey. They were both being held in loving, all-powerful hands. He jumped up from the couch, startling Ivan who had been dozing beside him. Reaching down, he hugged the Siberian exuberantly.

"Did you know you were an angel sent to guide me?" he asked the dog, who tilted his head as though considering the question before delivering a lick to Mackenzie's face. He laughed, rubbing the dog's head. "And so was someone else," he said. "Someone I need to talk with."

A small knock sounded on the sliding doors, and Mackenzie turned to them curiously. A quick glance at the clock on the mantle told him it was close to two in the morning. He moved to pull the blinds back and smiled. He unlocked the doors, slid them open, and reached out a hand.

Karlee laid her hand in his and stepped inside. Her glorious hair was pulled back with a Christmas ribbon, her eyes were shining with tears. And love. He felt it almost like a physical blow. It washed over him, warming him inside and out, leaving his head spinning with the intensity of the experience.

"I'm sorry to come by so late," she said softly. "But I saw the light and wanted to see if there was any news on Lindsey...." Her voice trailed off as she met his gaze.

"You did all this, didn't you?" He indicated the decorated room, and a slight flush filled her cheeks. She nodded. "Why?" His gaze held hers.

"I wanted you to come home to Christmas," she answered.

He reached out a tentative hand to touch her cheek. She placed her hand over his, her gaze never leaving his. For a moment he couldn't speak.

"You're in love with her!" Amanda's accusation rang in his head, and he knew. Knew as certainly as he knew his name. She was right. He was completely, totally, irrevocably in love with Karlee McKay. With her glowing eyes, her laughter, flowing hair, her unique outlook on life, her sweet spirit...every crazy, illogical, absurd thing about her called to him. All he had to do was respond.

"It worked," he said, aware of the rough huskiness of his

voice. "I came home." He felt tears stinging at his eyes and a gladness swelling in his heart. "To Christmas, to God."

Joy lit her face. "Oh, Mac, I'm so glad!"

"But now I want to know something." He hadn't intended to say this, hadn't even realized he would go into this. But he knew as certainly as he knew God loved him that it was right. "I want to know if I can come home...to you." She drew in a stunned breath, and his heart threatened to pound through his chest, but he went on.

"My life has been crazy over the past few weeks, but one thing has remained constant. Seeing you, talking with you, spending time with you...that is what brought me joy." He cupped her face gently. "*You* brought me joy. And a sense of peace. I thought at first I was just relieved to have you around to help with Ivan. But that didn't explain why I was always so glad to see you, why I always felt so good after we'd been together. Tonight, I realized God had worked a miracle. He brought my faith and my heart back to life. He showed me that my faith belongs to him." His hand caressed her soft cheek. "And my heart belongs to you. I love you, Karlee. I don't want another moment to pass by without you knowing how I feel."

He saw his answer in her eyes, read it in her face, but he still wanted to hear it. She didn't disappoint him. "And I love you." Her eyes shone with tears, but her glowing smile assured him they were tears of happiness. "When God put you in my heart, I thought it was for you. To help you see him. But now I know it was for both of us."

He nodded. "Immanuel."

She smiled, understanding. "God with us. Now and forever."

He drew her close, cradling her in his arms, resting his chin on her head. "I don't know what will happen with Lindsey. But I do know God is here, with us. With me. And I'll be all right because I have him. And I have you." Glancing up, his eyes

285

came to rest on a small sprig suspended from a string. He looked down at her with a grin. "I see you didn't forget the most important decoration of all."

She colored. "It isn't really Christmas without mistletoe."

"Well, we can't let it go to waste, now can we?"

Her gaze held his as she shook her head. Slowly, savoring, anticipating, he lowered his head until his lips met hers—and as her arms slid around his neck, he could almost swear he heard angels singing all around them.

"Glory to God in the highest, and on earth, peace, good will to men!"

Epilogue

❧

I wish Christmas would last forever, don't you, Zsuzsi?"

Karlee St. John reached down to pet the Komondor's corded head and felt her other hand nudged impatiently. "Now, don't you go getting jealous, Ivan," she said, scratching his soft ears. "You know I love you both."

The husky plopped down beside her rocking chair with a sigh, and Karlee laughed. She gazed down at the Bible in her lap.

"See, the Sovereign Lord comes with power.... He tends his flock like a shepherd: He gathers the lambs in his arms and carries them close to his heart; he gently leads those that have young."

Gladness and gratitude filled Karlee, and she hugged the Bible to her chest. What a gift. What an amazing gift God had given them. She could hardly wait to tell Mac.

Thank you, Father, that you gently lead those that have young, she prayed. *Lead us now into this wonderful new adventure you've given us. And show me the best time to tell Mac—*

"What are you smiling about, sweet?"

Karlee looked up to find Mac leaning on the back of her

chair, a tender smile on his face as he looked down at her.

"Christmas," she answered. "The wonders of Christmas."

"Hmmmm, why am I not surprised?" The indulgent gleam in his eyes warmed her. "But you'd better get cracking. Lindsey is expecting us for dinner in half an hour."

Karlee stood, setting her Bible on the chair as she did so. "She's really doing well, isn't she, Mac?"

He nodded, pride evident in his expression. It had taken several weeks, but Lindsey had finally come out of her coma. Though she had a long road of recovery, they had all rejoiced that God had preserved their family. Now, nearly two years after the crash, Lindsey was amazing everyone with her progress. "There's still the question of long-term impairment." Mac's eyes softened. "But she's still with us and I can't thank God enough for that."

Mac held out Karlee's coat, waiting as she slid her arms into the sleeves, then wrapping it around her for a hug.

"Lindsey will make a wonderful aunt," Karlee said with a smile as Mac directed Zsuzsi and Ivan into their crates.

"Absolutely," he agreed, closing the doors and tossing treats to the dogs. "She'll be the best—" He broke off suddenly and spun to face her. "An aunt? Lindsey will be an aunt? But that means…I mean, we'd have to be…parents!"

Karlee grinned. "There's that keen sense of the obvious ag—" She didn't get the chance to finish her teasing. She was too occupied with Mac's crushing embrace, and his sweet, tender kiss, which was just fine with her.

PALISADES...PURE ROMANCE